The Road Home

For my Mother

The Road Home

My American Journey
in Search of Inverness

Mike Edwards

With very best wishes,

Mike Edwards

KESSOCK BOOKS

First published in Great Britain by Kessock Books 2018

A CIP catalogue record for this book is available from the British Library.

ISBN 978-0-9957453-1-5

Text design and typesetting by Stanford DTP

Printed and bound in Great Britain by CPI Group (UK)

Contents

About the Author

Twice a day, every day, for the last twenty-five years, Mike Edwards has entered into the homes of millions of people across Scotland.

Mike is Senior Reporter at STV News and, in his own inimitable and respected style, he has covered every story of significance to have broken over this period, including politics, sport, humour, personalities, crime, tragedy, travel and much more.

He is a Major in the Army Reserve and has served in Iraq and Afghanistan. He has also written a novel, *Friendly Fire*.

Mike was born and brought up in 'the one true Inverness' in the Scottish Highlands, and he currently lives near Glasgow.

Acknowledgements

This project would never have come to life without the expertise, guidance and, moreover, patience of many people.

I owe a huge debt of gratitude to Rab MacWilliam, Iain MacDonald and all at Kessock Books for believing in my idea and making it a reality. They took an unwieldy and travel-weary manuscript and polished it into something special.

At STV I am indebted to Rachel Pike, Nancy Taggart, Bryan Wotherspoon and Linda Nelson for their help and forbearance. There is no way I can adequately describe my love and gratitude for Ron and Debbie MacKenna, my closest friends, for their support. Good Caley men Gordon Fyfe and Billy Urquhart will always be heroes of mine, but I thank them again for filling in a few blanks in blue and white.

I am deeply indebted to Scotland's First Minister Nicola Sturgeon MSP for taking time out from running the country to read my manuscript and for her comments, and to Scotland's foremost historian Professor Sir Tom Devine for dropping other more notable tomes to read mine. Thanks, too, to Sanjeev Kohli for his valuable comments. I'm still trying to persuade his character Navid to stock this book in his shop in 'Still Game'.

A huge vote of thanks goes to everybody I met on the road across the USA, those whose hospitality I was humbled to share and those who patiently answered my interminable questions.

But my greatest debt of gratitude is for those closest to me, those who put up with my absence and presence alike and who gave me the support without which this book would still be a bundle of crumpled papers alongside all the others in the 'ideas box' on the shelf: my mother Margaret, my wife Emma and my little boy Pete, who wait for me at the end of the road home.

Prologue: Wanderlust

The soporific sound of the train stopped suddenly and I awoke to the jerk and rumble of sleeping cars shuddering to a halt. The only sound now, the snoring of my father on the top berth.

Above me, there was a tiny azure night light. I clambered out of my bunk and felt my way to the window. Gently, I slid the blind up a few inches and I pressed my nose against the cold glass. I could see sidings packed with wagons, car transporters and fuel tankers.

This was Mossend marshalling yard in deepest, darkest Lanarkshire. It was a grim landscape, not far from the massive mines and steel mills which were then Scotland's staple industries. Today, it is an industrial wilderness where work is now done in call centres or in labs where microchips are made. I smiled to myself. I always woke up here.

In the middle distance I heard the familiar rhythmic beat of two diesel engines: Class 26 locomotives, for the rail enthusiast. They were tethered together in tandem, and had taken me south from my home town of Inverness. Here, they would unhook from my train to be replaced by an electric locomotive, a Class 86, which would take us on to London. It was at Mossend that the new world began.

South of Mossend, railways had two tracks instead of the single line of the Scottish Highlands They were electrified, with thick copper wires bearing 25,000 volts of alternating current hanging over them. The signals were the coloured lights of the modern era, and not the semaphore arm of my Highland branch line.

The Class 26 diesels rattled past my window. With their irregular tempo, the engines sounded as though they each had a piston loose. It was an odd noise, yet it was somehow comforting. Whenever I heard it I was happy, as it meant that I was either about to embark on an adventure or was returning home after one.

As a small boy heading off on the annual family holiday, my excitement was at fever pitch. What made it even better was the fact that, although usually a strict disciplinarian, my father, Donald, had written to my headmaster to tell him I was being taken out of school for two weeks during term time. He argued that being immersed in a foreign culture and language was of more educational value to a young boy than was sitting in a classroom in Scotland.

In my imagination, the Class 26s would now scurry off to a Mossend siding and sleep there. Later, the process would be reversed, and they would latch onto our northbound sister train, newly arrived from London behind its electric loco. Then these short stubby diesels would power their friends, the coaches, over the mountains and home to Inverness, making short work of their journey over Druimachdar Pass, the highest point on Britain's rail network.

The trains, northbound and southbound, were called 'The Royal Highlander'. I thought that was a grand name, and one which, even today, holds an important place in my heart. As a wee boy, I used to imagine the locos winking to each other as, near Carlisle, they passed in the night.

To this day, I have never slept as well as I did on those old sleeping cars. I was rocked gently to sleep by the noise and the motion, so it was no surprise that I woke every year without fail when we stopped at Mossend to change locos. In later years, when flashbacks and nightmares kept me awake or woke me in a cold sweat from fitful sleep, I would think back to those sleeper journeys.

I love my job, but there is plenty to keep me awake at night.

*   *   *

I was the duty officer in a massive tent in the middle of the Kuwaiti desert, just as the operation to liberate Iraq got underway. In front of me was a map table, with red and blue pins carrying little flags inserted at key points. That morning I had watched the advance of the British armoured division (the blue pins), and had seen the enemy (the red pins) removed one by one as they were destroyed. I was a Major in the Territorial Army, called up from my civilian career, in the desert about to go to war.

On my belt was a gasmask in its case. In my rucksack was a thick charcoal-lined oversuit, designed to keep out the chemical and biological agents we believed Saddam Hussein possessed. My radio headset crackled into life and I heard a man's voice at the other end speak clearly and slowly. He said only three words, but these words caused me to freeze.

They were the codewords which told me that Iraqi scud missiles had been launched, and were heading for us.

LIGHTNING.

LIGHTNING.

LIGHTNING.

Peter Tobin was already a serial killer when I first encountered him. The press bench at the High Court in Edinburgh was directly behind the dock and, as he was led in from the cells every morning, he would fix me with his eyes.

On the first day I looked away. But the next day, my anger rising, I stared him out. I did so every day of the six weeks of his trial for the ghastly rape and murder of Angelika Kluk in a Glasgow church.

I was determined that this vile bastard, who preyed on weak and defenceless women, wasn't going to spook me. I hated him. But I couldn't let that show in my reports on the STV News every night. It was the most dramatic, sensational story I have ever worked on.

The sickening scene-of-crime video, showing Angelika, naked and punctured by multiple knife wounds, was played on big TV screens high up on the walls around the courtroom. I knew that the last thing she saw, as Tobin repeatedly plunged his knife into her, were his cold, inhuman eyes.

*   *   *

I was close to death. I had overstepped the mark and I would pay the price. I had said the wrong thing at the wrong time to the wrong people, and my usual irreverent humour was not going to get me out of this one. Quite the reverse. It had got me into it.

They had now cornered me. They were led by a man who was ridiculously dressed, but in Kabul anything goes. He wore a sports jacket and a threadbare pair of trousers. His shirt was caked with dirt and his sockless feet were clad in ancient shoes, several sizes too big. I was serving at the NATO, headquarters and my uniform was clean and my boots polished.

As he screamed in my face in his broken English, I realised I was in deep trouble. I was alone in a room with forty angry Afghans who had me pinned in the corner. I thought I might headbutt him and make a run for it, but what about the other men? I didn't stand a chance. For all I knew, he may have been about to whip out a machete.

My arms were outstretched, my palms flattened towards the crowd as I apologised. Slowly, gently, so as not to anger the mob any further, I dropped my hands to my side. I brought my right hand forward a few inches, and with my thumb I flicked open the flap of my holster where I kept my personal weapon, a Browning 9mm High Power pistol. Only as a last resort would I cock it and, only if I felt I had no other option to save my life, would I shoot.

My thumb did its business and I slid my hand into the nylon holster. But my heart stopped beating for an instant. I saw flashing lights before my eyes and heard wind rushing in my ears. The holster was empty.

*   *   *

The news editor screamed down the phone at me to hurry up. I tried telling him that the cameraman was driving as fast as he could, but he wasn't listening. He'd never been a TV reporter. He simply didn't understand.

Somebody had phoned STV News to say there had been a shooting in a quiet suburb of Glasgow. There were only a few minutes before our lunchtime news programme, and the satellite truck was seconds behind us. Very shortly I would be standing before the cameras, broadcasting live to the nation from another Glasgow gangland hit.

The caller had said his neighbour had answered a knock at the door, and was then shot several times. The victim had crawled outside and tried to hide under his car in the street, before the gunman delivered the *coup de grâce*. This had happened in broad daylight in front of the man's pregnant wife. This sounded like a great story for the News, and I jumped out of the crew car, preparing my lines as I did so.

We had arrived there earlier than usual. There wasn't yet a police cordon, far less a tent, to protect the crime scene and from which white-suited forensic officers could work.

I nearly jumped back into the car when, just feet away from me on the pavement, dripping into the gutter were the victim's brains.

*   *   *

He had taken the bait. I'd written to him on impulse, hoping for a reply.

In my letter I was gently probing while also gently massaging his vast ego. I had asked him several questions, and he had answered them. We then began a correspondence which I would use as a news story, or as part of a longer piece, when the bastard died.

A colleague had brought that first letter to my desk from the mailroom. 'Looks like you've got fan mail from a bunny boiler there, Mike,' she said pointing to the scrawled address. I knew instantly who the letter was from.

I locked myself away in a room at STV and carefully sliced open the envelope. The contents were dynamite. Knowing that I was fingering paper which had been touched by the most evil man in Britain, I immediately photocopied it, envelope and all, and locked it in my safe. Then my boss and I sat down in a quiet room with the photocopies.

'Wow! This is one for your memoirs,' she said, looking down at the spidery signature of Moors murderer Ian Brady.

*   *   *

The Royal Highlander would arrive at London's Euston Station at around 8am. An hour later we were at Victoria, about to board the boat train to Folkestone. That train used to hurtle through Kent until the blue of the sky met the blue of the English Channel.

The train emerged from a tunnel, and then stopped in a siding before reversing slowly down a single line through the town of Folkestone to a tiny harbour, where we would board the ferry for France. As she slipped her lines and rolled away from the quay, the seagulls shrieked above me and the salty spray splashed my face. I couldn't have been happier.

An hour and a half away, across the English Channel, we could see the beaches of France. A thousand wartime stories lay there, some involving my father, who had served in both the RAF and the Royal Navy during World War Two, before returning to Inverness to work in the railway.

I'm not religious, but I prayed that my father, who had passed away fifteen years earlier, would keep me safe when I was at war, and that he'd make sure I went home to my mother. When I narrowly escaped with my life from that baying mob in Kabul, and after the hideous bombardment from scud missiles when I sat baking inside my protective suit waiting for anthrax, botulism or plague from the warhead to waft towards me across the scorching desert, I again said his name under my breath as I waited to die.

*   *   *

Because of my father's job, I grew up on the railway. While I never wrote down an engine number in my life, I loved trains and everything about them, but French trains were not like ours. They were different colours, for a start. They were sleeker, they were cleaner, they had names, they had character, they had drama, and they had romance. And, best of all, each carriage possessed a board stating its destination. Ancona. Moscow. Port Bou. Berlin. Irun. Trieste. Vienna. Belgrade. Istanbul. Warsaw. Nice. Rome. Naples.

The train I usually boarded at Calais after disembarking from the ferry from Folkestone was called the Flanders-Riviera Express. It headed to Paris before continuing, after some marshalling, to the South of France.

*   *   *

The next morning the sun would blast into the compartment, and the first vista out of the window was the golden beaches and blue seas of the Côte D'Azur. It was usually hot. The final destination of Nice was still some hours away, but the train always stopped for a while in Marseilles. Here, my mother would rise and walk to the head of the platform, returning with coffee and croissants for us all.

At French railway stations in the 1970s, men rolled little trolleys about, serving steaming hot drinks to start passengers' Riviera days. We would joke that this was a brave thing to do for a woman alone in a rough town like Marseilles, where we believed unaccompanied females were frequently kidnapped for the slave trade.

Travelling, broadening my horizons, and encouraging my attempts to understand other cultures and to speak their languages: these were the greatest gifts my parents gave me.

The smell of the coffee is lodged in my memory, alongside the sound of the Class 26 diesels, the scream of the Folkestone seagulls and the spray of the English Channel. Two days and two nights travelling was nothing. Sleeping with snoring strangers was an irrelevance. Grime, fatigue and inconvenience were all meaningless. The adventure was all.

*   *   *

Looking back on my childhood, I realise that these journeys were the best part of it: the Friday night sleeper departures from the one true Inverness to London and beyond.

The electric loco hummed towards the head of my train and gently nudged onto us, ready to mother us south to England. Soon we would be rocketing through the night to adventure. It was time I returned to my bunk.

I realised that it was here at Mossend, a dirty little nothing place from where I headed year after year for the magical continent of Europe and beyond, that my wanderlust began.

'Every line of strength in American history is a line coloured with Scottish blood.'

Theodore Roosevelt
26th President of the United States

'To a Scot the past clings like sand to wet feet, and is carried about like a burden. The many ghosts are always a part of them, inescapable.'

Geddes MacGregor
Scottish philosopher

'You're a tourist in your own childhood.'

Sick Boy
Trainspotting 2

CHAPTER ONE

Inverness, California

Working all day, and the sun don't shine.
Trying to get by, but I'm just killing time.
I feel the rain, fall the whole night through.
Far away from you, California blue.

Roy Orbison

'I'm writing a book about Inverness,' I said pleasantly, as she plopped my cappuccino down on the marble-topped table. The waitress said nothing, but gave me a half-smile in response. I moved my ancient laptop a few inches to allow the cup some space.

Audrey Hepburn looked down on me from all around, with pictures of her, all black and white, on the walls and ceiling. I was in the Café Audrey, after all, on Las Palmas, just half a block from Hollywood Boulevard.

If I couldn't find the inspiration to write here, just a stone's throw from the cocaine-fuelled, pounding heart of the world's cinema industry, I couldn't write anywhere. In fact, if I couldn't write here, I just couldn't write.

Soon, mine wasn't the only laptop under Holly Golightly's gaze. A young man in polo shirt, baggy shorts and flip-flops entered and opened up his Apple. It was slimmer, shinier and, no doubt, much lighter than my steam-driven machine. Our eyes met across the café, the way gunslingers' eyes might have done. Who would tap first, who would lay down the opening words of his magnum opus, who would be ambling along the red carpet on Oscar night, clutching that screenwriter's trophy?

'Cream and sugar is over there.' The waitress, clearly oblivious to the situation, was chivvying me along. It was lunchtime, and she didn't need a writer clogging up a table for hours nursing a single coffee when there were power lunches to be sold to the movers and shakers of the movie world.

Some kind of smoothie or milkshake appeared on his table. It looked much more exciting than did the sadly flaccid froth on my cappuccino. I already felt locked in competition, and I hadn't written a word.

Suddenly there were two more laptops on tables around him, their custodians hunched over them, hoping to get that Hollywood buzz, that motivation from the location to sprinkle stardust on the words. I felt better, cranked up the cats' whiskers and valves in my ancient laptop (or, as I prefer, my 'ageing lapdog') and started to write.

Up on the main drag live the stars. Well, they don't, really. They live in Beverly Hills or Malibu or New York or Aspen. But the stars do reside on the sidewalk of Hollywood Boulevard, about a foot and a bit across, sunk into the concrete and edged in gold. Each has a little emblem, like a film strip or a gramophone stylus, telling the passer-by to which milieu the name belonged.

An intriguing part of Hollywood Boulevard is the Chinese Theatre. People of my vintage will know it as the place where a spotty youth parked the Pink Panther's futuristic car in the children's TV series of the 1970s. I grew up loving that opening sequence because it heralded an hour's worth of entertainment. 'How did he get a job like that?' I used to wail to my dad. 'It's Hollywood, son.' he said sagely. 'Nothing is real in Hollywood.'

What is real, though, is the pagoda outside the Theatre. Its red gables catch your attention as you approach. The only other indication of the Theatre's presence is the crowd of people standing outside. It is small and unremarkable when you see it for the first time but, like everything in LA, it has a back story.

Sid Grauman and his father travelled to the Yukon in search of their fortune. They made it, but not by finding the mother lode. Where they struck gold was in bringing entertainment to the masses of people who were mining and prospecting. First, Sid sold newspapers. Then he put on shows. Finally, he and his father built and ran theatres. The Gold Rush over, they moved to the east coast and then back to San Francisco, where they set up a vaudeville theatre called the Unique. It was going great guns until it was destroyed in the devastating earthquake of 1906. Grauman, ever the entrepreneur, salvaged a movie projector from the ruins, borrowed a marquee from a church in nearby Oakland, and again set up shop.

With the burgeoning Hollywood film industry just a few miles down the coast, Los Angeles was host to his next venture. He was backed by Adolph Zukor, who would go on to form Paramount Pictures. Sid imported fixtures and fittings from China and he employed Chinese artists and builders. The Chinese Theatre complete, the stars soon rushed to see and be seen there.

The hand and foot prints in the concrete outside the Theatre is now one of the most famous sights in LA, but Sid maintained it was all an accident. Mary Pickford, it is said, was going to see the new building and stood on the sidewalk, not realising that the cement hadn't quite set. Sid thought this was an excellent idea, and he selected many of the famous people of the time to do likewise.

As well as the footprints and handprints of the stars are indentations formed by sundry other articles, such as George Burns' distinctive round spectacles and Groucho Marx's cigar. You marvel at the petiteness of Judy Garland's hands and Marilyn Monroe's feet.

Sid became part of the Hollywood establishment and could count Charlie Chaplin as a close friend. Movie premieres were held at the Chinese Theatre and, although he eventually sold out to Fox for many millions, he wrote a clause into the contract which meant he'd be the managing director for the rest of his life.

Hollywood is a dirty, tacky, tourist-filled area of Los Angeles. But the name is, of course, synonymous with the movie industry. Hollywood, however, is a thing, not a place. Just like most of the world's major landmarks – the White House, the Great Pyramid and the Eiffel Tower – the neighbourhood just a street or two away is far removed from the gloss and glitz associated with the name. There are drugs, prostitutes, pick-pockets and poverty here.

But the real power in Hollywood isn't here in Hollywood, it's in 'Hollywood', if you follow. It's on the lots elsewhere in LA. In Burbank, or Glendale. The Warner Brothers lot, for example, is a vast studio complex and has umpteen gates, each with a barrier and security. It employs thousands of staff but is located miles away from Hollywood.

*   *   *

Noel Coward said television was for appearing on, not for watching, and I agree. Certainly, today's television is different to the quality broadcasting with which I grew up. I wouldn't thank you for most of the rubbish that appears on our screens apart, of course, from the news programmes, Champions League football and the occasional documentary with high production values. Because too many people on the planet are starving, I abhor cooking programmes, and the notion that you can become a celebrity for not winning a talent show or a reality TV series is risible.

While I would criticise parents of today for allowing their kids to sit for hours at a time on their phones or in front of computers, I should remember that TV played an important part in my upbringing. I think, though, that programmes were so much better in my day, and I learned a lot from them.

I grew up on decent dramas like 'Colditz.' The kitchest thing I ever watched was 'Dallas.' And, in between, there were dozens of other classics. My family seldom watched ITV because of the adverts, which is somewhat ironic given that, for the last twenty-five years, I've made my living out of adverts on Scottish Television.

My tastes and views on TV programmes became well developed at an early age. Perhaps because my father had been a good photographer, I was aware of lighting. I knew which scenes of a drama had been shot on a set and which on location. I could tell which actors had been classically trained because of their voices and the way they delivered the lines. Being a TV viewer as a boy honed my senses for working in the business in later life.

Our first TV was an old walnut cabinet which sat in the corner of the living room. You changed channels by rotating a small disk on the side and, if the signal was fuzzy, you played with the thin fronds of the aerial on the top of the set. I thought we were a really happening family when my father hired somebody to clamber onto the roof and bolt an external aerial to the chimney stack. But we became really happening when we bought our first colour set.

This was a magical moment in my life, and I remember racing home from school to see my first colour TV programme. However, because of some issue concerning the local transmitter at Rosemarkie on the Black Isle, colour programming didn't start until 7pm and was only available on BBC2. We had to watch our normal programmes in black and white, then switch over for the technicolour. I saw this as yet another disadvantage of living in the Highlands of Scotland. Although there were many advantages which outweighed this racist outrage, this internecine slur, at the time I was gutted.

Los Angeles first came onto my radar about twenty-five years before I visited the city. When I was a youngster I was a fan of police drama series and films on TV. I became quite discerning and, although I had never visited the USA, I knew which programme belonged in which city. I only needed to see a few frames of the start of each film before I knew where it was set.

'Kojak' was set in New York and Michael Douglas obviously pounded the beat on 'The Streets of San Francisco'. I remember watching the Hitchcock classic 'The Birds' and deciding it had been filmed in California. However, I didn't know it had beeen shot in Bodega Bay, north of San Francisco and only an hour away from my first Inverness.

'Hill Street Blues' never claimed to be set in any one city. It was largely shot in Los Angeles, but the producers wanted viewers to think it was set in Chicago or Pittsburgh. Before it became my favourite US crime show, I used to park myself in front of the TV to watch 'Starsky and Hutch'. But by the time 'Hill Street Blues' hit the screens I was a teenager, and I understood the subtleties of the plots and the relationships between the characters. 'Starsky and Hutch' whetted my appetite. And it introduced me to Los Angeles.

The rough parts of Los Angeles portrayed in each episode weren't particularly rough, and the programme was fairly jolly. It had some drama, but it also contained light moments and the kind of camaraderie between the two main characters for which, as an only child, I often yearned. It also engaged with some American taboos, which added to my understanding of life and, I suppose, my education. There were drugs and references to prostitution. Captain Dobey was a black man, as was Huggy Bear. So Starsky and Hutch were characters in stories with a black boss and a black informant.

Starsky and his pal Hutch set my heart on 'the city of the angels'. I loved the palm-lined boulevards of Los Angeles, that special blue Hollywood sky, the sunshine and the laid-back coolness of the city I was watching on TV. I vowed that one day I would go there.

*   *   *

The 'Hollywood' sign is nowhere near Hollywood Boulevard. Its crooked white teeth smiled at me out of the smog as I drove along the freeway. It used to say 'Hollywoodland', and it was erected in 1923 by realtors on the 2,000-feet-high Cahuenga Peak overlooking the city to advertise a new housing estate.

The Hollywood scuttlebutt says the sign was only ever meant to be in position for a year or so. But it quickly became a recognised part of the LA skyline, and when it was due to be torn down there was such an outcry that it was left *in situ*.

There are continual local rumours that the land around the sign is to be developed by realtors. It's enough to make Los Angelenos want to kill themselves. If they do, they could always choose the method used in 1932 by Hollywood actress Peg Entwistle. She was so sickened by the way her career had gone south at the hands of the big studio moguls, that she climbed the hill to the sign and threw herself to her death from the top of the letter 'H'.

Beneath the sign sit thousands of houses, lining narrow, steeply inclined and twisting roads. The homes range from tiny flats to mammoth mansions, and all seem to have either a front or back view over the canyon under the sign. The demand for these abodes is high, matched only by the rents and the salaries of those who can afford to live there.

I was on my way to visit friends who live in the shadow of the sign. They have a house with a wooden-decked balcony built on stilts overlooking the gorge, the sign and the city. Parking here is a problem, especially as the Americans drive on the wrong side of the road. But once I'd locked the Chevy's wheels against the kerb, stuck a couple of boulders under them to stop it rolling down the mountain to the freeway, and shoved the shift into park, I felt much better. When I say 'shoved the shift into park', what I mean is that I left the bastard in gear. And I was joking about the boulders, but once or twice in this part of LA I would have felt more comfortable with a couple to hand.

'Somebody had a brain fart a few years back and put the sign up,' said Frans Evenhuis, gripping my hand and ushering me out onto the deck. 'I guess I kind of take it for granted because I live here. I look at it every morning and sometimes I suppose I don't even see it.' We stood and gazed at it for a while. The view was panoramic, and certainly one I'd never tire of.

The view inside was none too shabby, either. Their house was built in 1960, and it was cool and furnished in modern minimalism but with quirky touches here and there.

Frans was a freelance graphic designer who created covers for the DVDs of Hollywood blockbusters, and his wife Cherie was his business partner. They were clearly doing well enough to earn the kind of bucks you need to live in a place like this, but were the most unassuming people you could meet.

Frans took me down to his studio. I counted a handful of computer monitors, including one big one which I took to be the main attraction, the canvas upon which he created his masterpieces. Along one wall were hundreds of DVDs, each one bearing his artwork. We chatted about his studio, which I loved. And if he got stuck (we artists are such delicate flowers and can dry up, you know) all he had to do for inspiration was pop out onto the balcony and look at the view. Or maybe not.

'It can have its pitfalls, working at home,' he said. 'Once I start in the morning, I get my head down and get on with it. It would be too easy to pop out for a cup of coffee or ask my wife something. You have to be very disciplined to work this way but I'm quite good at it now.'

Cherie had a similar office at the other end of the building, but with a chaise longue and French doors leading out onto a terrace with that view. On her desk was a vase of flowers. On his was a hi-tech reading lamp. Beside her chair was a pile of magazines. 'The UK edition of *Hello* is regarded as a style bible among Hollywood ladies,' she said, earnestly. 'The images of the stars are much better than in the LA edition. Frans buys me a subscription every year as a Christmas gift.'

We moved upstairs again to the deck, and I felt more relaxed than I had been since I arrived. It was baking hot outside, but we were so high up that there was a gentle breeze, and all around the minimal sound of an LA Sunday. Now and again, there was a buzz of a helicopter taking tourists up to see the sign, but in the main it was tranquil.

'So you're in television?' she asked. I am, but I felt petty talking about it here, beneath that sign.

'Are you in back?' This is an American way of saying behind the scenes.

'No, I'm an in-vision, on the road, foot-in-the-door reporter,' I replied.

'Really?' There was an awkward silence. She said it as most people do, with a surprised tone. I can't be that ugly, surely.

'Have you been up to the sign yet?' she asked, after a time. I wanted to say no, that I am far too cool, too much of an old LA hand to bother with such tourist-trap trappings. But I couldn't.

'You can walk up there if you want, but you have to do it from behind the hill. Don't just go straight up the hill or you're in trouble.' Frans waved expansively towards the sign, so close to their decking that I felt I could have touched it.

'There are cameras and loudspeakers up there, and when people get close the security people start screaming at them in this menacing voice, it's really alarming. Lots of tourists get into trouble, it's steep and hot and if you get heat exhaustion then the Fire Department have to come out to rescue you. It's not pretty.'

I wanted to stay. Hell, I wanted to live here. Their life seemed idyllic, so special. I don't doubt that they worked very hard, but where would you rather work hard? And much as I love my Inverness, the one true Inverness, I would happily have a go at Hollywood.

'I came here for a look thirty years ago and I stayed,' he said. He was a fresh-faced man in his late forties. 'I was bold and brash then, I was inquisitive, keen and hungry. I got a job, kept it and just got my head down.'

'Getting his head down' included producing a coffee table book called *Hollywood Poolside* which shows stars pictured at their lavish swimming pools. It features movie legends from Marilyn Monroe to Bogart and beyond. We chatted about writing and I felt like a million bucks. Here I was in Hollywood with a Hollywood player who was also a friend and he was asking me about my book, this book, *The Road Home*. I tried to stay cool, and explained it was a work in progress.

We chatted books for a while, but I was conscious I was eating into their downtime. Hollywood players like Frans and Cherie would cherish every moment of R&R and I didn't want to disturb them any longer. I thanked them for their hospitality, bummed some directions back to the freeway, and headed out in to the sunshine.

I retrieved the boulders from behind the wheels of the Chevy and jumped inside. Following the notices to the Hollywood sign, I drove off. There were people polishing their cars or blasting leaves away from their front lawns with fiendish blowing machines, and I wanted to stop and ask them the way. But every one of them gave me that look, as I slowed down, which said 'don't ask the way to the sign, OK?'

Close up, you can't really see too much although, if you're intrepid, you can get right up to it and amble through the letters. Your best bet is to head downhill until, eventually, you hit a crescent which affords a perfect vista of the letters on one side and the city on the other, if it isn't too smoggy. I was in LA for a week and it was only smoggy twice: once for three days, then for four days.

The Chevy drew to a halt, and I stepped outside. The road here was level and there was no need for boulders behind the wheels. There was a small reservoir, complete with dam, but obviously in need of some rainfall. Beyond that, was the downtown area of LA, a cluster of high-rise office blocks, and beyond that was the Pacific Ocean.

I have been to Los Angeles many times but I have never felt any need to go to the downtown area. It holds no attractions and is somewhere you whizz past on the freeway on your way from the airport to Hollywood or Venice to Pomona. Why would you want to go there unless you worked in LA? I made a mental note to drive through it one day, in case it was lonely or something.

At the foot of the canyon beneath the sign is the 101, or the Hollywood Freeway. There are five lanes of traffic in each direction and, no matter the time of day or night, it is busy. Los Angeles is another city that never sleeps. And you would never sleep if driving among madmen bothered you. You would lie awake fretting about the freeway, especially during the rush hour, especially at night. To survive driving in Los Angeles you have to do what they do, be what they are and drive the way they drive. I think the word is 'robustly'. I wended my way onto 101 and headed north towards Pasadena.

Thing is, as the Americans say, after a while driving in LA the whole Hollywood aura rubs off on one. There is something about the light, the air, the smells and the sounds. I gather the film industry set up here because of the quality of the light. And the air and the sounds are unique. You often get a waft of what I consider the LA smell. I have asked many people what it is, and they just say it's the smog from car exhausts. Except it isn't. It's more like a scent of trees or bushes or something. There is a kind of hush, a stillness about the place, too, unless you're driving on the Hollywood Freeway during the rush hour.

Pasadena became a real home from home for me during many holidays. It is a haven, an oasis in the midst of the sprawling megalopolis that is Greater Los Angeles. Friends live here, and I was fortunate enough to visit annually for twenty years. Hotels are one thing, but being able to unwind in a family home is another. I've seldom felt more relaxed anywhere in the world.

The town retains a kind of 'olde worlde' charm. Its palm-tree-lined main street is on Route 66, the road made famous by those escaping the Midwest 'dust bowl' poverty during the drought of the 1930s. There is no freeway numbered 66 as such: it's a series of roads which starts in Chicago and ends in Santa Monica on the Pacific Ocean, a few miles from Pasadena.

The dust bowl resulted from poor farming techniques during a period of sustained water shortage and high winds. Farmers were ruined in their thousands during three waves of droughts in the Great Plains area of the USA and Canada between 1934 and the US entry into World War Two in 1941. Some areas experienced nearly a decade of drought.

Increased mechanisation prompted farmers to use combine harvesters and ploughing machines to cultivate already dry prairie. In so doing, they dug up grasses which held the soil together and which stored moisture, even in extremely dry periods. Replacing those grasses with crops exacerbated the problem. People took to the road in their tens of thousands, the words 'go west, young man' ringing in their ears.

Around about the time I first came to Pasadena, I had just seen the Robert Altman film 'The Player'. The film is a delicious satire on Hollywood, with dozens of A-listers making cameo appearances. The fact that I recognised many of the locations in the film made it a favourite of mine. To this day I drag out the DVD now and then, and pore over it. This was the LA of which I wanted so much to be a part. I wanted to live here, to write fiction and have my stories turned into films. I wanted the Pasadena life, the quiet Sundays, that LA smell, and streets with great names in my satnav. It's a dream I'm still chasing.

In Pasadena, the pace of life is laid back. In fact, it isn't laid back, it's positively supine. The people who live here are wealthy professionals. The houses were built in the 1930s and have survived fire, flood and earthquake. Each has a strip of lawn at the front, room to park three cars, and a pleasant if not expansive garden at the back. One or two have swimming pools. They are all roughly the same height: one storey tall. I am not sure if this is down to planning regulations but it makes perfect sense. If you look up here, all you see are palm fronds and the glorious blue California sky.

Graham Lewis was born and grew up in Inverness. His house in Pasadena occupied a couple of acres, and the surrounding grounds were, to say the least, lavish. The kitchen alone was bigger than many people's flats. I counted half a dozen sinks in there, as well as two cookers. Or was it three? The fridge was the size of a garage. Graham's garage was the size of a house.

'Did you feel the earthquake last night?' he asked. I shook my head slowly. I don't think I will ever live down the fact that I have been in LA during an earthquake and slept through it. 'It was quite a biggie. You kind of get used to them here. You only really remember the really big ones.' We were in his well-stocked bar. I was sitting on a stool, munching cashews and sipping a much-needed cold one, ahead of a barbecue in his vast garden.

'You can tell when one is coming. It's quite eerie. The animals tend to sense it and give you a kind of warning. Everything goes quiet, like the lull before the storm, then the dogs start howling because they know something is wrong. There are shifts in the air pressure and their senses are far more attuned to that kind of thing than ours. Then it hits. You know it's coming but you never know how strong it's going to be. You just have to hope it's not a biggie.'

Graham was a marine engineer and knew about things like air pressure and turbines and the like. My knowledge of these matters is basic and my understanding less. I asked him about building design here. Very few buildings are more than a storey or two high, except in downtown LA. I asked if this is because of the earthquake threat.

'I don't think so because these buildings, the bigger ones especially, have fluidised foundations so they can take the hit and move around with the tremor. I've been in one of those buildings when a quake hit. It wasn't very pleasant. It interrupted the meeting and I realised it was time to go. If I'm at home when it happens, I'm told you have to jump under the bed. I can't because my bed is one of those solid jobs.' Only in LA could you have a solid bed in a building with fluidised foundations

He was born and bred in the one true Inverness, and he went to Inverness High School, as I did. He grew up in Dalneigh, just a few streets away from where I lived as a boy. He had travelled the world and his accent was from everywhere. But from time to time he lapsed into a word or two of Invernessian. I felt homesick, and my trip had only just started.

'I remember there was an earthquake in Inverness when I was a boy,' he said. 'But it was a sideshow compared to the ones you get here.'

Graham was in his fifties. He was dressed in shorts, open-necked shirt and sandals. His blond hair was swept back and his tan was deep and healthy. He left school and went to Southampton University to study navigation. His parents met in the RAF during the war and, after they married, they were posted to what was then Ceylon. Graham spoke fondly of the passage there and back on ocean liners. I sense it was on these voyages that he fell in love with the sea. After he graduated, he joined the Merchant Navy and travelled the world on cargo ships.

'On my first voyage we took steel from the UK to Australia and New Zealand. Then we took cars back to Europe. That was just the start. I was still a cadet then. It was two years before I saw Inverness again. I don't really get back that often and when I do I hardly recognise the place.' He's not alone.

'Did you have a girl in every port?' I asked. He laughed and sipped his cocktail. 'Not quite, but it was a fabulous lifestyle.'

There may not have been a girl in every port but there was a girl. He transferred to passenger ships where he met his wife. Gretchen is an artist and choreographer who produces shows on cruise ships. Above Graham's mammoth garage was Gretchen's dance studio, mirror-walled and kitted out with a grand piano and the latest sound system. In another part of their mansion was her design room where she creates the costumes and routines. There was an architect's drawing table littered artfully with costume designs and swatches of cloth.

Unfortunately, Gretchen was at sea when I visited. As Graham and I started a barbecue outside, she was sailing from Dubai back to Europe, putting her latest creation into action.

While I had missed Gretchen, I was very lucky to see Graham. The week after my visit he was off to Australia, where he was going to work on a ship which was in dry dock in Brisbane. He picks and chooses his jobs, and doesn't spend nearly as much time at sea as he once did. He mentioned something about her twin screws and rudders and Lloyds, the world's shipping insurers, but I'll be honest: I didn't understand a word of it.

The house was impressive. Every space was tastefully finished, and every corner and hallway had something to catch the eye. In some houses, spaces are overcrowded, but not in this one. This was finished just right. My bathroom had a sunken marble bath and sink with gold plated taps and ornate mirrors. I always thought a shower was pretty much a shower until I stayed there.

There was a rustle and a growl, and my fork stopped midway between plate and mouth.

'Oh don't worry, that's just the skunks and racoons,' he said.

We sat quietly and watched half a dozen of the monochrome creatures surround a dog bowl, and eat away together happily. The racoons delicately picked up each dog food pellet in its little claws and ate as a human might eat a sandwich. Suddenly, a skunk thrust his tail into the air. It opened up like a fan.

'That's a sign,' said Graham. 'You don't want to get too close. If you get sprayed by him, you'll know about it. Rotten eggs doesn't come close. If the dogs get hit you have to buy a chemical called 'skunk-off' and blast them with a hose to get rid of the stench. The dogs love it ... not.'

We sat drinking and chatting late into the night. This was a boy from Inverness who had made good. He had worked very hard and deserved everything he owned. He had a great job which saw him travel all over the world. Hell, he even knew Bill Gates. Yet, despite it all, he was the most unassuming man. I hadn't seen Graham for a couple of years and, when I left in the morning after a comfortable night, we had a good manly hug and backslap.

'Give my regards to Inverness – all of 'em,' he said as we parted.

I drove off the freeway onto Santa Monica Boulevard, and headed west. Managing not to slam into any oncoming traffic, I leant over, rummaged in the glove compartment and whipped out a CD. I slid it into the player just in time for Roy Orbison's amazing voice to start singing 'Pretty Woman,' as I nosed the Chevy on to Rodeo Drive. It was a cliché, I know, but Hollywood is full of them.

Rodeo Drive is not a long street but, lined with designer clothes shops and jewellers, it is impressive. It was a major attraction long before the 1990 Richard Gere and Julia Roberts film, which took the name of Orbison's song, and it is a 'must see' for visitors to LA. I found a parking space outside Salvatore Ferragamo, and I pumped the meter full of nickels and dimes, giving me an hour to walk around. Perhaps I should not have been surprised that, in the space next to the Chevy, was a yellow Rolls Royce Phantom Drophead Coupe. It was gaudy and tacky, but lovely. The top was down (the temperature was in the 80s), and its interior was finished with the kind of wooden decking and leather you get on plush yachts. It kicked the Chevy into touch.

I stood beside it, fumbling in my pocket, pretending the car was mine and that I was looking for the keys. Soon, a crowd gathered. There was an outbreak of nudging and murmuring from people who clearly didn't believe that someone such as I could be associated with such a piece of machinery.

Some of Rodeo Drive's designer shops have their doors locked to discourage paupers. Instead, their clientele make appointments. I'm not really a designer label kind of guy, even though I work in the supposedly glamorous world of television. While I have to be smart before the cameras, my clothes are more robust than anything else. Apart from a couple of handmade examples from a decent tailor for special occasions, my work suits are from Marks and Spencer.

On Rodeo Drive you would pay as much for one small accessory as you would for my entire wardrobe. Still, it was fun to be there. The sun was splitting the sky, and the mood was upbeat. The traffic on the road was busy, with people coming here to pick up that special little number, and people like me, here to rubber-neck and enjoy the day.

At the foot of the road is an unmissable E-shaped building, which is instantly recognisable as the Beverly Wilshire hotel where much of the 'Pretty Woman' film was set. Down Wilshire, the road which runs at right angles to Rodeo Drive, is a shop with which I was more familiar and comfortable. Saks Fifth Avenue is top-drawer, but it is a shade more human than some of the designer boutiques which line Rodeo. Some wag named the coffee shop therein 'Snaks', which I thought was quite a wheeze. I ordered a coffee and a pastry and sat down to rest my weary non-designer-shod feet.

Coming to a place like this also gave me the chance to use the loo, which is an impossibility pretty well everywhere else in this part of town. Could you imagine hurrying into Yves Saint Laurent cross-legged and asking to use the bathroom? Aye. Good luck.

You visit Beverly Hills and you don't want to stand out as what you are: a tourist trying to do things on the cheap. I tried to blend in and look the part. I adopted mild eccentricities, such as a gentle twitch and a soft lisp. I got chatting to the young waiter who served me. He was black with an unusual hairdo. He had dreadlocks, except they weren't really long enough to be dreadlocks. They kind of shot out and headed off into the air. And, like so many other people (and let's not kid ourselves here, myself included), Matthew wanted to make it in Hollywood.

'You have to be alert all the time,' he said, as he poured my coffee. 'There are a million people here who will step in front of you and take the limelight if you give them half a chance. The thing is if they take the limelight then they might also take your break and that would be unforgiveable.'

We chatted for a while, and I gave him my card. I told him I was writing this book and explained all about the Invernesses. As soon as I said that, I got the impression that he thought I might be able to help his career to take off. I began to feel a bit guilty, because he seemed to be hovering around my table and ignoring other customers. Then he disappeared. He said he was a gym instructor and told me he wanted to be a personal trainer for some of the big names in Hollywood. Then he returned.

'Hey man,' he said, slapping my back. 'I've just Googled you. You're famous, man! You're on TV every night. Do you know what that means here? That's awesome. It's a pleasure to meet you.' He pumped my hand.

Flattered, I thanked him, but I wondered if he'd be so impressed if he knew that I stood about in the pissing rain for a living. It is very doubtful that I could do anything for him, but I am burdened by an inordinate sense of fair play and, of course, I will if I can. So, if any Hollywood impresario is reading this, first of all you have to make this book into a film. Second, there is a guy called Matthew working in the coffee shop at Saks off Rodeo Drive, and you should talk to him.

North again on Hollywood Boulevard, and I hung a quick left onto Mulholland, beginning a snaking run up into the hills. The view was occasional now, and there was a layer of smog between us and the San Gabriel mountains on one side and the Pacific Ocean on the other. The road was narrow, twisting and high-sided, and there were lots of hairpin bends. Occasionally, there was a glimpse of LA to the left or the mountains to the right. I couldn't enjoy the view as my beady eyes were fixed on the road ahead. I turned left and rolled out onto Ventura Boulevard. This was not an accident. I was leaving Los Angeles now and heading to the coast for the long drive north to my first Inverness.

Having ditched Roy Orbison pretty well the moment I left Rodeo Drive, I now had Tom Petty on the Chevy's sound system. I love his song 'Free Fallin''. Every time I hear it, it takes me to LA, to the heat, the blue skies, the long freeway drives and life in this exraordinary city. In it, he speaks of Mulholland, Reseda and Ventura Boulevard, and it was fitting that it was playing as I drove.

Tom Petty and the Heartbreakers are my favourite band. As a child I flirted with ABBA, as did most children of the 1970s. I transited through the Boomtown Rats, the Stranglers and the Clash during my teenage rebellion (such as it was) and, as I matured, my tastes were also changing. I went to see the Rolling Stones in concert, and I've had mild flings here and there with other bands and other types of music, but Tom has long been my 'bestie'. That relationship grew serious when I lived in Switzerland and saw him in concert for the first time, and it was cemented when we became friends on the roads of the United States of America.

Unknowingly, my best pal Ron MacKenna and I both had girlfriends studying on the same course in Aberdeen while we were reporters at the *Press and Journal* in Inverness. We travelled back and forth independently of each other for weeks until the four of us met by chance at the Press Ball in the Drumossie Hotel just outside Inverness. Thereafter, we were inseparable.

Ron and I would head to Aberdeen two or three times a week in his red Fiat Panda or my blue Nissan Micra. We had barely left the town when Petty's 'I won't back down,' belted out from the cassette player. This was particularly appropriate during the bitter year-long strike at the paper, when we were both on a picket line for a year. Tom's gig at the Velodrome in Basel in 1992 was two hours of raucous rock and roll, interspersed with no little subtlety. That band holds something special for me, there can be no doubt.

Shortly after I picked up the guitar and managed to bang out a few chords, it was his songs I learned. The day I stood in front of a mirror and strummed out that amazing chord sequence at the start of 'Free Fallin'', I felt like a million dollars and I was instantly teleported to Ventura Boulevard. It's not my favourite song of all time, far from it. But no other piece of music can affect me in quite the same way.

At Malibu, where I saw the Pacific properly for the first time since I arrived, I had no option but to slide Tom out and Billy Joel in. As the Chevy's wheels hit the Pacific Coast Highway for the first time, he exhorted me to 'Say Goodbye to Hollywood'. This I did, somewhat reluctantly. The first leg was over.

I pumped north up the coast towards San Simeon, San Francisco and the first Inverness. My plan was to travel the Pacific Coast Highway, the road that hugs the sea and joins California's two major cities and which, after Route 66, is arguably the most famous and picturesque road in the USA.

There are large areas of poverty in Los Angeles, but Malibu isn't one of them. In truth, most Los Angelenos don't go near them. They just drive on by on the freeway, and on my many visits I haven't spent much time in them either. I once had to find a petrol station in a hurry and, while I was 'pumping gas', as the Americans call it, I looked around to see that I had chosen to top up the tank in the rough area of Inglewood in south central LA. The attendant was in a small shack, which looked like the kind of police station you used to see in Northern Ireland, all corrugated iron and barbed wire. She sat behind a grille with, I imagined, a loaded machine gun across her lap. She took my cash first, through a tiny slit in the bottom of the barricade, then flicked a switch to allow me to get fuel. 'You're not from around here, are you?' she said.

Where I most noticed poverty in LA was in the shops. Of course, I don't mean Rodeo Drive and places like Glendale mall, just a few miles west from Pasadena, and the Santa Clarita mall, a few miles east, which are clean and posh. The clientele there ranges from the rich bitch to the middle class. There, you have the big shops: the Penney's and the Sears and the others. Mobility is the key in LA, and public transport doesn't really encourage those who don't have a car to get to the posh parts. If you have a job, then the chances are you have a car. If you have a job but no car, then I don't give much for your commute. The place is vast. People may come to these malls to shop, or they may just come here to hang out. The poor don't shop here.

As a good Scotsman, I love a bargain, and good bargains proliferate at shops like K-Mart and Walmart. These stores are massive, and often contain a supermarket as well as a hardware store, a DIY store, a clothing store, a gun shop and much else. I love them. Everything is of good quality and reasonably priced. They stock fashionable things, but with unfashionable labels at seriously unfashionable prices. The shops are generally situated in working-class areas of towns and cities, and almost always on a bus route.

Every now and then, I receive an e-mail entitled 'Walmartians' with a link to pictures of the poor souls who shop at K-Mart's rival, Wal-Mart, highlighting perhaps a bizarre hairdo or outlandish fashion statement. Sometimes these people have a trolley full of doughnuts or dogfood. And while these pictures are superficially, and grotesquely, funny, whenever I see these emails I pause and think about the humanity behind them. I am lucky. I have a good job and the ability to travel. I love and am loved. Most importantly, I have my health.

There is a K-Mart in the Rosemead area of Los Angeles, which is the one I have used the most. On one of my visits there, I noticed a queue of people waiting to use the free internet terminals. I suppose this is another way of gauging poverty here: no TV, no car, no job, no internet. I watched as a Hispanic family of three took turns to surf.

The mother was young, beautiful and pregnant again. She looked up images of cheap, gaudy jewellery. When it was dad's turn, he downloaded images of sports cars. The child, predictably, looked at cartoons. An hour or so later I saw them laden with bags of shopping and waiting at a bus stop across the main road.

There are no K-Marts in Malibu. Instead, off to the left is the Pacific
Ocean and mile after mile of white beach beneath high cliffs. It was in
Malibu that Jim Rockford and his dad Rocky lived in a caravan in the
1970s TV series, 'The Rockford Files'. That made sense, because there's no
way anyone other than a millionaire is going to afford a home here.

The houses are remarkable, with some perched on stilts and others
embedded precariously in the rocky hillside. Some are modern designs
which might suit the taste of trendy types. Others are more traditional.
All have that priceless view out to the west over the endless ocean. Every
day is blue sky and blue sea. Every night is a sunset to behold. Turning left
is a hazard, but I eventually managed to avoid the oncoming traffic, cut
across the highway and drive down to the shore.

Paradise Beach was not a misnomer, and I thought how lovely it would
be to stop and have lunch at the restaurant here. I was put off somewhat
by the $4 charge merely to park the Chevy. Similarly the 'Minimum $20
spend' sign stapled to the menu was off-putting. The restaurant was on
the beach. The food was great and the service fine. However, I couldn't
help but think that your visit was more about making them money than
serving you as a customer, which is not something you can say too often
about America in general and California in particular.

The beach was busy. There were suntans aplenty. Some bathers were
bearded and ponytailed, many were elderly. There was a proliferation
of tie-dye t-shirts and cut-off denim shorts and, of course, dozens of
surfboards. The sand was clean and the sea blue. The waves crashed up
the beach, and I was tempted to strip off and hurl myself into them. As
a consolation, I slipped off my deckshoes and wandered along barefoot,
relishing the sand and seawater between my toes. It would have been
lovely to lie there for the rest of the afternoon, but I wanted to see as much
as I could of the Pacific Coast Highway in daylight. To drive this road at
night was a waste.

The ocean teased you. You got a glimpse now and again, then it was
gone for an hour and more. You ducked and dived and bobbed and
weaved up the road until, at last, you paralleled it again. Heading north to
San Francisco and the first Inverness, I was full of hope and ambition and
happiness. How could anyone fail to be happy here?

Roy Orbison was on the CD player again with a track called 'Windsurfer'
which fitted perfectly with the view: the high cliffs, the golden beaches
and the waves crashing onto the shore. I raced away from Los Angeles,
through Oxnard, Ventura and Santa Barbara.

The sun was sliding gently away to the west, and the light was golden as the afternoon slipped into evening and the evening passed into night. I needed to stop because I was full of emotion and very tired. This road is a full five-sense experience. To travel north towards San Francisco while looking at nothing more than the tail lights of the car in front would be heinous. There aren't too many inns on the route, so I booked ahead and checked in at the Morgan hotel in San Simeon.

I was 'plumb tuckered out', as the Americans say. What I needed was a few pages of the Frederick Forsyth I was reading, a hot shower, a splash of Brut, a clean shirt and, like any good Scotsman, a drink. I had worked up a thirst and, happily, next door to the hotel was a Mexican restaurant called El Chorlito, with a tempting menu and, more importantly, bottles of ice-cold beer glistening in the heat.

The Morgan is a splendid hotel which was named after Julia Morgan, an American architect born in the 1850s and who designed more than 700 buildings in a prolific career. An avowed feminist, many of her designs were for organisations such as the YWCA, but critics say the highlight of her career was the work she did here at San Simeon. I was heading to see it in the morning.

The hotel rooms are decorated in pastel greens and yellows. The furniture is dark wood and there are fireplaces in the corner. On the walls of the lobby, corridors and rooms are prints of plans she had drawn up for her many projects throughout her career. The prints are fascinating, and in keeping with the genteel theme of the whole place.

This is what I now know to be a 'boutique' hotel. That's modern speak for 'quite posh'. By now, you'll know that I'm an unreconstructed Scotsman and posh hotels don't impress me. All I need in a hotel is a clean bed and a shower. A lock on the door would be a bonus, I suppose. I wouldn't thank you for a TV, because I never travel anywhere without a small transistor radio and several books. I'm quite happy in one of the many chains of unspeakable motels you get in the United States.

I rolled out onto the freeway, briefly heading south again, back towards LA, through the dun-coloured fields. My next port of call could just be seen, seductively peeking out from a cluster of buildings surrounded by palms, atop a serious hill. It's not as well signposted as it might be, given it is a major American attraction. The brown arrow hits you as something of a surprise as you roll down the freeway. A few hundred yards off the main road is the visitor centre and car park. This must have been my sixth visit to Hearst Castle, but I didn't care. I couldn't wait to get inside again.

'And where is your accent from?' asked a man in leathers and a Harley Davidson cap. He must have heard my voice as I bought my ticket at the entry point.

'I'm from Scotland,' I said, puffing out my chest proudly and hearing Frankie Miller sing 'Caledonia' off in the distance somewhere. Before they could tell me that they too were Scotch (or Irish or Welsh), I asked them where they were from.

'Washington,' he replied. 'My wife and I are riding home after going down to San Diego to see our daughter. This is the weather to be on a Harley.' I got the impression I was meant to say 'Gee, it's a long way from Washington to California', but even I know the difference between Washington State, up the coast, and Washington DC.

We jumped on a bus at the base station and rolled up the hill towards the Castle. The road was narrow and twisted and turned through the grounds, and shortly we saw the Castle perched on a cliff. Then the bus twisted and turned away, and it disappeared again. We passed the private airport, complete with mile-long runway and hangar, before heading off through fields towards the summit.

Hearst Castle belonged to William Randolph Hearst, a billionaire newspaper magnate who grew up on a ranch nearby. He loved animals so much that he built the biggest private zoo in the world, which at one point housed sixty species, including lions, bears and llamas. Now there are just four, among them zebras. But the zoo was just one of his many indulgences.

Long before he could inherit his millionaire father's fortune, Hearst set about making his own. He started in newspapers but quickly branched out into the new media of the day: radio and the movies. He spent six months of the year at his Castle and invited A-list guests to stay. His particular favourite was Marion Davies, a Hollywood star who became Hearst's lover while his wife was safely out of the way in New York. Their relationship was long and complicated, and he had something of a fixation with her. Latterly, they lived together openly at a time when such extra-marital affairs were rarely conducted publicly.

The Castle was started in 1919 and, despite Julia Morgan's best efforts and an unlimited budget, Hearst's excesses and flamboyant desires meant the project was never finished. When the couple first met, he told her he wanted to build a chalet on the hilltop because he was too old to camp there any more. When Hearst hired Julia Morgan, she asked how long the contract would be. His response was that she would be on the staff for a couple of years. It didn't work out that way. He was the worst of men: an obsessive-compulsive with billions of dollars in the bank. He changed things repeatedly. The upshot was that she stayed with the project for twenty-eight years until 1947, when he left to live in Los Angeles because of ill health. He died in 1951.

It's difficult to describe the place. It's not a castle, it's not a palace. It's a collection of buildings which Hearst confusingly referred to as 'The Ranch' and officially named 'La Cuesta Encantada', Spanish for 'The Enchanted Hill'. Hearst travelled far and wide, especially to a Europe shattered by war, and swept up artworks which nowadays would be considered priceless and untouchable by private collectors. Sometimes his purchases dictated the scale of the buildings, not the other way round. He bought some ceilings which were too big for the rooms which Morgan had designed. There are incongruities everywhere: modern fixtures and fittings beside medieval tapestries. The Castle and its estate occupy a quarter of a million acres, and were gifted to the state of California in 1957. His art collection is still largely intact, although he has sold many millions of pounds worth of artefacts.

'Where is the visitor from Scotland?' asked a guide. I am quite shy, despite my day job in front of TV cameras, and I nervously shuffled forward and timidly lifted my hand into the air, cursing the bikers from Washington. Word must have got out.

'I have leaflets in Hebrew, Serbo-Croat, Cantonese and Polynesian French. Sadly I have none in Scotch,' said Robert Watson, our tour guide, slapping my back with a battering ram.

I bristled instantly, but my anger quickly dissipated. He had worked here for thirty years and commuted every day from San Luis Obispo, just down the coast. 'Maybe one day I'll get a proper job,' he quipped. 'People often ask me what that lake is over there,' he chuckled, pointing towards the azure Pacific Ocean. 'Someone else asked me why Hearst built this place so far away from the visitor centre. You've got to laugh.'

Bob's patter continued as we walked. 'I was doing a tour once and this man was on his cellphone. I was listening with half an ear to his conversation. "I'm in California," said the man. "I'm in a big house, it used to be owned by the guy who made millions in the car rental business, you know, William Randolph Hertz."'

'I love Scotland,' said Bob, as we parted, 'but I haven't got as far as Inverness. I'd sure like to go though. I cycled around Scotland but the summer of 1980 wasn't great for cycling. It was a little moist. Still I can say that I went up the Wallace Monument in Stirling before Mel Gibson did, and I know you don't pronounce "Milngavie" the way you spell it.' Good old Bob, I said to myself. I could have cheered. My kind of American.

*   *   *

Hearst was to American newspapers what Lord Beaverbrook was to Britain's. Our family home was always full of newspapers, and this may have been what prompted me to become a journalist. My mother had Beaverbrook's old broadsheet *Scottish Daily Express* delivered every day and the *Inverness Courier*, where I started my newspaper career, was delivered on Tuesdays and Fridays. Being a good Labour man, my dad would bring home the *Daily Record* every night. That pile of newsprint was augmented by the *Sunday Express* and the *Sunday Post*. I was never short of reading material.

This was long before daytime television, so my father's old Marconiphone radio was always on. I would get home from school at lunchtime just in time for the 'World at One', presented by William Hardcastle. I implicitly trusted his tobacco-encrusted voice, which took me through the day's events while I ate my lunch. I would return to school at 2pm having been fully briefed about the fall of Saigon, Watergate or the latest strike by British miners. I found it fascinating. It whetted my appetite for finding out more about the world and what was going on where. I had a good, hard news nose by the age of ten.

I loved toys, football and my bike, and I played as much as any kid. But I always wanted to know what it was like in Rhodesia or Bangladesh or Argentina. I would lie on the floor in the living room with the *Express* open and I would read it as best I could. Occasionally, I'd ask my parents what 'free collective bargaining' or 'unilateral declaration of independence' meant.

The radio was never on when I came home from school. Instead, I would watch kids' programmes on TV before the news came on at 6pm. Watching something else was never entertained by my parents: they were avid news viewers. I grew to love it. One day, I imagined, it would be pretty cool to work in television news.

*   *   *

I slid the shift into drive and headed north again along Route One, through fruit fields and vineyards, with the Pacific to the left. I crossed the Bixby Bridge, a spectacular concrete structure built across the gorge at Big Sur around the time Hearst was at the peak of his powers. It's one of the tallest single-span arch bridges on the planet, and was a feat of engineering well ahead of its time. The view of the bridge from a distance is startling and is often seen in car commercials. It adds to the landscape rather than scars it, and the vistas from its arch out to sea is awe-inspiring.

You don't think the beauty of the coast can be bettered, but you change your mind pretty quickly when you roll into downtown San Francisco. When I first visited in the 1980s, I was a wide-eyed boy. Today I am a grizzled veteran of 'the city by the bay'. But it still makes my jaw drop.

There were no available hotel rooms in San Francisco, so I navigated onto the Bay Bridge and rattled over to Oakland. This was a good thing because it meant a splendid view of the city by the bay, from the city across the bay. My unspeakable motel chain had a branch here, and there were plenty of vacancies. It offered me a waterfront room with a view out to a marina, ferries dotting back and forth across the water, the bridge and San Francisco itself. But the bridge was small beer compared to the daddy of all bridges, the Golden Gate, beyond which lay my goal: the first Inverness of my trip.

San Francisco has a decent public transport system, but the best way to see the city and its environs was in the Chevy. Downtown has the same gridiron pattern as most US cities, but it also has a few interesting twists and turns. What stand out are the steep slopes on which are built many of the city's roads. A vista like the one afforded to the first settlers wasn't going to be squandered by something as paltry as a couple of hills. They didn't build somewhere else because it was a shade too steep here. They just dug in their heels and started driving piles.

Today, the colourful wooden board houses which line the residential streets are a joy to behold. Those on the many crossroads all seem to have a turret room with a window on the corner. Above each thoroughfare are spiders' webs of electricity and phone lines criss-crossing, while below are the steel rails of the streetcars which ply their trade up and down this old city.

I drove around the most famous neighbourhoods. such as Haight Ashbury and Nob Hill, surveying the properties and that view out to the bay, with dozens of white-sailed yachts bobbing on the blue water, the Golden Gate Bridge and Alcatraz.

Alcatraz is the subject of myth and lore, of film drama and crime fiction. But right out there in the bay, staring back at me, is the long, thin island with a cluster of buildings, a water tower and a couple of chimneys, which bears that dreadful name.

I turned the Chevy out onto Van Ness, the main north-south avenue, and headed north to the waterfront. Gradually, the real San Franciscans were replaced by tourists, camera-slung and guidebook-hugging hordes from across the planet. They, like me, were heading for the city's main visitor attraction, Fisherman's Wharf.

It is worth seeing, and I guess that in San Francisco you should at least pass through it. But Fisherman's Wharf is entirely man-made and wholly tacky and, while it serves its purpose, it is the kind of place I would happily avoid. It has rows of shops and restaurants which are crammed into the wooden environs of an area of the San Francisco waterfront. They are all nautically themed and have unlikely pseudo-maritime names, like 'Neptune's'. And, while they look pleasant enough, they are very expensive and gaudy and not the kind of place where I would want to spend time, far less money. But it's from here you take the boat trips out into the bay, to Alcatraz and the Golden Gate Bridge beyond.

Most endearing here is the wildlife. In the little marinas which surround Fisherman's Wharf, there are dozens of wooden pontoons upon which lie colonies of seals. The tourists coo and cluck at the animals, which respond by honking. They honk in every sense. The stench of seal urine is overpowering.

Having been here many times before, I gave the brown mammals a cursory glance before joining the lengthy queue to buy a ticket for the boat trip out to Alcatraz. On the main road opposite Fisherman's Wharf stand hundreds of less official and therefore much cheaper tourist shops. I think this sort of place is more human and much less contrived These buildings were once waterfront warehouses, and each time I see the wooden structures I think of John Steinbeck's *Cannery Row,* although the book was set down the coast in Monterey.

Despite the bright sunshine, it wasn't too warm. San Francisco has its own micro-climate, which prompted Mark Twain to opine that the coldest winter of his life was his summer here. As the tourist boat headed out into the bay, I felt the cold once again. When the daunting shape of Alctatraz loomed ever closer, it made me shiver.

You vie for sea room in San Francisco Bay with any number of vessels from tiny yachts to warships to huge bulk carriers. Alcatraz is little more than a mile away from shore, and you are afforded views of San Francisco city, its skyline dominated by the Transamerica Pyramid and Coit Tower. To the east you can see Berkeley and Oakland, to the north the little town of Sausalito and, to the west, the Golden Gate Bridge.

Alcatraz has been many things: a lighthouse, a military camp, an arsenal, a nature reserve, a prison and now a museum. The bay was first charted in 1775 by Juan Manuel de Ayala, a Spanish naval officer who played a major part in European navigation and exploration in California. He was the first European to enter San Francisco Bay, and he named the island 'La Isla de los Alcatraces', Spanish for 'the island of the pelicans'.

Your angst increases as the boat nears the island. You feel that you have left the civilised world behind as you disembark. The landing stage is the only part of the tour which affords you any kind of comfort, with a small shop, a smoking area and a toilet block. The rest of the place pulls no punches.

The first role Alcatraz enjoyed was as a lighthouse station but, when the island was acquired by the United States from Mexico after the Spanish-American War, President Millard Fillmore decreed that it be used for military purposes. He had a point. The island was well placed to provide bombardment against shipping which attempted to enter the bay, or a defence against ground troops who tried a landward assault on the city. The obvious problems it faced, however, were its propensity for being besieged and its issues with resupply if San Francisco ever fell. Initially, around 200 soldiers and a battery of cannons were stationed on the island, but that was increased dramatically during the Civil War. In the end, however, no military gunfire ever came from Alactraz.

Its lasting use was as a prison. The first inmates were brought here during the Civil War when Confederate sympathisers and soldiers were imprisoned. In 1933 the island was first used as a federal penitentiary, a role it held until 1963 when cost forced the government to close it.

Alcatraz was considered to be escape-proof. San Francisco was so close and, on the face of it, prisoners had a short swim to freedom. But even in the height of summer the water is desperately cold and, regardless of the temperature, the currents are so severe that even the strongest swimmer would drown long before he reached dry land. And there were sharks with which to contend. But, before they were able to dive into the water, would-be escapers had to get out of their locked cells, escape from the high-security buildings and cut through or climb gates and fences.

During its existence as a prison, there were fourteen attempted escapes involving thirty-seven prisoners. Two dozen were captured before they had managed to get very far. Another thirteen died in the process. Two were known to have drowned during their attempts, because their bodies were found. Another five entered the water without leaving it on the other side, and they are officially listed as missing. Six were shot dead.

Also frequent were the deaths on the rock. Eight prisoners were murdered by other inmates, and five killed themselves. Fifteen men died of natural causes. Given the desperate and violent men incarcerated here, it was obvious that there would be tensions. To keep racial aggravation to a minimum, Alcatraz operated a strict segregation policy, with black men occupying a cluster of cells. They ate together, exercised together, and even had their hair cut together by black barbers.

More than 1,500 inmates could be held there but the jail was never full. The average number was 260, the highest 320. The two most famous prisoners in the rock's history were Chicago gangster Al Capone and Robert Stroud, the so-called 'birdman of Alacatraz'.

Oddly enough, Capone was not sent to Alcatraz because he was a violent gangster. Prosecutors couldn't pin that on him but finally secured his conviction on tax avoidance. The Supreme Court ruled that illegally-earned income was taxable and, as Capone had paid nothing, he was jailed for eleven years.

Aged just thirty-three, and with an estimated wealth of more than a billion dollars by today's standards, Capone faced challenges even greater than over a decade behind bars. He was ill with syphilis and gonorrhea, and he had a cocaine addiction which caused severe withdrawal symptoms.

It became evident during his time on Alcatraz that his illness was more serious than previously thought. He never sought treatment for his syphilis because he didn't want his wife to know about his serial philandering. Consequently, it spread to his brain, eroding much of his mental capacity. Following his neurosyphilis diagnosis, he was treated at a number of hospitals in the United States after his release, and he died peacefully in his luxury mansion in Florida in 1947, aged just forty-eight.

Robert Stroud was also sent to Alcatraz for unusual reasons. Like Capone, he was a brutal man who killed many men without batting an eyelid. He took his first life in 1909 when he was a teenage pimp in Alaska and murdered a bartender who had failed to pay one of his girls for her services. Stroud handed himself in, and was jailed for twelve years.

Although he showed little signs of remorse, while at Leavenworth Prison in Kansas in 1920 he found a nest containing three injured sparrows, and he nursed them back to life. He developed an interest in ornithology and a new governor encouraged this interest, hoping to show that his establishment was a progressive prison which helped inmates to rehabilitate. Stroud was allowed tools, and he built bird cages. He began to breed hundreds of canaries which were sold to inmates, guards and visitors.

He wrote a book called *Diseases of Canaries*, the manuscript of which was smuggled out of jail and published. It became regarded in ornithological circles as an expert work, and his research, all conducted in his solitary confinement cell, led to the discovery of a cure for septicaemia in his favoured feathered species.

However, Stroud was eventually incarcerated in solitary confinement on Alcatraz between 1942 and 1959 and was never allowed to keep birds on the rock which, ironically, is today a bird reserve.

The cell blocks contained hundreds of cells on three levels. Light was provided by a narrow strip of glass tiles in the ceiling. There were four blocks. No cell on Alcatraz was built against an outside wall. If you stand in a cell and stretch out your arms, you can touch each wall. Each contained a steel bed, a porcelain toilet and a sink. The only modicum of creature comfort came from a tiny steel bench embedded in the wall behind a tiny table. There was no privacy for inmates even on the toilet, as the cell front was comprised of bars with a sliding door.

In Alcatraz there is an all-pervading sense of sadness. There was little hope of getting out, and the only chances a prisoner had of leaving were medical transfers, or to be well behaved for long enough to merit a move to a general prison.

At one end of the cell block there is a barred window with a view across to San Francisco. As I gazed out, a small yacht cut across the bay, its white sail billowing gracefully in the wind. I stood there for a minute or two and thought about how despairing it must have felt for inmates, particularly those with no hope of freedom, to have had this glimpse of the outside world.

I boarded the ferry back to San Francisco, and said farewell to Alcatraz. The small yacht had passed under the Golden Gate Bridge, and I shifted

my gaze to squint at the bridge through the setting sun. My excitement
was mounting. Tomorrow I was heading for my first Inverness.

I couldn't tell you how many times I have driven over the Golden Gate
Bridge, and neither could I tell you about the views.

I have been trammelled by stark panic on each journey, petrified that
I might be involved in a multi-vehicle pile-up and end up in the ocean
below. I am sure the seascape is scintillating, but I have been too busy
keeping my eyes on the car in front, the road ahead and the rear-view
mirror. You are aware of the vast red metal structure, the azure blue of
the sky and the dark greeny-blue of the sea, but beyond that I can tell you
little. One day I will go across as a passenger, sit back and relax.

The last stop before crossing the bridge heading north is a visitor centre
and a car park, where you can take pictures of the Bridge, drink coffee
and buy tacky souvenirs. This is possibly the last contact many people
have with humanity before they hurl themselves off. The Golden Gate
Bridge is a favoured suicide location, and you can understand why. It is
starkly beautiful, and offers at least momentary solitude. And there can
be no doubt about the result.

Well, this is what I thought, until one morning I was listening to the
radio news and I heard an interview with a man who had jumped and
had survived. It was one of the most startling pieces of radio I have heard.
The reporter was Maggie Shiels, who started in broadcasting, like I did,
at Moray Firth Radio in Inverness. She is now a BBC correspondent in
Los Angeles.

The man spoke passionately to her about his depression and about why
he felt his life was so worthless. He described walking up onto the bridge,
and then pausing briefly to say goodbye to the world before he leapt off.
But then came the really interesting part. He said that the moment he
jumped, he changed his mind. He realised how precious his life was and,
as he fell, he understood that he had made a disastrous mistake.

He believed that strong winds arrested his fall and, although he hit
the water at great speed and suffered multiple fractures in the impact,
he was rescued by a passing yachtsman and rushed to hospital, where
he underwent emergency surgery. Nowadays, he works as a suicide
counsellor, trying to talk people out of jumping by telling them his story.

Immediately to the north of the Golden Gate Bridge is the little town of
Sausalito, which gives a splendid reverse view of the Bridge, Alcatraz and
San Francisco. There is clearly money here. This is where city dwellers

come to relax or park their yachts. The waterfront is serene and perfect. It leads to a smaller road which takes you to a viewing point under the Bridge, affording more views of San Francisco Bay. I vowed to pause longer on my return journey. Right now, a strong magnet was pulling me north.

Los Angeles and San Francisco are fascinating cities. I have visited both many times, to the extent that I seldom need a map any more. By comparison with these conurbations, my destination on this visit is small fry. But to me, this first step was a profound one.

I was on a journey of self-examination which was starting here in California. In a way, Los Angeles and San Francisco had been sideshows: tasters and warm-ups for the real deal. My lengthy trip would see me cross this continent and visit five special places named after my home town. I wanted to see the country for myself, meet the people, feel the heat and cold, and smell the smells of the United States. And, between here and the Atlantic, and across this great nation's four times zones, I would not fly.

Route 101 is a continuation of the Pacific Coast Highway, the main north-south highway which cuts through California. The sea views had now largely gone, gradually giving way to pine forests. The weather, which in my experience is seldom all that warm in the San Francisco area, was now even cooler. I didn't need to scan the map. I had virtually memorised the atlas and, as I cut off 101, a major freeway, the landscape changed once more. I was again on a normal road with one lane in each direction, and it twisted and turned dramatically. As I approached my first Inverness, the weather was becoming colder and wetter, and there was a particularly Scottish mist drifting in from the sea.

Then I saw water again, but this time it was the Pacific on my left and not San Francisco Bay on my right. Suddenly I felt ill, similar to the motion sickness I have felt many times flying in an RAF Hercules. On board these aircraft you sit facing inwards rather than forwards, and they have no windows. I must have been paying too much attention to the road and not watching the horizon, and I thought I was going to throw up. I cracked the window and rummaged in my pocket for a mint. This wasn't good. I knew my first Inverness was just a few miles away, and on my arrival I didn't want to be vomiting out of the Chevy window.

As quickly as it came, the queasiness went. The road was straight and shining and, like a green beacon ahead of me, was the road sign I'd been looking for: Inverness.

It is small. I counted two shops, two restaurants and a post office. And, well, that's it. I sat down in Priscilla's Café on the main drag and ordered half a dozen oysters. I made like I ate oysters all the time, but anyone watching closely would have seen right through me as I gagged my way through my bucket of cold seafood. Still, I'd heard of their aphrodisiac properties.

I got chatting to a likeable couple who were visiting from San Francisco. We sat on the terrace of the restaurant and shot the breeze. Duncan Seibert was in IT, and his wife Gail sold insurance. On previous visits, the United States was the land of plenty, and I was exhorted to buy what I liked on credit, eat as much as I could, throw away what I couldn't eat, and waste fuel if I wanted because there was always plenty more, and there were always enough jobs and money around. Not any more. Now the TV was full of ads about cutting costs, saving fuel and finding work.

'Nobody wants to see people suffer, not ordinary people,' he said. 'But bankers made a lot of cash out of selling mortages and giving credit to people who couldn't possibly pay it back. Now it's the bankers who are getting a dose.'

The couple come to Inverness from San Francisco for the weekend because they like the beaches, they like the cycling and they like the oysters. I tried not to gag, and I rallied a bit when Duncan told me that he liked Scotch whisky. With a Christian name like his, I would have thought so.

Next door was Vladmir's Czech restaurant. I've been all around the world but I don't think I have ever eaten at a Czech restaurant, even when I was in the Czech Republic. When I visited Prague, I don't recall eating anything at all, focusing instead on drinking beer. Vladmir's was closed, but I earmarked it for dinner later on. Also closed were the Post Office and Bellwether shop next door, which sold expensive wooden toys, clothes and leather goods. So I padded across the road to the Inverness General Store and had a good look round.

It appeared to be the centre of the local community. It sold everything from books and groceries to alcohol and DIY accessories. There was a stream of customers during the ten minutes I was inside. I didn't want to distract him from business, so I bided my time before I collared the owner for a chat. I'm glad I did, although after a few seconds his accent had floored me. I gave up. I couldn't place it.

Raj Parmar was originally from Richmond in south-west London. He grew up in the USA and married in the UK. He now lives in Inverness, and is settled here with his wife and two children. He goes back to Richmond once a year.

'Life in Inverness is very good. It's very different from anywhere else in California. It's very safe and the ideal place to bring up children. There is a fantastic atmosphere here and that is because it's a tourist town. I've been here for twenty-five years and although I love going to London every year for a few weeks, this is home and I wouldn't want to go back to the UK permanently,' he said, confidently.

Raj was busy. I didn't want to get in his way, so I said a silent cheerio and ducked out onto the main street. Actually, calling it a main street was doing it way too much justice. Downtown Inverness California comprises a cluster of five buildings.

I stood in the middle of the road and looked up and down. I wouldn't say I was thinking the first Inverness was a bit of a disappointment, but I had imagined there would be a lot more to it than this. Raj told me there were between 600 and 700 houses in and around Inverness, but most of them were rented out. I didn't think there were that many residents. In the summer season though, with the surf high and the sun hot, it was probably very different. These houses were obviously scattered around the countryside.

I toyed with the idea of sending a postcard of my first Inverness to my mum in the one true Inverness, with a stamp bought and postmarked in the post office here, but it was closed. As I peered through the glass to try to see any signs of life, I noticed a couple of notices pinned to the outside of the building. One of these made me jump. The first was a pretty standard warning to residents to be sensible about watering their gardens because 'our creeks are drying up'. The other was written in bold black type and had the look and feel of a government public information office warning.

It spoke of a mussel quarantine affecting the western seaboard of the US from Alaska all the way down to Mexico. It added that mussels were only to be used for fish bait and were not safe for human consumption because they may contain poison. The notice was signed by the Marin county health officer, on behalf of the California department of public health. I gulped. Did this quarantine cover the six phlegmy oysters I'd scoffed down at Priscilla's? I stood still for a moment, listening hard for any tummy chortling, but thankfully there was nothing.

I jumped back into the Chevy, which I had parked behind Raj's place, and drove off to explore. In Inverness itself, the weather had brightened up and it was very pleasant. However. the moment I pulled away it became cold again, and clouds appeared. Rain flecked the windscreen.

There wasn't much else to Inverness. I passed St Columba's Episcopal church, with a sign outside which invited me to join the worship on Sundays and Wednesdays. Then there was the Inverness Yacht Club which also had a sign outside. While the church wanted you to come in, I got the impression that the yacht club didn't. There was a big 'Members Only' board outside and another little board of club rules attached to the gate. Thanks, but no thanks.

I drove on along Sir Francis Drake Boulevard and continued out of town. The reason the road was named after Sir Francis quickly became evident, as just a few miles away is Point Reyes, the windiest place on the Pacific Coast and the second-foggiest in the USA. It was here in 1580 that the English nobleman landed during his circumnavigation.

During the drive to the end of the peninsula, I passed another sign which made me scratch my head. It was a board indicating that I was about to pass the 'Historic Lifesaving Station Cemetery'.

The further I drove, the more rugged became the terrain and the worse became the weather. The mist descended and a film of rain covered the windscreen. I stuck the air conditioning on to heat for a minute or two. It was that bad. Out to my left was the Pacific Ocean showing me an occasional white-capped wave. I was more than happy to be a landlubber in a nice warm, dry Chevy rather than an ancient mariner out there with nothing but a star to steer by.

I didn't last long up at Point Reyes lighthouse. I stuck my nose outside the Chevy for a minute or two, for the sake of form if nothing else, and then dived back inside. I wasn't dressed for these conditions but dozens were, and there were crowds of outdoorsy types from San Francisco and beyond who were here for the weekend, taking the vapours. I saluted them, and drove back to town.

On the way back to Inverness, it became evident that the landscape – the greenery, its proximity to the water on the landward side and, of course, the weather – was strikingly similar to that of the one true Inverness. It reminded me of Loch Ness or Loch Duntelchaig, the reservoir from which the town drinks. I started to feel a shade homesick. I also started to feel a shade hungry, having only had six shells full of phlegm at lunchtime. I wanted to get back to Vladimir's to try whatever Czech delicacy was on offer. Sadly, I couldn't sample any Czech beer, not with the Chevy to pilot home.

The restaurant looked great from the outside. It was festooned with US and Czech flags, and had a railing around its terrace like the ones to which cowboys lashed their horses. There was a large sign showing an ancient flag-waving horseman atop a white charger and, in a bizarre touch, the posts which held it up were festooned with skis. I would soon find out why.

I scanned inside for Vladimir, expecting to see a man with high cheekbones and swirling moustaches. I racked my brain trying to remember what Czech people looked like having only been to the Czech Republic once to see a Scotland football match in 1999. I'm ashamed to say that apart from a brief visit to the Charles Bridge, I spent pretty much the whole week in one bar or another with the tartan army.

Sitting down at a red-and-white gingham cloth-bedecked table, I asked if Vladimir was in tonight.

'I am Vladia,' said the waitress. 'My father died some years ago.'

My first experience of Czech cuisine was memorable. I had a starter of borscht, a beetroot and cream soup, with salad and dumplings, followed by lamb shank. But the best part of the evening was sitting with Vladia and chatting over coffee after the last customer had left.

'I was born in Inverness and lived here until I was nineteen,' she said. 'It was a dream world for a kid, the ideal place to grow up. We swam in the bay and we walked barefoot in middle of road because there were no cars. It was like a playland. Like all things in life, I didn't realise quite how good it was until I left.'

I thought about what Raj had said earlier, and remembered my own childhood in the one true Inverness. It too had been an idyllic upbringing in the most beautiful of places. I felt homesick once again, and thought back to those memorable days when the summers all seemed to be scorching hot and the winters long and snowy. My first Inverness reminded me of home. The surroundings were so similar.

Old Vladimir Nevl had been quite a boy. In 1956 he came from Australia to California, where he met his future wife who hailed from Inverness. He started what would be the family business in 1960. Prior to that, the premises had been an English pub called the Drake Arms. Before that, it had been a general store and a candy store, then it had burnt to the ground.

Vladimir had tried to escape Nazi-occupied Czechoslovakia, and he crossed the mountains into Germany on skis, thus the unusual sign outside. But things didn't go to plan. He was picked up by German soldiers who, understandably, thought he was a spy. He was interrogated and thrown into jail before being sent to a concentration camp. After a time there, he managed to convince the authorities that he wasn't a spy, and he got a job in the kitchens.

After the War he made it to France but returned to Czechoslovakia just in time for the Soviet invasion in 1948. Cursing his luck – and his timing – he left again, this time to Australia.

'When I was young I heard there was another Inverness, in Scotland, and that it looked similar,' said Vladia. 'At school we learned all about the Loch Ness monster. You will have seen it, right?'

Actually, I have. I was only a baby, but technically I have. My mother's family were from Glenurquhart where they had a holiday cottage, which we went to frequently when I was a child. One day, when driving back to Inverness from Drumnadrochit, my mother saw something in Loch Ness. She stopped in a layby and pulled out a cine camera, which my father had bought to record my first steps. Holding me in the crook of her arm, she tried to film the water. In the end, the camera recorded only wobbly shots of the Loch, although it was sent to the Royal Zoological Society for analysis.

My mother's story has never changed in fifty years. What she saw that day in the Loch was long, hump-backed and most definitely a living creature. Obviously, I was there and would also have been looking out over the Loch, but I can remember nothing.

'I studied the local history,' she added. 'I believe some of the original settlers here were from Inverness in Scotland and that's where the name came from.'

I asked her about the Inverness she came back to when Vladimir died and she took on the family business.

'It's very sleepy here. Lots of people from Berkeley bought their second or summer homes here and there are some who live here all year round. The population doubles in the summer and the main street, although small, can get very busy. There used to be another restaurant and a gas station here and there were more visitors then.

'Some call Inverness an island in time because there's only one way in and one way out,' said Vladia. 'There are people up in the hills you never see and you don't even know exist. It's a nice place. My dad was a pillar of this community, he was an icon, an institution.' She stopped talking, and giggled.

'He was quite a character and very forthcoming. He didn't hold back, he said what he thought. If you weren't dressed properly to come in here', she gestured around the place, 'he'd tell you.'

By the time I left Inverness, my first of the trip, I was choking for a beer, Czech or otherwise. That, though, would be a luxury I'd have to reserve for my unspeakable motel and my looming date with my ageing lapdog. My route back to San Francisco wasn't a short one and I had much to mull over on the way.

Was this journey across the USA via the towns named after my home town, simply a middle-aged man's vain indulgence? Was I using the journey to find myself and, in so doing, save myself the cost of a ticket to India where that kind of discovery usually happens? Or was it just something that would be purely and simply fun?

The first Inverness was not a disappointment, far from it. But it had not been what I had been expecting at all. It had been much smaller than I had envisaged. It was no less lovely for its size and, as I drove out of town back towards 101, the Golden Gate Bridge, San Francisco and what some might term civilisation, I promised myself that one day I would come back here during the season and go hillwalking and birdwatching.

*   *   *

Radio as much as television formed my personality and tastes and, while those Mossend sleeping berth moments were my favourite childhood memories, they weren't my earliest. Somewhere deep in my subconscious is an image of myself as a toddler, sitting on my mother's lap in the living room of the family home in the one true Inverness. She is wearing a brown tweed skirt. I had that image in my mental databank long before I found an old family photograph album, which showed a picture of her in that precise garment. From memory, we weren't just sitting there, we were listening to the Marconiphone radio, and in my mind's ear she is singing along to Simon and Garfunkel.

That Marconiphone was a survivor. It was still on top of the sideboard in our house until a few years ago. My dad was parsimonious, to the point sometimes of being 'penny wise, pound foolish', but he was a real gadget freak. We were the first family I knew who had a cine camera and a colour TV. He insisted that we get a microwave oven and, when domestic stereos came out, he was first in line to get one. It was the same story with his digital watch. The microwave was so big it looked like a TV set and the stereo was a far cry from the digital appliances of today.

But it was switched on from first thing in the morning until we all left for work and school and, long before the advent of breakfast TV, it provided information and entertainment for a couple of hours every morning. Like so many people of the time, we tuned into Terry Wogan's breakfast show on BBC Radio Two.

Of course I knew there was jazz and I knew there was classical, folk and country and western. And while Terry played a broad spectrum of music, and introduced me to different artists and genres, he also unearthed songs which were quirky and gave them prominence. Without Terry Wogan we would not have had 'Floral Dance' by the Brighouse and Rastrick Brass Band, which got to number two in the UK charts. So he introduced me to brass bands. Without question, Fiddler's Dram and 'Daytrip to Bangor' would never have been the smash hit it was (number three in the charts) without Wogan, so he introduced me to folk music. Neither would songs like 'Lucky Stars' by Dean Freidman (number three) or 'Car 67' by Driver 67 (number seven) have made an impression on people.

However, his biggest protégé was probably one he'd rather forget, although clearly he had no influence on the timing of it all. Ultravox were on the scene. The New Romantic movement had quickly filled the void left by punk, and Midge Ure and his colleagues had started pumping out clever songs: well-produced, melodic and backed up by the new medium of the music videos. One of their first hits was the haunting ballad 'Vienna' and the accompanying black-and-white video showed Midge and co wearing long trenchcoats and doing their thing on glistening wet cobbles in the Austrian capital.

The song was released to critical acclaim, and rightly so. This was January 1981 and nobody had heard or seen anything like it before. It rocketed up the charts, destined, it seemed, to hit the number one spot. At the same time, Terry Wogan started playing the catchy but otherwise vacuous 'Shaddap you face' by Australian-Italian Joe Dolce, which unbelievably knocked John Lennon off the top spot and pipped Ultravox to number one. It stayed there for three weeks, by which time tastes had moved on and Roxy Music had taken over.

Wogan introduced me to so much more. Nat King Cole, Neil Diamond, Barbra Streisand, Hank Williams: the list goes on. The artist who had the most profound impact was Canadian singer-songwriter Gordon Lightfoot. He was in his forties when I first heard him and already a well-established artist. His guitar playing and intuitive lyrics had me hooked, and I love his music to this day. It gives me great pride to be able to lift a guitar now and play some of his songs, and I told him so when I met him after a gig in Glasgow.

Because I loved music, and was starting to understand more and more about different styles, my parents wanted me to learn an instrument. They granted me free access to their record collection, some of which I adored, and I was allowed to buy records when my pocket money had reached a sufficient level. And so it came to be that I would listen to my dad's James Last albums, my mum's Burl Ives records, then my own Abba 45s on the Marconiphone.

I vividly remember the day my mum took me to the Record Rendezvous in Inverness, an independent shop on Church Street, which survived for years into the download era, and bought me a copy of 'The Planets' by Holst. I couldn't wait to get it on the stereo. I was equally surprised when my overtly 'square' parents bought me a Boomtown Rats album that Christmas, without my even suggesting it.

The Record Rendezvous is now a café, and I am pleased that it has retained its large, orange LP-shaped doorhandles. I'm not bitter that it is no longer a record shop, because it has survived a lot longer than I thought it would in a world of Amazon and MP3 players.

I wanted to learn the guitar but my father said no. When I told them my second choice was the bagpipes, my parents just looked at each other aghast. Inverness had a piano teacher who was hugely popular and getting a spot with her was hard, although one was eventually secured. My parents sent me to many things as a kid – clubs, sport, arty stuff – and I dutifully went. But these piano lessons were hideous and I hated them from the start. I dug my heels in and begged to do anything else, but my parents refused.

The lessons were on a Monday afternoon at 4.30, and I just had enough time to get home from school and practise for ten minutes before heading back out the door again. I used to make myself ill over the weekend, knowing that this half hour was looming. By Sunday evening I was a wreck, and on Monday mornings I'd rather have climbed the gallows than go to school.

The teacher was an old dragon who had not an ounce of humour or warmth in her. And, even though I was a polite and happily co-operative little boy, she sparked a little fire of rebellion in me. I loved music but I didn't love her music. I wanted to go home and listen to Holst. Unbelievably, I went to her for years and even passed exams under her tutelage.

Then one Monday evening the phone rang, and she was on to my mother demanding to know where I was. To this day I swear she had told me there would be no lessons for a fortnight. But that particular afternoon she said the wrong thing at the wrong time to the wrong person.

'I can assure you my son is not a liar,' mum said. 'I don't appreciate that kind of tone,' was another response. 'If that's the way you feel, perhaps Michael should go to another teacher. Good afternoon.' The phone was slammed down.

At a cousin's wedding, round about the same time, the best man bottled out of doing his speech, He had had far too much to drink to calm his nerves beforehand, and was unable to fulfil his duties. My dad was volunteered to do the business, and stood up to speak. Totally unprepared, totally unrehearsed, clutching cards and telegrams he'd never seen before, he delivered a flawless gag-laden speech which was better than many a stand-up routine.

It was pitched perfectly for the bride and her family, the po-faced minister, and even the kids. People were rolling with laughter. As he sat down after proposing the toast to the bridesmaids, I can remember looking at him and thinking how proud I was. I felt exactly the same when my mum told the piano teacher to shove her lessons where the sun didn't shine.

Smiling smugly, thinking I'd won a watch by never having to endure the agony of piano lessons ever again, my mum brought me crashing back down to earth. She immediately lifted the receiver and phoned John MacLean, her cousin, who was the organist at the Methodist Church in Inverness. Within a week I was down at the church hall battering away at an old upright.

He was a lovely old man whom I'd known since early childhood. He and his wife lived in a corrugated iron bungalow beside the Culloden railway viaduct, a magnificent red sandstone structure which spans the River Nairn a few miles east of Inverness. I loved going there when I was a boy. It was near Culloden battlefield, it was in the woods and it was beside the railway!

After my first lesson, John led me through a maze of dark corridors into the body of the kirk. My jaw dropped open when, at the flick of a few switches, he illuminated the massive church organ. He beckoned me to sit, and soon my notes were filling the nave. It was awesome. Thereafter, I looked forward to my piano lessons because I knew that the last fifteen minutes of the hour would be spent like this. To this day I love listening to church organs. Equally, I adore the swirling sound of the Hammond organ, used by many rock, country and folk artists, including my man Tom Petty.

John was an elderly man but he knew popular culture. He loved football and, as a native of Fortrose, was a Ross County man. They are Inverness Caley's sworn enemies and we ribbed each other mercilessly. In his day he had been a great tennis player and knew the sport inside out, telling me discreetly one day that he had a crush on Tracy Austin. More importantly, he was well versed in modern music and knew about the Skids and the Stranglers and the Boomtown Rats, bands I listened to at that time.

He helped me re-discover my love of music and turn it into something physical and, for the first time in my life, piano lessons became fun. I am eternally grateful to him. Sadly, schoolwork got in the way of my music lessons, and after some years I had to concentrate on tedious things like O Grades and Highers. The piano in our house was sold when I had to shift my attention towards my books.

Decades later, I saw an advert in the paper for guitar lessons at Langside College in Glasgow. I had long since mastered the air guitar but never thought I would be able to play the real thing. I signed up. On the first night the classroom was full, but every week thereafter the numbers dwindled. The attrition rate is notoriously high in evening classes. But I stuck it out, and plucked and strummed my cheap guitar every week for the duration. It was a beginners' course but the teacher, Stef McGlinchey, was a first-class musician and knew exactly how to pitch it. When the first eight weeks was up, I signed on again. In all, I did the course four times.

I am nothing more than an adequate player but I love the guitar. For my fiftieth birthday I was given a Fender Telecaster and an Epiphone acoustic twelve-string. Nothing pleases me more today than picking them up and howling out a bit of Tom Petty or Gordon Lightfoot.

On the train home after each lesson with Stef I would think back to my piano teacher who nearly spoiled the whole thing for me, and to cousin John who rekindled the fire. I only wish my dad's love of electric gadgetry had extended to Fenders and that he'd agreed to what I'd asked. Instead, he had broken my heart by echoing the record company which had auditioned the Beatles in 1962 and knocked them back, saying guitars were on the way out.

*   *   *

The time had come to say goodbye to many things. First and foremost I
would no longer need the Chevy. I had other ideas. Farewell, too, to my
first Inverness, to San Francisco and to California. I was on foot again,
and I would have to find my own way across the bay by myself. I dived
down into Civic Centre metro station during the rush hour and joined
the throngs of people going home for the night.

It must be something about me. I must attract them. At the next station
a group of about eight Irish people, complete with dreadlocks, piercings,
tattoos, guitars and dogs, joined the train. We hadn't gone very far when
they burst into song. They looked very odd, and they were regarded with
horror by the commuters, but we had quite a jolly singalong as the train
trundled off towards Oakland.

When I got off at Lake Merritt station and trotted up to surface level, it
was my intention to hail a cab. An hour and more later I was still standing
there with my arm in the air, like some kind of Caledonian Statue of
Liberty. It was dark now and the bustle of the sidewalk had all but gone.
The commuters had disappeared, all safe and sound in their homes to
be replaced by night people, by beggars and rough-looking types. I am
no lily-liver, and I have seldom felt threatened in the US, but I knew
that the longer I waited here for a taxi, the more I stood out and the
more menacing the atmosphere was likely to get. I should have walked
while there was still some daylight because it was only three miles to the
unspeakable motel. Thankfully, a cab finally arrived.

I had asked at the metro station for the number of a taxi firm, and I
dialled it from a payphone. But the dispatcher was not hopeful. All the
cars were busy, she said. I was on their plot but she couldn't guarantee
when, or indeed if, they'd get to me tonight. This was desperately bad
news. Nearly two hours after I got off the metro, Ray came by and saved
my life. So grateful was I, that I was able to hail him (actually I ran
screaming into the traffic waving like crazy when I saw his light) and I
immediately hired him for the next leg of my journey. He dropped me at
my unspeakable motel, where I slept fitfully until 5am.

The first fingers of light were touching the sky in the east as I stood
in the chill outside the motel. My bill had been paid and my alarm call
booked the night before. But where the hell was Ray? Having promised
him a big tip, I couldn't believe for a second that he wouldn't show. My
sigh of relief was audible across San Francisco Bay when the lights of his
large Ford Crown Victor swung into the motel car park.

We were tootling along the freeway when he started to talk about himself. I immediately felt heart sorry for him. He was originally from New Delhi. He came to California in 2001 and lived in a trailer, a big caravan, with his mother, wife and three daughters. He told me he worked from 7am to 10pm. Every day. Now, I had already promised him a big tip the night before if he would pick me up, so I'm not sure if this was a sob story or not.

As Ray and I rolled towards the sunrise, I realised that he was another immigrant knocking his poor pan in while trying to make a better life for his family. I couldn't imagine the poverty he must have escaped in India to make this lifestyle attractive. I thanked him profusely and gave him $20 on top of the fare. I knew that if he had been late, or had not turned up at all, I would have been totally stuck.

Without Ray the next leg of my journey, my next Inverness – all of them, in fact – would not have happened.

CHAPTER TWO

Inverness, Illinois

Chicago, Chicago, that toddlin' town.

Frank Sinatra

It rolled into the station: silver, shiny and ten double-decker cars long. At its head were three locomotives, their power awe-inspiring, and their angry bellow a malevolent rumble as the train coasted to a halt along the length of the platform. This was the California Zephyr.

San Francisco has no main line railway station. Instead, trains head east from across the bay. My case had already been checked in, airport-style, here at Emeryville, and I would see it next in Chicago three days hence. I had only a small carry-on with me which, I would discover, was just as well.

As a railway addict, I felt a burst of excitement. This was virgin territory for me. I had flown and driven all over the USA and, while I had hopped on commuter trains here and there, this would be the first real American rail journey I had ever taken.

Bill Heath was one of those men who, when you meet for the first time, you feel you have known for ever. Moreover, you know that his friendship will be unselfish and understanding. He also reminded me of somebody. But who?

At six feet six inches tall, he was an imposing man, but the term 'gentle giant' could have been written for Bill. He was the attendant for sleeping car 0632 and a thirty-five-year veteran of Amtrak. He clipped my ticket and showed me to my tiny compartment, my home for the next three days.

Why is there never a cat around when you need to swing one? The compartment comprised two seats facing each other and a small table between them, with just enough room for my ageing lapdog. Printed into the table was a chessboard, or a 'checkers board' to Americans. Above the two seats was a bunk, propped at an angle and ready to be lowered into position when the time was right. Given my taxi-fuelled angst, I hadn't slept well the previous night and I felt that I would be hitting this bunk early tonight.

There was a power socket above one seat, ideal for the ageing lapdog, and, above the other, controls for the air conditioning, lights and PA volume. There was also a yellow knob which would ring a bell, should I need Bob's ministrations at any time.

'You're a lucky guy,' he said, as I surveyed my new home. 'There ain't nobody sharing with you and the place is yours all the way to Chicago.' Those were exactly the words I needed to hear. It was tiny, grimy and pretty threadbare, but it was all mine, and I wanted to enjoy this journey in peace and quiet.

I stashed my jacket in the tiny closet, removed the ageing lapdog, plugged it in and then buried my bag beneath the seat. That, and the holder for a coffee cup, was the sum total of my storage space. I then realised that the two seats folded down together to make another bunk. This room was for two people? A couple living in a room like this would find it challenging, especially if they were total strangers.

Pretty well the first thing announced over the PA system was the meal timings and where you could find the dining car. The train hadn't even yet left the station. I sat in contemplation.

One Inverness down, four to go. Since I'd flown into Los Angeles, I'd driven 1,500 miles. But now the Chevy was in the tender care of another hire car driver and, to reach the next Inverness, I was about to embark upon a 2,500-mile swing across the United States with someone else at the wheel. Although I have never written down an engine number in my life, the whole train experience completes me. My father was a railwayman all his days, and I grew up around trains. Every early adventure on which I ever embarked started and finished on a train.

Somewhere outside in Emeryville a whistle sounded, and big Bob shouted 'all aboard', just as they did in the movies. The three angry mammoths at the top of the train bellowed to be set free. Their master granted that wish, and let slip the leash. He pushed open the throttle and suddenly we were rolling. Rolling, too, were my tears. For some reason, I was whisked back to my childhood, to those adventures which started on the overnight train from the one true Inverness to London, and to my father, the funniest man I ever knew, who was taken from us far too early.

*   *   *

My father would only say so much about his wartime experiences. Like many servicemen, there were some things, about which he would not talk. But he was a great storyteller, including some of his own war and the yarns he made up when he was putting me to bed. He had a vivid imagination and encouraged me to read and write. He wasn't a great reader, but my mother was.

The family's bookshelves were similar to our record collection: many and varied. In time, we would read the classics at school, but at home I was exposed to a wide selection of fact and fiction. I had access to the usual children's books, but I recall seeing them off early and moving onto fry bigger fish. We also had *Reader's Digest* delivered to the house and, as a young boy, I'd pore over each edition.

Not long after I'd watched the film 'Where Eagles Dare' on TV, I was surprised to find a copy of the book, written by Alistair MacLean, at my mother's bedside. I snaffled it, and with some difficulty started to work my way through it. What made it all the more interesting for me was that MacLean was brought up in Daviot just outside Inverness. Soon I devoured his books. They had everything a young boy wanted. There was action, intrigue, well-defined hero and villain characters, and great storylines.

MacLean had been in the Royal Navy during World War Two, like my father and, also like him, he had served on convoys. *HMS Ulysses* was his first and probably his most brutally stark work. Many others followed, and some were made into films, such as *The Guns of Navarone*, and *When Eight Bells Toll*. This latter work had an unlikely hero in Anthony Hopkins who, along with a portly Robert Morley, investigated the hijacking and disappearance of merchant ships off the west coast of Scotland. They battled baddie Jack Hawkins, who lived aboard a white motor yacht called Shangri La. The yacht was known in real life as the Maureen Mhor, and was moored for years on the Caledonian Canal in Inverness.

One Hogmanay, my parents took me to first-foot a neighbour. Iain Cowie's tales had me enthralled. He had been in the Palestine police during the War, and had lived through a great deal. I loved men like him, and my father, being a bit older than my friends' fathers, knew loads of them. In their company I would sit and listen open-mouthed to their tales, speaking only when spoken to.

'What kind of books do you like son?' he asked, after my mother had told him that I was a voracious reader. 'Adventure,' I replied. When we walked home down the snowy street early on Ne'erday, I had a bundle of Iain Cowie's paperbacks under my arm. I started with Desmond Bagley before moving on to Len Deighton and Gerald Seymour. I still had years to go before I left primary school but, by the time I did, I knew these writers well.

As a young man, Bagley set out to see the world and find adventure. He travelled overland to South Africa and settled there, working in mining, before becoming a journalist and novelist. His books had a special resonance for me. Because of his background, he spoke powerfully about the earth and the environment long before it became fashionable. When he approached publishers with a manuscript, his opening gambit was 'I write books like Alistair MacLean's'. He was taken on by Harper Collins in Glasgow, and went on to sell millions of copies.

In later years I loved Len Deighton's *Berlin Game, Mexico Set* and *London Match*, and also Gerald Seymour's *Harry's Game*. I can recall Seymour working as a reporter for ITN in the early 1970s. His 'Gerald Seymour, ITN, wherever' payoff is still burned in my memory.

But the daddy of them all was Frederick Forsyth. His stories were the most adult in subject matter, but in a way they were the easiest to read because Forsyth's style is so uncomplicated. I trawled through *The Day of the Jackal*, pausing only to ask my parents sometimes embarrassing questions about the sexual content.

Even at that early age, I recognised Forsyth's ability to keep the twist in the tale right to the end. His storytelling and his attention to detail are beyond compare. I came to understand that this is because he trained as a journalist. I have flirted with John le Carré and I hold Graham Greene close to my heart. I love Evelyn Waugh's books and EM Forster's. But Forsyth is the only writer for whose books I counted the days until publication.

It was these men who did it, with their tales of derring-do, their uncomplicated manly heroes and their dastardly villains. Inverness's own MacLean, adventurer Bagley, spy-obsessed Deighton, former TV newsman Seymour and Frederick Forsyth, the master storyteller: they all gave me a taste for adventure and made me want to become a writer.

* * *

For the first few miles the Zephyr hugged the coast, as if unwilling to say goodbye to the ocean. There was light to heavy industry here, alongside the glorious little boatyards and marinas which hove into view. Occasionally, there were glimpses of the deep blue Pacific, then suddenly it was gone.

We passengers quickly became a community. There were those leaving or boarding at Reno and Salt Lake City or Denver and Omaha. But I was there for the long haul, and was on the Zephyr until it pulled into Chicago's Union Station three days hence. We long-termers began to stick together, bound by our destination.

'I've got pictures with both of em,' said Bob. His little compartment was directly opposite mine, and we were to be next-door neighbours all the way to Chicago, his home town. 'They wouldn't sign autographs because you can sell them on the internet and make a lot of money, but they were happy to pose for a picture.'

He was talking about former President Bill Clinton and civil rights figurehead Rosa Parks, who grabbed the headlines in 1955 when she refused to give up her seat to a white man on a bus in Montgomery, Alabama. Both had been on his train in the past few years. His chest swelled with pride as he spoke, making him seem even bigger.

'She did such a lot for us African-Americans, allowed us to do so much. I am deeply grateful to her. We all are. She was a great lady. What struck me about her was how meek she was despite everything she had done, and there we were, chatting away on my train.

'She was an old lady and to be honest she didn't say a great deal. But how important was she? To people of my background she was a heroine. And she just stumbled into history. There she was that day, her feet were sore and she didn't want to go and sit at the back of the bus like she was meant to. But what happened then in Birmingham unlocked the door for people like me. She allowed me, a black kid from Chicago, to go on and work on the President's train.

'I thanked her that day, how I thanked her.'

I asked Bob what Clinton had been like, but perhaps foolishly, I used the term 'slick Willie'.

'There ain't nobody got the right to be mad at him but his wife and daughter,' he said, hotly. 'He was a man, a human being and he made a mistake. Look at Roosevelt. Look at Kennedy. Look at how they lived their lives when they were in the White House. They had a lot of fun. When I met the President he was very personable. He spoke to each and every one of us and made us all feel very special.' More than once Bob caught me staring at him. I just couldn't for the life of me remember of whom he reminded me.

We had left the coast and had turned inland, heading north-east to Sacramento. Many believe that either Los Angeles or San Francisco is the capital of California, but the state's most famous governor Arnold Schwarzenegger, 'The Governator' as he was known, had his desk in Sacramento for two terms of office.

Because of the age of the track, the top speed of the California Zephyr was 79 mph. But, as Bob correctly pointed out, if you want to travel any faster, fly. As we headed north-east and started to climb, the speed dropped to 35 mph and the gradient became noticeable. The earth was redder and drier as we left the coast, and I saw some kind of hare or rabbit with long ears, startled by the train, bound off into the trees.

Along the way, we flirted with the freeway. This was Interstate 80, a road I had driven along many times. Hell, I am sure I had seen this train from my hire car in previous years. I had many thousands of miles yet to drive on this trip to get to the Invernesses, but for the moment I was happy to relax and let someone else take the strain. With every mile that passed, I felt the stresses of daily life in a busy TV newsroom waft away from me. I was in a steel cocoon. I could do nothing except eat and sleep, and read and write. And relax.

As we climbed towards the Sierra Nevada mountains, the speed dropped further. At several points I swear I could have run faster than the train. Here the gradient was 2.4 per cent. The line rose nearly two and a half feet in every hundred.

Americans' panacea for everything, crawling trains included, is food. We were summoned to the dining car where breakfast was being served. The orange juice was so cold it had a layer of ice on it, and the coffee was so hot it steamed away in the air-conditioned cool. Amtrak call it 'community seating', and anyone in parties of fewer than four could expect company at the table. While I was keen to travel alone, I was more than happy to share meal times with fellow travelers.

I was joined by a sweet elderly woman, and I could have spoken to her all day. Ethel must have been in her late eighties, and wore a hairstyle which Scottish people know as 'an orange rinse'. She was going all the way to Chicago and would prove to be excellent company. She was from California, and was a retired industrial chemist from Oakland. In her day, when not working in the petrochemical industry, she had been a yachts-woman and had raced up and down the coast. It was so refreshing to talk to her. She had even been to Scotland.

We rattled along through little picture-book towns like Colfax. This place reminded me of something you would see on a child's model railway. It had a station house, or depot as they call them here, a couple of stores and a saloon. I expected to see a horse or two tied up outside, the swing doors bursting open, and some unfortunate wrangler tumbling down the steps and rubbing his chin. Instead, there were SUVs, kids eating ice cream, police cars and all the other things you see in small-town America.

The Union Pacific railway was built in the 1860s, largely by Chinese labour. In total, 35,000 workers, what we Scots would have called 'navvies', came here to work on the embankments, cuttings and tunnels. They used hand tools and black powder to dig and blast their way across the Sierra Nevada mountains, and were soon respected by locals as hardworking, faithful and patient people. When the railway was finished, many members of the labour force settled in San Francisco, which to this day has the biggest Chinese population in the United States, after Hawaii.

Elsewhere in the USA, the railways were built by African Americans, Hispanics and, of course, Europeans. The 'railroad', as they called it, was crucial to the creation of the USA, and many Americans regard the men who built it as a proud symbol of the New World's patchwork quilt of ethnic backgrounds.

The Zephyr continued to climb, and we could have been in Scotland. The railway was lined by tall pine forests, and every now and then there was a glimpse of crystal blue water below us from lakes and rivers. As we climbed towards the summit high in the Sierras, you could see the track which we would occupy once we began our descent. It ran hundreds of feet beneath us, at right angles to our current path and ready to take us away from the mountains, away from California and into Nevada.

Actually, although I compare this to Scotland, it might also have been Switzerland because everything was on a similar scale. The trees were tall and luscious green, and the mountains dominated the landscape. We reached Blue Canyon, named because of the smoke emanating from the lumber mills here back in Gold Rush days. Railway legend has it that the water was so good here, that the Union Pacific used it in all its dining cars.

Next stop was Emigrant Gap, named after those hardy souls, the pioneers who headed west to California in the 1840s to find fortune, but who had to dismantle their covered wagons and lower them down into the valley below on ropes when they found no way through the mountains.

By this time they had already traversed Donner Pass, a similarly hazardous area on the route to the west coast. It was here that a party of pioneers, suffering from the so-called 'westering fever' of the times, became stuck in snow when trying to get through the mountains. Of the original eighty-seven members of the party, only forty-seven made it out to the other side. Infamously, they resorted to cannibalism to survive.

The group was made up of a number of families, among them the Reeds and the Donners. It was the latter family which gave the location its name. I was about to take up the matter with Bob, but I found him checking his watch and pressing his nose against a window. Suddenly, a silver shape bulleted past.

'There goes Isaac,' he said, and waved. 'Isaac?' I asked. 'He's my brother. He's on the sister train heading west. We always wave at each other when we pass. Depending on our work schedules, it happens twice a month.'

*　*　*

Central Primary School in Inverness is a place I went for seven years. I went, that's all. I was neither happy to be there, nor hated it. I was neither a dullard nor a stellar pupil. I did all that was asked of me, and I then left to go to Inverness High School.

My teachers were all women, the formidable kind of Scottish women you would expect in a primary school housed in a Victorian building. One was named Ethel Black, a Capstan-smoking spinster from rural Aberdeen-shire, who took no prisoners. She was a good teacher, though, and many salutary lessons, mainly about respect, were learned from her.

I was average at my lessons. I wasn't good at art. I was enthusiastic at sports, if not accomplished. But I loved reading and writing stories, and I made friendships which endure today. Those were the positives. There were negatives too, in abundance. I hated the way Ethel battered the Bible into us. It's possibly why I loathe religion now. I was given the belt for absolutely nothing one day, and I resented it for years. She also once reprimanded me fulsomely and publicly for drawing Moses as a black man. And I can recall to this day her broad Doric tones giving me the row of my life for mumbling while reciting poetry.

'You'll never get a job reading the news,' she lambasted sternly if inaccurately.

Those days were uncomplicated. The school week was bookended by weekends spent with my parents, weather permitting generally outdoors. My father was a keen gardener, and we would often head out in the car looking for sand, leaf mould or stones for his rockery. He rarely went to a garden centre, preferring to drive around the countryside until he found what he was after, and fill the car boot.

My mother Margaret was a nurse and worked shifts. She'd started as a staff nurse, then became a midwife before being promoted to sister. She ran A&E wards and operating theatres, and ended her career as a tutor, teaching the next generation of nurses. Generally, her weekends were spent feeding and watering the family, preparing us for the week ahead, and resting. She was never happier than when surrounded by books and newspapers, as I played with my toys on the living room floor and my dad was in the garden.

When it came to toys, I had the same tastes as most boys my age. Although I begged my parents for a train set, my father was always dead against anything which might see me follow him into the railway. He only acquiesced when, aged fifteen, I was desperately ill with bronchial pneumonia. I loved books and was lucky enough to receive any title I asked for. Birthdays and Christmas usually saw me inundated with book tokens.

But my favourite toys came to me in an unusual manner. My father's cousin was a fascinating man called John Ross who became a scientist with Ferranti in Dundee, doing sensitive things with lasers about which we were never fully told and which were never discussed. His father was a bank manager in Gairloch, and we often went on Sunday drives to see them. John was much older than I, and more often than not he was away at university when I came calling. But one Sunday we drove home to Inverness with the boot of the car packed with tea chests full of his books and toys.

John's toys were from a different era, indeed a different world, and the books he read were far removed from my toys of the early 1970s. He had crazy things like electric motors, gyroscopes, indelible pencils and invisible ink. These were toys which were educational as well as fun. They gave me years of pleasure and I still have them all safely packed away in the family home.

There were no colouring-in books, no comics, no football annuals. His were all about science, spaceships, planets and the like. I'm sure many kids my age would have thrown them to one side. Instead, I was spellbound. There is a collection of *Eagle Annuals* on a shelf in my mother's house in Inverness, which may well be worth quite a lot of money but I would never be parted from them. They were a huge component of my growing up and my education, and I still look at them today. I was reading about Dan Dare and Harris Tweed while my classmates were reading the 'Dandy'.

I had a bike. I built model kits. And, of course, I loved the beautiful game.

Caledonian Football Club came into my life around then, and I would spend Saturday afternoons at Telford Street Park watching the boys in blue. The summers seemed long and hot, the winters long and snowy and, in my childhood memory, Caley swept all before them. Trophy after trophy went onto the boardroom sideboard. They played fast, attacking football, with players who were beyond compare: each man was a legend. Caley had a thriving supporters' club, and coaches would be put on for fans who followed the team home and away. If there was no coach, dad and I would just jump on the train.

We were the team to beat in those days, and we were guaranteed a good game when we went to Brora, Nairn, Forres, Elgin or Keith. We'd end up in a pub afterwards, even though I was a wee boy. It was all magical. I loved everything about those Saturdays, and the experience was heightened in later years when some of the players I idolised, such as Billy Urquhart and Gordon Fyfe, became friends. My dad used to take me to the Caley Social Club on Greig Street after big games, and I remember the many times the team came in around six o'clock, clutching the latest piece of silverware. The cheers were deafening.

They played in the Highland League and were so successful they would get into the Scottish Cup virtually every year. I saw Caley play the big guns of Rangers and Hearts, and also travelled to far-flung places like Berwick and Methil to watch them in the Cup. These annual forays were *Roy of the Rovers* moments, and I used to lie awake at night wondering which teams we'd come out of the hat with. I don't think many people looked forward to the first week of January as much as I did, because it was then the Scottish Cup draw was made.

My sixteenth birthday was on 21 April 1981, but it is memorable not because I got married or had sex: something much more important happened. That night, Caley went to Keith needing a victory to win the Highland League title. Because Kynoch Park then had no floodlights, the kick-off was at 5pm. Although it was a huge game, few fans would be able to get off work so Caley didn't run any supporters' buses. This didn't affect me because I would be at school.

Unbelievably, my father stepped in. I would never have predicted his actions, because he was usually a stickler for the rules. I was then approaching my O Grades, and school time was vitally important. But when I came home that lunchtime, he broke some amazing news. My dad was a big Caley fan and he was also a regular attender at the Social Club. The club secretary Gordon Smith was a pal of his.

'If you catch up on your studying tomorrow, you can take the afternoon off school to go to the game,' he said. I looked at him askance. This was fabulous news! But how was I going to get there for a 5pm kick-off?

'I've got you a seat on the team bus.'

To say I floated down the road that afternoon is an understatement. This was a world first. I'd seen the players at close range in the Social Club and frequently mumbled an awestruck 'hello' to them. But, beyond a 'how's it going, wee man?' none had ever acknowledged my existence, far less spoken to me.

I touched base with Gordon outside the club and thanked him profusely. There were only about a dozen supporters allowed on that coach, the rest of the seats being occupied by club officials and, of course, the players. Today I would sit among Gods.

But as we hit the A96, it was clear that many Inverness employers would be short of staff that afternoon. There may have been no supporters' buses laid on, but there was a lengthy convoy of cars, bedecked with blue-and-white scarves and flags, heading east.

Caley destroyed Keith that night, but the game remained goalless with ten minutes to go. I can't describe the tension. The experience was destined to end in frustration, because a draw was no use. Then, with seconds to go, stocky striker Neil MacKintosh, now the coach of the Scottish schoolboy team, popped up in the six-yard box to bundle home the winner. The title was ours.

A sizeable Caley crowd went bananas. We even invaded the pitch. How it happened I don't know to this day, but I was clearly emboldened by the events and ended up in the away dressing room with my naked heroes. The champagne flowed. Manager Alex Main, a journalist with the *Scotsman*, was carried aloft by the players and unceremoniously dumped in the bath. It was fantastic. As mayhem was developing all around me, I sat on a bench among the hanging blue blazers and grey flannels and drank in the atmosphere.

Soon I became aware of the pile of blue-and-white kit in the middle of the floor, liberally bedaubed with mud, blood and snotters. I wouldn't have got away with a jersey, nor a pair of shorts, but in a drawer at my mother's house in Inverness today lies a pair of blue-and-white Caley socks liberated from that victorious dressing room.

On the desk in my study as I write this, is a stone from Mount Tumbledown on the Falkland Islands and a piece of marble from Saddam Hussein's River Palace in Basra. Whenever I experience something that's out of the ordinary, I like to take away a souvenir. I wore those socks playing football for many years. I told myself they made me a better player. I doubt that they did, but I still have them and would never be parted from them.

The players staggered onto the coach and very quickly included me in their boozy party, despite the fact I was two years away from my first legal drink. I doubt any of them could bite their fingernails, such was the level of their inebriation. John Docherty, a magician with the ball and a favourite of mine, carried a case of lager onto the coach. As he walked up the aisle past my seat, he dropped two ice-cold cans in my lap.

'Don't tell your dad', he said.

Caley won a place in the *Rothmans Football Yearbook* thanks to their phenomenal record. It reached the stage where I nearly became bored of winning. Never in my wildest dreams then, as I followed Caley home and away, did I ever think that my home town team would decades later, become a new club in a different league. If you told me that when I was fifty we would win the Scottish Cup at Hampden and play in Europe, I'd have sent you off to lie in a darkened room. My two teams, Caley and Scotland, have given me so much more than I could ever adequately describe in these pages.

But all too soon my love affair with Caley, and football generally, came to a juddering halt.

* * *

The Gold Rush witnessed crazy days, ruthless days and violent days. And it wasn't just a case of panning for gold or even digging for it. For a time, hydraulic mining saw people blast away at the landscape with high pressure hoses to try to find a seam. The damage to the environment was scandalous. The man-made erosion of vast tracts of land can never truly be repaired. Eventually, nature took over again but the place never looked the same. Union Pacific even had to employ special police to protect the railway line, because the miners wanted to wash away the ground under the track in their quest for the mother lode.

The business of the Sierras was complete. We were up and over and dropping down the other side into Nevada. The territory here was very different. The railway and the freeway paralleled each other on a plain between two giant mesas. Cars raced the Zephyr and many pulled away, leaving us in their wake. We could open the throttle here, but never beyond 79 mph.

Nevada was about an hour old when the sun slid away to the west. I was left gazing out onto a moonscape of rounded grey rocks, pinked by the sunset. I wondered whether there had been volcanic activity here, or if glaciers had formed the shapes of the mountains.

When I returned to my cabin after dinner, I found that Bob had transformed it into a bedroom. If anything, it was even smaller than it had been during the day, but by then I didn't care. I slid under the sheet and blanket and let the gentle motion of the California Zephyr rock me to sleep like only trains can do, as it rolled on into the night.

*   *   *

Inverness High School was so close to my home that I could get out of bed at ten minutes to nine, brush my teeth, have breakfast, get dressed, read the paper, walk to school and still be early. In later years I would admire its art deco frontage, but at the time it was just a school to me. It had previously been known as the 'Technical High School', because it offered a series of engineering courses. But by the time I went there, it was one of Inverness's handful of secondaries.

When I moved to Glasgow I would discover what rough housing schemes were all about, and Inverness had nothing by comparison. The High School drew from Dalneigh and the Ferry, the roughest areas Inverness had to offer back then, but in reality they were not very rough by today's standards. However, much of it was quite daunting for a wee boy like me.

Secondary school enhanced my love of books, and my English teachers were my favourites. One of them was Lillian Asher, who would marry my father's cousin John Ross whose toys from a different era had taught me so much. Although she never once showed me any favouritism, what she did show me was a new world of authors. When I told her about the latest Desmond Bagley I was reading, she gave me a Thomas Hardy. I mentioned Len Deighton, she showed me Evelyn Waugh. My Frederick Forsyth became her James Joyce. I read these in my spare time, in addition to the books we studied as part of our classwork.

The school had a thriving network of clubs called 'High Society' and I joined the drama club and the debating society. I was keen on sport, too, and joined the badminton club, something I love to this day and with which I should have persevered, for I was always a far better badminton player than a footballer.

The drama club threw me together with someone who is today a world-renowned literary figure. Ali Smith was barely a teenager when she wrote her first play and her talent and intellect were obvious, yet she remained down-to-earth. She grew up in Dalneigh, as close to the school as was my own home. The drama club produced her play 'Peanuts', which played to packed houses every night for a week. My character was called Joe Press, a journalist with dubious morals. Good old Ali. She knew me well, even then.

The drama club was a great place to be, but I took more than a degree of abuse from school enemies because I was the only male member of the club. But their aggressive questioning of my sexuality didn't last long when I started dating my leading lady, who was two years my senior and gorgeous. I quickly lost any childish inhibitions by appearing on stage and delivering my lines, and I came out of my shell thanks to Ali and others, including that leading lady.

The school years sped by, and I passed and failed exams in equal measure. I was never particularly studious, and I had to work exceptionally hard to get even the barest pass marks. I loved English and French and adored Geography, and swept straight As there. I was tolerably good at Mathematics, but other subjects just passed me by, especially Art. I had no interest in Science whatsoever, and drew the wrath of my Chemistry teacher, while banging on about protons and electrons one day, by asking him the same question repeatedly: not 'how?' or 'what?', but 'why?'

I had not even reached my sixteenth birthday, when my life changed. That day started as a schoolday, like any other, but I went home at night knowing that something major had occurred and that there would be no going back. Because we were approaching the tickly bit of our school lives – when we would make decisions which would shape our futures – our careers teacher had organised work experience trips. I had already endured a few, and the best that could be said for them is that they afforded the afternoon away from the monotony of classwork.

One had been to the offices and workshops of AI Welders, then one of Inverness's main employers. The company had a global reputation, and pieces of metalwork used in construction and industry the world over proudly bear the company's plaque to this day. I had no desire to work for AI, but I took the tour anyway, and ambled around the firm's sizeable factory in the town centre.

I had no clear idea of what career I wanted to follow. In my heart of hearts, I wanted to be a pilot or an astronaut but, without science O-Grades, I realised this was not going to happen. Equally, I knew that never being good enough to play for the school football team meant it was unlikely Alex Main would lift the phone and ask me to sign for Caley. I could do what Desmond Bagley did and start a new life as an adventurer and travel to some of the places I saw on the news every night but, without any money, this was going to be difficult.

Also, my previous experience of travelling had been limited to family holidays. It was not going to be easy suddenly to swap the sleeper and sunloungers of a Mediterranean beach for a penniless trek across Europe or the USA. Anyway, that suggestion went down particularly badly with my parents, who wouldn't entertain the idea of me leaving school and not studying for a degree. So I kind of banked on going to Aberdeen or Glasgow universities to study English. After that, I had no idea. But everything changed on that work experience afternoon.

In the 1970s my mother, father and I always watched 'Reporting Scotland,' on the BBC because, although Grampian TV was supposedly our local station, it was based 100 miles away in Aberdeen. We lived in the Highlands, and nothing identified us culturally with Grampian at all. Even the name repelled us. We became fed up with 'North Tonight' and its Aberdeen-centric stories about the booming oil industry, new traffic lights in Inverurie and the price of fish at Peterhead. Grampian's news agenda baffled and alienated me, even at my young age.

There was nothing about the programme that to me said glamour (far less humour) or hooked me in to watch. 'North Tonight' was like a programme produced by state TV in the Soviet Union of the 1950s, with item after item about tractor production and crop yields. I was only a boy, but I couldn't believe anybody, apart from dull Aberdonians, would watch it. I would rather tune into the BBC to see what was happening in Dumfries than watch a Grampian TV story about lamb prices in Newmachar. To cap it all, Grampian didn't even have a reporter and camera crew based in Inverness.

So, when it came to radio, I was already predisposed to the BBC: in particular, Terry Wogan in the morning and the 'World at One' at lunchtime. When a new commercial radio station started in Inverness,

I paid scant attention. I was interested in local news, but I couldn't see myself listening to a programme which played adverts every few minutes. How wrong I was.

My work experience trip was to this new station, Moray Firth Radio. So few people wanted to go that afternoon that we went in a teacher's car rather than in the usual coach. The mode of transport didn't register with me when we went, but when we came back I realised that it suited me: less competition!

The entire radio station – including three studios, office space, a record library and an engineering area – occupied the floor space of an average family house. The main open plan office housed the desks of the presenters, the producers and the newsdesk. It was this last area that caught my attention.

Huddled over half a dozen huge Olivetti typewriters, and battering away feverishly, was a group of men and women. One of the first things I noticed was that, when somebody telephoned the newsdesk, all the phones rang at the same time. Two teleprinters chattered away, churning out reams of paper. Somewhere in the background I could hear the screaming noises of audio tape being played at high speed. The voice of the on-air presenter crashed out from a huge loudspeaker bolted to the wall near the door, telling listeners, over the dying notes of a record, that the news headlines were next. The noise was deafening.

With just seconds to go to the top of the hour, one of the men ripped the sheet of paper from the platen of his typewriter with a violent tug, grabbed a bundle of reel-to-reel tapes, and sprinted away round a corner. Moments later the newsroom was filled with a booming voice. 'Moray Firth Radio News at three o'clock, this is Alan Saunby'.

We stayed for an hour or so. Instead of asking questions, as did my three co-visitors during the tour, I remained silent, watched and listened. The wall of the newsroom was covered in part by a map of the station's broadcast area, a wide swathe of the north of Scotland from John O'Groats in the far north to Peterhead in the east. The rest of the wall was covered with the phone numbers of every police, fire and ambulance station, coastguard centre and local council office in the area. In the corridor which led to the three studios, the record library and the engineering space, was an Ordnance Survey map of the extensive transmission area.

The atmosphere was electric. There was a real team spirit about the whole place. Everybody seemed to be having great fun and getting along well with each other. I suddenly realised I wanted to work here. I wanted to work here more than anything else in the world. When we were about to leave to return to school an hour or so later, I did have a question for the station's managing director, Thomas Prag.

'Any jobs going for a trainee reporter?' I asked, hopefully.

'Afraid not,' he said.

But I wasn't going to let it lie. I had never been so profoundly affected by anything before, and I was determined to set the wheels in motion for my return. The visit was on a Friday afternoon, and I fidgeted all weekend until I could go back to school and speak to the careers teacher. I also abandoned Terry Wogan and 'The World at One', and re-tuned the Marconiphone to MFR.

The careers guru was Fraser MacKenzie, another of my English teachers and a man who taught me much about literature and life. He was a shinty player from Glenurquhart, and hard as nails. But he also possessed a sensitive side and an innate ability to teach. There was never any carrying-on in any of his classes, even when he left us alone for a time, not because we were scared of those caman-wielding biceps but because the work he gave us was so interesting. He treated us like adults and we behaved as such. He was fascinating to listen to, and we would sit rapt and absorbed by his lessons. Early on the Monday morning, I waited by his door.

Inverness High School had a reputation for being rough but, while the fabric of the classrooms behind that exquisite art deco exterior may have left a lot to be desired, and some of the pupils were a bit ragged, there could be no doubting the high quality of the teachers.

Our conversation was brief. Fraser assessed the situation in an instant. The school was farming pupils out on work experience hither and thither as they approached their career decisions. I went back to see him during the lunch break, by which time he'd phoned head of news, Alan Saunby, who said I was welcome to spend Wednesday afternoons on the newsdesk at MFR. I punched the air.

Every Wednesday lunchtime for the next two years until I left school, I borrowed a pal's bike and creaked up the steep hill to Scorguie where MFR's studios overlooked Inverness. I did very little to start with. Again, I just sat and watched and listened. In later life Alan Saunby, who hailed from Middlesbrough, would become one of my best friends. When I joined STV as a reporter a decade later, he was the business correspondent and one of Scotland's best-known journalists. He had an incisive intellect and could talk in depth about any subject under the sun.

He was also the hardest-working man I've ever known. Alan was the first head of news at MFR and had an admirable pedigree in the business. He'd worked for Granada Television on their famous 'World in Action' investigation programme, and had a background in newspapers and radio in Canada. When he spoke, I listened.

The first thing I did for MFR was a round of check calls. This involved phoning the police, ambulance and fire service to find out if anything was happening. In a broadcast area the size of MFR's, this took some time. I was allowed to write very brief and carefully edited news stories about issues of little importance, which made it onto the end of news bulletins, if at all. Obviously, I was desperate to write the lead story and then sit in the newsreader's chair and broadcast myself, but that was going to be years away, or so I thought.

The trainee was Maggie Shiels, later of Golden Gate Bridge fame. She was probably well aware that I was after her job. But I was still a spotty teenager who could barely write his name, and she knew she was safe from me. She may well have been the trainee, but she was already a battle-hardened veteran who had started life in local newspapers and knew what she was about. Above all, she was also very tough.

The other reporters were Lindsay Taylor, a talented man who would go on to work for Channel Four news and win awards for his journalism. Among these was a Sony award for his coverage of the Kings Cross fire in 1987. He'd witnessed events at first hand while working for Independent Radio News and, by chance, had his tape recorder with him when he travelled home on the tube that night. Isabel Fraser was the other journalist who would be Grampian TV's first Inverness-based reporter, before joining the BBC. But it was Maggie who took me under her wing on those Wednesday afternoons.

I quickly realised that there was a lot more to this reporter lark than just enthusiasm. It was hard work, and the knocks were numerous. But every week I picked up a little more experience. I learned how to edit tape with a chinagraph pencil and a razor blade, and was taught my way around the world of radio.

Thomas Prag was upfront. There was no way he could take me on straight from school without any experience and, although I was gutted by this, I fully understood. He and Alan said that to work at MFR I had to go to university or get a job in newspapers, and preferably both. I was heartbroken at first, but soon set my mind to doing something about it. And time was passing.

Because I lived so close to school, I could run home at break time or during study periods and use the phone. I used to make a pest of myself with the editors of every newspaper in the Highlands by ringing them every few days, asking if there were any jobs going for a trainee. At least they knew I was keen and that this was not a whim. This went on for months without success, until I had another break.

The editor of the *Highland News*, Inverness's weekly paper, was a great guy called Willie Wilson. He was exactly what you'd imagine a news-paperman to be: he smoked like a chimney, drank like a fish and was a larger-than-life character. His 'WW' column in the paper was well regarded in the Highlands. I'd phone him every week and to be fair to him he always took my calls. Instead of saying 'Hello', he'd always answer, 'What's the story, Mike?' And I loved that. The conversation would dip thereafter, however, and he never had any vacancies. Then one day I called him, and he paused before he answered. 'Come and see me at 10 tomorrow.'

I nearly fainted. I was sixteen. I didn't have a shirt and tie, far less a suit. After school that day, my mother dragged me to Marks and Spencer and spent a fortune on my outfit. I was scrubbed, polished and twenty minutes early when I appeared the next morning at the paper's offices in Diriebught Road in Inverness.

The building was totally different to MFR and was a real newspaper office. There were papers and notebooks strewn everywhere. The air was blue with cigarette smoke. It was intoxicating and I could feel the excitement swell in me. I loved this. I wanted so badly to be a journalist.

Willie took me into his office and sat me down. We chatted about what was in the news, and I was well briefed, locally, nationally and globally. He was impressed. He lifted the phone to the newsroom and called somebody in to join us. Mike Hurry was six feet plus, with bright blue eyes, long red hair and beard and a hooked nose. All that was missing was the horned helmet and sword. It didn't surprise me when I learned he was from Orkney. To this day I've never met anyone who looked more like a Viking. And to this day I've never met anyone who has had a greater impact on my working life.

The offer was a simple one. On Mondays and Thursdays from March to September, Inverness had a thriving amateur football league, in which dozens of teams fought it out at the town's Bught Park. Would I like to cover it for the paper this season?

During the many phone conversations I'd had with Willie over the previous six months, he was well aware I liked football and that I knew my stuff. I'd even played a few games in the league myself. The week before, the regular correspondent had left to start a new life in Australia. The role was mine if I wanted it: they'd even pay me.

'When would you like me to start?' I mumbled. I could barely speak. 'Tonight,' said Mike.

Although I loved every minute of it, my new job was a tough gig. The Bught Park was big enough for a dozen football pitches, and there were six games a night. I would try to watch as much as I could of each match and compile the basis of a report, which I'd pad out later. I became well known among the coaches and players, and I was well treated. The standard was quite good, and some of the games drew large crowds. For me, there was no better way to spend the evening.

All kids talk the talk but how many walk the walk? When I was eleven years old I had wanted to write a book. I told my mum that I had a plot in mind and characters developed, and I gave her a rough outline of my story. She lifted the *Courier* and scanned the small ads. A minute later we were in the car *en route* to an address in Inverness where a lady was selling an Olivetti portable typewriter. Mum paid cash.

Within the hour I was tapping away on the dining room table, working on my first novel, which was a story about pirates using an oil tanker to hijack merchant ships in the English Channel. The old Olivetti was now getting good use, and I would drop my copy through the *Highland News* letterbox the night before deadline. It was a great time for me, but it was destined to get much better.

One night, the doorbell rang and another Inverness journalist called Hamish Black stood there. He introduced himself, and asked if he could speak to me with my father present. He said that he had seen my copy in the *Highland News* and asked if I'd also consider filing for his paper, the *Evening Express*. I said I'd have to check with Mike Hurry, because the *Evening Express* was a rival, but if he said it was OK, I would do so.

Mike laughed. 'You've opened a can of worms for yourself because you'll have to write a different version for the *Express*!'

Mike taught me so much about writing for newspapers, how to deal with the people I was writing about, and how the industry worked in general. He was patient and dedicated, and I think he saw in me a shade of that same dedication.

Another of my many breaks happened shortly afterwards. I can't remember the reason, but I had to phone Mike to ask him something about that week's games. I was astonished to hear from the receptionist that he had left the *Highland News*.

'But, he can't have,' I wailed. 'Where has he gone?'

'Moray Firth Radio,' she said.

I hung up and dialled MFR. His opening gambit changed my life. 'How do you fancy coming up on Saturday and help me put together the sports programme?'

This was a watershed moment. Usually I would head for Telford Street Park on a Saturday and watch Caley. It would have been easy to say, sorry I can't make it, I'm going to the game. But I realised that, if I was going to be serious about this, what I did for fun was irrelevant. If I was going to make journalism my career, then the career came first and, regrettably, Caley came second.

To make matters worse, the ground was on the way to the MFR studios and I remember passing the stadium with a lump in my throat that first Saturday afternoon as the crowds queued to get in. I kept on walking. In later years I would miss holidays, hospital appointments and liaisons with beautiful women because of my job. I learned to suck it up because it was part of being a journalist. The story comes first. Always.

Because I spent Wednesday afternoons at MFR, I already knew how the technology worked. I was an accomplished tape editor, and was more than capable of recording interviews and reports from the phone onto tape. One of the things that makes broadcasting so appealing is the mix of writing and using technology. I still love it, although the technology of today is a far cry from that of MFR in the early 1980s.

Mike and I would produce an hour-long sports programme which went on the air at five o'clock every Saturday afternoon. It was crammed with news and features about a dozen sports, which we spent the day putting together. I had no interest in shinty or golf, far less cricket, rugby or curling, but it was great fun. The football section was presented by two guys. Sandy Young was a bank manager and an ex-Caley player himself, and Ken Thomson was a businessman who, although a big shinty man, later became a director of Inverness Caledonian Thistle.

Football had changed for me. It was no longer a sport I loved to watch. It was now part of making a living. Even though I missed watching Caley every Saturday, I was learning my trade by the week and I was also growing in confidence. After a time, I was treated as an equal although I was significantly younger than the others.

I was well short of the legal drinking age when Mike tapped me on the shoulder after one Saturday programme and asked me to join them for a pint. I was in the team! I was one of the boys! After two pints of lager shandy I was drunk as a skunk when I lurched home that night, and my mother threatened to ban me from future MFR visits. But my dad smiled knowingly. He knew that alcohol was closely associated with journalism, but he knew also that I was sensible and realised that those Saturday afternoons provided me with experience which money couldn't buy.

Then one Saturday afternoon I turned up at the studios to be met by Mike Hurry who, for once, was in a terrible state. 'We've got problems,' he wheezed. 'I've got the flu, Sandy is on holiday and Ken's been called away on business. You have to present the programme.' To say I was nervous is an understatement. But I did it. And I did it so well that Mike asked me to present the programme the next week and the week after. In fact, he never stopped asking.

One Monday, Thomas Prag phoned me at home to congratulate me on how well I was doing. MFR was starting a new sports bulletin service on weekday mornings, and he wondered if I'd be interested in being the presenter. It meant getting up at 5am. Many of my pals had jobs, and some had jobs which required getting up at 5am to deliver newspapers. But nobody else was on the radio.

I recall being overwhelmed with gratitude at all these opportunities but, at the same time, I felt I was taking them in my stride. I was comfortable doing what I was doing. It was sport, so it wasn't very controversial, and there was little I could get wrong. But when I sat down to think about it, I scared myself shitless. I was writing for two newspapers, producing and presenting an hour-long Saturday sports programme and morning sports bulletins on a mainstream commercial radio station while I was still at school. I was also making more than £100 a week!

The next big date in my diary was my seventeenth birthday.

* * *

We had left Nevada and had rolled into Utah during the night. In so doing, we had crossed from Pacific time to Mountain time, and our watches went forward an hour. The train cut through imposing red sandstone canyons and mesas. This was Western country, and I looked to see if John

Wayne was cresting a hill and waving us past, before tying his horse to a tree and lighting up a deadwood fire to heat up some coffee and beans.

I was also half expecting to hear a cartoon 'beep beep' and see the dust trail of a road runner being pursued by the hapless wily coyote who, as every cartoon fan will tell you, was never quite wily enough. Beneath pretty well every red rocky outcrop was a boulder field. Down the years – hell, down the millennia – the wind and rain and ice had eroded the mesas, and rocks ranging from pebbles to boulders the size of cars had fallen from them.

I had barely said good morning to Utah when we crossed into Colorado, and the train again began to climb. We were about to cross our second major mountain range, the Colorado Rockies, on the long trip to Chicago. However, we were about to cross much more than the Rockies.

The Continental Divide is an imaginary line which runs south from Northern Alaska, through Canada, along the Rockies, through the USA into Mexico and South America. Rainfall along that line has two very different destinations, and raindrops which land only a few millimetres apart end up in different oceans. Whatever falls to the west rolls down the mountains to end up in rivers which takes it into the Pacific. Whatever falls to the east rolls, eventually, into the Gulf of Mexico.

I looked out to see a thin covering of snow on the mountains. Yesterday in California it was in the 80s. It was much colder here, not least because we were high up. Down below the train was the Colorado River. Here, it was just a relatively narrow but fast-moving stream which eventually cut its way down to the Grand Canyon. This was tunnel country. There are twenty-seven tunnels on the last stretch of the line into Denver. Moffat tunnel is just over six miles long and, at 9,239 feet, the highest point on the trip.

*   *   *

Today, there is an elegant sufficiency of media studies courses. I must be honest and say I don't rate them. I've known graduates with honours degrees from these media studies courses, and many of them can't spell or punctuate, far less write a news story. Being a reporter is not like being an architect. There is no template you can apply to this business. It's not something you can teach, apart from law and shorthand, it is something that is learned on the job, preferably somewhere else. If you want to be a journalist, you should travel, live some life and study for a degree at university. Avoid media studies courses. A degree will do you much more good.

Ron MacKenna became the political editor of the *Daily Record* without a media qualification. He has three degrees: maths, geography and law. Lindsay Taylor had a degree in music, for God's sake. Another former colleague, who was a fine reporter, had a degree in physiology. Why am I so prejudiced against media studies courses? Because I went on one.

They are everywhere now but, in my day, there was only one in Scotland – at Napier College in Edinburgh – and the competition for places was high. I had good grades in my Highers and a couple of years working in the business, admittedly part-time, to show I was deadly serious about this. But, while I had done exactly the right thing in writing for the papers and working at MFR, I wasn't alone in that, and it took me three years of trying before I won a place.

I was desperate to be a journalist and I thought Napier was the way to do it. It was a two-year course, whereas university degrees took twice as long. I couldn't afford to be out of the loop for that length of time because I was petrified that someone would get a big break which should have been mine.

I loved Napier, every minute of it, but I now know that I should have gone to university and studied English. I would have been a better journalist for it. Napier taught me shorthand and media law, but that was about it. The rest was froth. University would have matured me, and taught me more about myself as well as my subject matter.

So petrified was I that someone would steal my MFR spot that, every Friday night, I'd catch the train back to Inverness, arriving around ten at night. I'd collapse exhausted into bed and be up early the next day to go to MFR for the Saturday shift. I'd spend the Sunday with my family before getting the train back to Edinburgh that night.

To maximise time at home, I took the overnight train but, because I couldn't afford a sleeper, I sat up all the way. I would arrive at Haymarket at twenty to five in the morning, and I would stand exhausted in the cold waiting for a bus to my flat. To this day, a whiff of the malt smell from the brewery there teleports me back to 1984. I had two years of that weekend round trip and it nearly killed me.

Towards the end of my second year, in March 1986, I ventured down to Radio Forth, MFR's sister commercial station, and enquired about freelance work or the possibility of a full-time job when I left Napier. The news editor was called David Johnston who was widely known for being a quality, creative journalist, but with a short fuse. Radio Forth was a big city radio station, and it kicked MFR into touch. It had many more staff and a much larger audience, and tackled big city news and sport stories. It also broadcast round the clock.

I introduced myself to David and told him what I was about. Just as Alan Saunby had done years earlier, he said he wouldn't be able to offer me a job but that I was welcome to spend Wednesday afternoons in the newsroom. He'd obviously checked me out with Mike Hurry because, otherwise, there is no way he'd have made that kind of offer. But every time I went to the studios on Forth Street, the sports editor Vic Wood, the man I really wanted to talk to, was nowhere to be seen.

'He's in Mathers,' David would say, gesturing to the pub round the corner on Broughton Street. I wondered how he got away with that, because Johnston wasn't the kind of guy to mess with. There was a hard-drinking culture in newspapers in those days, but not so much in broadcasting because at the end of the day you had to sit behind a microphone.

Fed up of waiting, I would go and see him at the bar and buy him a pint. He repeated that there were no openings and, even if there were, the list of potential candidates was lengthy and they all had more experience than I had. I was dejected, but not surprised. However, I got the impression after a while that he was brushing me off. Undaunted, every Wednesday I would head down to the studios regardless and sit around until I was asked to do something. This was invariably doing rounds of check calls, or making the tea, or going to the bookies to put someone's line on. It was frustrating, but I did it because I would rather be there than anywhere else. And anyway, I might get another break.

Things were about to get serious again on the academic front. Apart from my weekly stint at MFR, I didn't have a job. Once the exams were out of the way, I would have to begin the business of trying to find one. But getting a start in journalism was always the hardest thing. I had done well to gain my broadcasting experience but, without a full time job at MFR or elsewhere at the end of it, it would all have been for nothing. And I was soon going to have to start working somewhere.

Nobody was looking for a trainee reporter and, with Napier about to turf out sixty graduates hunting the same jobs, finding one was going to be hard. Today, there are plenty of newspapers, websites, blogs, radio stations and the like. In 1986 the media world was very different. A town had a weekly paper and was covered by a radio station in Glasgow or

Edinburgh, Aberdeen, Dundee or Kilmarnock. The internet has changed all that.

My father had forbidden me from following him into the railway, but he had allowed me to work in the carriage cleaning depot during my summer holidays from college. If all else failed, my plan was to go back to the railway, despite his protestations, while continuing my weekend stint at MFR, until I got my next break. This came a week before my Finals.

This notion of 'Mum's taxis' had never existed in my life. My parents were of the view that I had legs for a good reason and, if I had to go anywhere, I should walk or cycle. In the light of this, you will understand my perplexity when I saw my mother waiting for me at the barrier of Inverness Station when I got the train home to study the week before my finals. She wasn't even in the car park. She was at the head of the platform. I was immediately concerned because my father hadn't been keeping well.

'Ron Lyon phoned me this morning. The trainee reporter at the *Inverness Courier* has just resigned.' She was so excited that she could barely speak. Paul Cowan, the trainee, was a friend of mine and had been on the Napier course the year before me. Ron Lyon was an Inverness-based reporter with the *Evening Express* and a great guy. He was one of the reporters I used to pester on the phone every week before I got a place at Napier.

His wife was a good friend of my mother's, and he well knew that I was still trying to break into the business. He'd heard on the grapevine that morning that Paul had quit, and he immediately called my mother. The train got in at around 12.30 that lunchtime. By 2pm, after a quick visit to Marks and Spencer for another suit, I was knocking on the door of the *Inverness Courier*.

In the late 1960s, developers had redesigned the town centre of Inverness. They had knocked down historic old buildings, and had replaced them with hideous concrete boxes which are to this day a blight on my home town. But, if you looked closely, tucked away on the river front in a corner surrounded by the carbuncles was a tiny red sandstone building. The developers had waved a chequebook under the nose of the owner, but she repeatedly refused to take what she saw as thirty pieces of silver. This continued for years, until the developers simply built around her.

She was an elderly spinster called Eveline Barron, the *Courier's* editor and proprietor, and I asked to see her that afternoon. The office was antiquated, both inside and out. There was an overwhelming stench of petrol which, I would later discover, was used to clean the printing presses in the basement. Everything was ancient, and the walls of the corridors were lined with bookshelves packed with dusty bound copies of the paper from the year dot. The prospect of becoming a part of this 'real' newspaper only heightened my nervous anticipation.

Miss Barron (to this day I still call her Miss Barron) was an enigma. She was not only 'old school', she was also from a different world. If the building and rooms were antiquated, her office was like something out of a Dickens novel. It was crammed with high glass cases packed with hardback books and more bound back issues of the paper. Her desk, which resembled a crime scene, was in the corner by a window, and she was so small that her chair was elevated on a wooden platform. She wore tatty old clothes and thick pebble spectacles and, when she read anything, her efforts were aided by a large magnifying glass.

As ever, I was polite and, while I didn't lie to her that afternoon, I didn't exactly tell her the whole truth. I said I was just about to finish the two-year Napier course and, because I was an Inverness boy, I wanted to start my career at the local paper. I added that I was an avid reader of the *Courier* and that I couldn't think of a better place to work. I didn't mention the intelligence I had received from Ron Lyon less than two hours earlier.

As she spoke, her eyes were like the spinning wheels of a one-armed bandit. 'Well actually, your timing is very good. A vacancy has just arisen for a position as the junior reporter.'

I smiled.

The *Courier* was a thriving business. The bulk of the paper was taken up with advertising and it made a sizeable profit every week. The fabric of the building was in dire need of repair and the equipment appeared to be in a similar state, but the staff were very well looked after. The salary she offered me to start as the junior reporter was a high one, and it would increase by a very welcome thirty per cent after six months probation. However, there were conditions. The offer was subject to good references. And to passing my Finals.

She didn't ask me if I could write and she had no desire to know what I had learned at Napier. When I mentioned all my broadcasting experience, she couldn't have cared less. The only question she asked me was 'might I know your parents?'

The next big date in my diary was my twenty-first birthday.

* * *

We emerged from the final tunnel and, some way below us at the foot of the Rockies, was a massive plain, on top of which sat the city of Denver. Its lights winked at us in the distance. It looked massive sitting there, like a huge sparkling omelette that had just been dropped on the kitchen floor.

As I marvelled out of the window, Bob walked past my cabin. 'Ain't she pretty,' he drawled. 'But make yourself comfortable. It's an hour and a half before we get there.'

I zipped into the tiny bathroom for a wash and brush up before dinner, although the Zephyr wasn't the kind of train on which you dressed for meals. There were people on board of all ages, but most of them were elderly or too infirm to fly. At least three passengers in my sleeping car wore oxygen masks and wheeled their black-and-white cylinders with them in little trolleys wherever they went. So, before dinner, many passengers simply put on fresh tubigrip or gave the oxygen cylinders a wipe.

Unexpectedly, the conductor came over the PA system and announced that Denver was a 'fresh air break', where you could leave the train for a few minutes for a cigarette. It felt odd to walk down a spiral staircase on a train (I've done it on a jumbo jet but never on a train) and step outside. Bob instructed us not to leave the platform, far less the station. It would be better, he said, if we stayed near the door, where he stood watching over us like a six-feet-six-inch sheepdog, as we pottered about stretching our legs and filling our lungs with fresh Colorado air or tobacco smoke.

It was 10pm on day two, and getting dark. We had crossed the Continental Divide and, when the train left Denver a few minutes later, we put our watches forward an hour. Bob shouted the 'all aboard', and we climbed back up the stairs to our little cabins. There was some shunting going on in the darkness: a locomotive was uncoupled here and another sleeping car was added there. By the time all that was finished, and the newly marshalled Zephyr had rumbled out of Denver, I was sound asleep.

Colorado had evaporated some time during the night and we were just out of Omaha, Nebraska on the home straight. From here on in to Chicago, the Zephyr powered over prairie lands, the Great Plains, America's breadbasket, the corn belt, the grain belt: call it what you will. The mountains were far behind us and, between here and Union Station in 'the windy city', there was not a hill worthy of the name. On either side of the line were fields tended by farmers who lived in white board houses which, in some cases, had the railway running through the back garden.

Dotted around the landscape were towering silos, ready to fill hundreds of trains or trucks. The fields groaned with wheat, soya, corn (or maize, as the Americans call it) or were left fallow and glowed green with grass.

Breakfast was with Janine, another singly. She was a thirty-something Australian and was also writing a book. She and I shared another connection: we were without question the two youngest passengers on the Zephyr. I asked her about her novel but she told me little. 'You can talk a book to death,' she said, 'like the last one I was working on and it didn't get written.'

It's set in Australia in the 1980s,' she said, 'a time and place I know all about.' And that was it. She told me no more. I was praying she'd ask me about my Invernesses project, but she didn't. We didn't even swap book small-talk. Instead, we spoke about our travels and our hopes in life. I think this was a gesture, a nod, towards being young and healthy, while all around us were older people, many of whom were infirm.

The fields were full of crops. Some looked brown and burned and dead, but I was assured that this was the best way to leave corn and that, despite appearances, it was perfectly serviceable when it was harvested. I was surprised to learn that less than one per cent of the corn grown in these breadbasket fields was eaten. Fewer than one in every hundred cobs ended up between forks and drizzled with butter. The rest was used for animal feed, seed or, more frequently nowadays, bio-fuel. This gives you an idea of the scale of things in this part of the US. The fields were huge, the farms were huge and the states involved were huge. Iowa, Indiana, Illinois and Ohio grow more than half of the corn produced in the USA.

At Burlington, Iowa, Janine and I watched as the Zephyr crossed a bridge spanning the mighty Mississippi River. It flowed beneath us, dark-brown and green, on its lengthy journey through the US heartland to the Gulf of Mexico. From its source on Lake Itasca in Minnesota, the river runs for 2,340 miles. All being well, I would greet the waterway again soon. Burlington was unremarkable, except that from the train there is a good view of the quaintly named Great River Bridge which parallels the structure carrying the railway line. It is an asymmetrical one-tower road bridge which was opened in the early 1990s.

'So that's what it looks like,' cooed a man somewhere behind me. 'I've driven over the sucker a million times but ain't never seen what she looks like coz I've been watching the road. Nice!'

Once across the Mississippi, we were in Illinois, the final state on the Zephyr's journey. We now began to observe flooded fields and the wrecks of caravans and buildings, as the river had recently burst its banks. Mindful of the carnage caused by Hurricane Katrina, the population of Burlington was on high alert. In the end, the floods killed twenty-two people, forced thousands of people from their homes, and caused a billion dollars worth of damage to property.

Across the Mississippi, in Gulfport, Illinois, 400 National Guardsmen had been mobilised, and 200 prisoners briefly released, to help strengthen levees on the eastern side of the river. When we rolled by, the flooding had all but receded, although there were patches of fetid water that looked as though they'd be there for several years to come.

Soon – all too soon – the passing trains began to take on a different appearance. Less frequent were the lengthy freighters, comprising eighty-plus wagons and hauled by half a dozen locomotives, carrying the foodstuffs and materials without which the USA would not function. These trains are the stuff of legend, the source of songs from the Gold Rush to the Civil War to Boxcar Willie. The beat of their exhausts and the cadence of the passing cars talked to me of times past, when people hopped a freight to escape their old life and start anew on the other side of the continent.

The multi-coloured oil tanks, grain hoppers and lumber wagons were replaced by shiny steel double-deckers like the Zephyr. But these weren't superliners upon which passengers sat for days at a time. These were commuter trains, taking the ulcered executives home to the "burbs". The light was fading. As the night approached, so did the destination. These trains heralded a new city. Chicago was near.

The plains and the fields of food and fuel began to evaporate. Slowly, imperceptibly, they were replaced by houses, then villages, then towns, then the city where the silver snake slithered into its nest. It seemed to be in a more fitting place now, among the concrete and steel. It would belong to someone else tomorrow, as it made the return journey to the west coast. It would no longer be my place of R&R, where I pushed back my seat, opened up my ageing lapdog, and surveyed the wonderful views for motivation. I had sensed waves of stress wash off me over the past three days and I have seldom felt as relaxed as I did on the Zephyr, but now we were about to go our separate ways. My tension levels would surely mount again in the windy city.

Two lines became four, then six, then eight, and soon we were down the throat of Union Station. The approaches weren't as bustling as the Gare Du Nord in Paris or as agitated as the Stazione Termini in Rome.

It had an American aloofness to it, a sort of calm, as if to say 'look, most people fly, but it's ok being a train. Let's just not get excited about it'.

I started to choke up about saying goodbye to Bob. He had become a friend, a confidant, a teacher even. He was a man whom I had grown to like immensely. The Zephyr was crawling now, and sneaked into the station as though it didn't want to disturb any of the other trains. There was no fanfare, no 'hoopla', as the Americans call it. The Zephyr slowed to a halt, and I felt a pang of sadness as the brakes hissed on. I tried to delay my departure from my tiny cabin but I knew that the longer I kicked my heels, the worse it would get.

I had only a small bag and it didn't take long to pack. I said a silent farewell to my compartment and trotted down the stairs onto the platform of Union Station. Bob was standing there, saying goodbye to people. It was then I realised who he reminded me of. It came to me in a flash. I stood before him, wanting to embrace him, when I snapped my fingers and pointed to him.

'Lawrence Fishburne,' I said.

'Man, I get it all the time. But I'm much better looking,' he quipped, crushing my hand in his big brown paw. We smiled and separated, he to six days off after eight days on, me to another Inverness.

* * *

Although never a great student, with the motivation I now possessed I crammed hard for those Finals. I finished at Napier on the Friday and started at the *Courier* on the Monday. I was so desperate to begin my career that I didn't even take a holiday.

The *Courier* was unusual in many ways. It is unique throughout the UK to this day, I believe, in that it publishes twice a week, on a Tuesday and a Friday. The job was perfect because it was a Monday to Friday gig with two late evenings per week on print nights, giving me the weekends free to continue my MFR sports job. Because nobody else wanted the 5am starts, I again took on the early morning sports bulletin shift, which added to the coffers and, when my *Courier* probation was up, I gladly accepted that substantial pay rise. I was now earning twice what my peers from Napier were taking home.

My first day at the paper was one I will never forget. I marched in with my chest puffed out and my head full of romantic notions about being a seeker of the truth. Best of all, on my way down the road that morning

I bumped into Raymond, our postman, who had a letter for me. The envelope contained my Napier results. I'd passed with flying colours.

The *Courier* news editor was Ian Ross, an ex-Fleet Street man who had a wealth of experience and who told tales which made my hair curl. The first thing he said to me that morning was this: 'Forget your ivory tower back in Edinburgh. Your training starts here.'

And he was dead right. The only thing I needed from Napier was my shorthand, and back then I had 120 words per minute. My handwriting has always been abysmal but my shorthand was good. As for my law lectures, it was months before I was allowed anywhere near a court, and then just the district court and only with another *Courier* reporter holding my hand.

My training was as it should be, on the job. I was sent out on little stories and came back to write them up. My first beat was the WRI flower show, then I graduated to the harbourmaster's monthly report, then to the giddy heights of the Kirk Session. Each time I would come back with my notebook crammed with spidery shorthand and I'd batter out however many words Ian demanded. Then he'd throw my copy back at me and tell me to do it again. And again.

My hit rate wasn't very good, and I quickly got the nickname 'Spike' from the *Courier* staff, because that's where the first few takes of my copy usually ended up. By now, my father had retired from the railway through ill health and, having heard my nickname, built me a beautiful wood and metal spike for my desk, which I treasure.

That desk was an old kitchen table which faced the newsroom wall. My typewriter was an ancient Olivetti which weighed a ton and must have been pre-War. But the *Courier* was the kind of place where men in overalls went around every day oiling machinery, and the Olivetti was always serviced to within an inch of its life.

The *Courier* was an unusual beast in so many ways. It didn't really resemble a newspaper at all because it was made up almost entirely of adverts. There were two news pages, but these were well inside the paper. One other idiosyncracy was that it carried no photographs. Down the first column of the front page were the births, marriages and deaths, and it was here that every Invernessian looked each Tuesday and Friday morning to see what had happened to whom. Right in the middle of the front page beneath the masthead was the listing for the La Scala cinema. Miss Barron's acerbic opinion columns were a high point of the paper, as were the readers' letters pages. The paper had looked like this for decades

This was 1986 and we were living in Thatcher's Britain. The newspaper unions had enjoyed years of lucrative but, with today's technology, unsustainable working practices, and were going head to head with Rupert Murdoch at Wapping. And they would lose, changing the newspaper industry forever. However, the *Courier* was still heavily unionised and there were work demarcation lines everywhere. It was a real eye-opener.

The *Courier* was an 'olde worlde' business, where people had worked for decades and would never consider leaving, and where there was universal deference to the managing director. Miss Barron was always called Miss Barron and never Eveline. Mr Tasker ran the front office, Mr Paulin the presses and Mr Beevors the commercial printing business. But the unions ran the main business: the production of the newspaper.

In those days, a newspaper was put together in a place called 'the case room'. The *Courier's* took up the entire top floor of the building and was a place into which I was grudgingly permitted to enter by the staff. However, if I had touched anything, there would have been an immediate walkout followed by a strike ballot. The printers, and there seemed to be hundreds of them, were all underworked, overpaid and locked in the 1950s. One afternoon, I naively asked why there were no computers there. I was asked to leave.

At one end of the room stood three large, complicated linotype machines. These were operated by chains, levers and pulleys, and clearly belonged to another era. Part of the mechanism saw an ingot of an alloy made up of lead, tin and antimony suspended on a line, melting into a crucible. Then the hot metal ran into the machine. The compositor tapped out the journalist's copy using a special keyboard, and a few seconds later a piece of metal called a 'slug', carrying the text in reverse, was ejected from a port on the other side of the machine. That was the end of that man's job.

A second man carried these slugs to an area where they were allowed to cool, and a third man would take it over to the stone, a large metal table, where a fourth man would place all the slugs in order to produce a part of a column. A fifth man would put all the columns together in a steel frame called a 'form', a sixth man would tighten all the columns in that form with special keys and a seventh man would hammer it all down with a mallet so that all the slugs were level. An eighth would carry the form over to a small press, where a ninth would roll ink on top so that a tenth could lay a sheet of paper on top and an eleventh press the paper onto it using a large weight.

A twelfth man would take the sheet, now called a proof, to a thirteenth man who would check it for typographical errors. Only once it was proofread would the form be lifted out of the proof press by a fourteenth man and taken down to the bowels of the earth, where a fifteenth man would lock it into the printing press. There, another similarly-sized team of men took over. It was ludicrous, but instructive to watch.

At 11am every day, one of the foremen would rattle a piece of metal against a steel column near the main staircase, and the entire building would stop for a teabreak in the canteen. After fifteen minutes, never a second more, never a second less, the rattle was sounded again to signify that the break was over. Foolishly, on my first morning at the paper, I sat there with the rest of the staff. There was a tumbleweed moment before one of the shop stewards (in the nomenclature of the printing and newspaper world he was called 'the father of the chapel') approached me and asked me to which union I belonged.

'I've just joined the National Union of Journalists,' I mumbled. 'This is a SOGAT and NGA canteen. You take your break somewhere else,' he said menacingly.

I had joined the NUJ and it would have a big impact on my life in later years, but I wasn't really interested in unions. I just wanted to get on with my career. However, the *Courier* was permanently locked in union fights. Members of SOGAT (Society of Graphical and Allied Trades) did certain tasks and members of the NGA (National Graphical Association) did others, and there was a constant battle to ensure that the twain never met.

Although I paint this bleak picture, it was actually a very happy time all round. My father was quite ill with a heart condition, but the three of us enjoyed some special times together. My parents were delighted that I had got my foot in the door of my chosen career and that I was working away quite happily. I loved the *Courier,* and every day brought a new challenge, to which I rose with varying degrees of success.

Miss Barron was irascible, Ian Ross punctilious, the printers rebellious and I was as happy as Larry.

Then one day I discovered that my cosy little world of being a journalist on the local paper was not all beer and skittles. I was walking across the main bridge over the River Ness to the *Courier* office first thing in the morning, when I saw the rainbow colours of petrol or oil pouring downstream. I estimated that it was about six feet wide, and it struck me as odd because the Ness water is usually clean enough to drink. I went home at lunchtime and noticed it was still there. When I returned to work after my break, the torrent had increased. I decided to act. I told Ian what I was about and, even though it hardly ranked with some of the stories he'd broken on Fleet Street, he was enthusiastic and sent me to investigate.

I thought I was Bob Woodward that afternoon, as I followed the oil slick upstream. It had grown to almost ten feet wide, and it showed no signs of stopping. I had no idea what it was, and wondered if somebody had struck oil in Loch Ness. It didn't take long to discover the source, and my presence was not appreciated in the slightest.

One of Inverness's loveliest features is a cluster of islands in the River Ness less than a mile south-west from the town centre. They're linked by bridges and you can cross from one bank to the other. As kids, the islands were often our playground, either on foot or on our bikes. We fished from there, we swam from there and, in later years, we would walk there with girls.

As I walked up towards the islands, I could see the unmistakable shape and colour of a JCB at work in the river. The machine seemed to be digging in the bed and dumping the spoil elsewhere. A cluster of men in outdoor clothing watched from the bank. Pluckily, I approached. I introduced myself and told them what I was about. Aggressive, abusive remarks followed.

Apparently, I was an idiot because I didn't realise that fishermen liked salmon to be in pools. When I asked if they had a comment to make about the JCB spewing oil into the Ness, I was told to shove my notebook up my arse. If I printed anything about this, they said, they'd come after me. As I walked away, one of them barged my shoulder with his own and said 'c***!' under his breath. I headed back to the office somewhat upset. So much for fishermen being a placid bunch.

In those days there was no such thing as SEPA (Scottish Environment Protection Agency) but Friends of the Earth existed and, of course, the local Council had a view. I got myself a nice piece in the next edition of the *Courier,* and was overjoyed to find that the *Press and Journal,* the Aberdeen-based daily paper which covered Inverness, followed it up in their next day's paper. After that I felt like Bob Woodward *and* Carl Bernstein.

Now that I was bringing in my own stories, I was sent to cover the Sheriff Court (alone) and Inverness District Council committee meetings. Things were taking off. Press nights were the best of all. We'd work late on a Monday and a Thursday to put the paper to bed, and the whole place bustled with energy. We'd have time even to attend Council meetings in the evening and write them up before the news pages were locked up.

Council committees were held in the imposing Town House in Inverness, a Gothic building which made history in 1921 when it hosted the first ever Westminster government cabinet meeting outside London. The Prime Minister, David Lloyd George, was on holiday in Gairloch when Ireland rejected direct rule from London. Lloyd George called an emergency cabinet meeting to discuss the situation and, because King George V was on holiday at Moy near Inverness, the meeting was held in the Town House. The attendees included Winston Churchill.

Above the press benches in the Town House to this day is a framed piece of paper which the Inverness Town Clerk, Mr William Bain, circulated as an attendance register at that meeting. It was signed by Lloyd George, Churchill *et al*, and I would gaze at it as the councillors droned on about Inverness's drains and streetlights.

You could see the myriad printers in all their glory on those press nights, not because they were a particularly efficient team but because they always wanted to get away at their allotted knocking-off time of 11pm. However, with twenty minutes to go before the end of their shift, they always made up their minds that they were staying on, and they would drag their heels lamentably until the top of the hour when a special overtime rate kicked in as a bonus.

And then that special moment came late in the evening, when the presses rolled and the whole building shook. I would be first in line down in the basement to grab a paper and take it home to my parents. When I presented it to them for inspection around midnight, it was still warm.

*   *   *

Chicago station was dark and noisy. I walked up to the head of the train and surveyed the mighty beasts which had hauled us all the way from the west coast. They were shiny stainless steel like the rest of the train. They were clean and new, but that slick, streamlined appearance belied a formidable power. I nodded some kind of thanks to them, and headed away from the train.

But, as I did so, my eye was caught by movement along the platform. It was a convoy like no other, made up of a dozen electric buggies carrying the elderly and infirm passengers, those who had taken the train because they were unable to fly. I suddenly felt a pang of sadness and realised how lucky I was to have my health. I stood rooted to the spot and waited until the sad cargo had passed. Then I turned and said a silent goodbye to the Zephyr.

After three sedentary days on a train, I really should have walked. But I arrived in Chicago as the rush hour was in full flow, and I couldn't face fighting through the crowds heading towards Union Station, or taking an El journey which carried with it the distinct possibility of getting lost. I bottled out, and took a taxi the few blocks to my hotel.

The El is a mystery I'd explored briefly on previous visits. The 'el' comes from 'elevated railway', the metro system which serves the windy city. No Inverness, of which I was aware, lay on an El line, so its further mysteries would remain unexplored by me. My next Inverness would be reached by another hired Chevy. The taxi journey from Union Station took only a few minutes, and I was quickly deposited outside the Palmer House Hotel on East Monroe.

My room was more than comfortable, but it wasn't my room that impressed me. The lobby was extraordinary. The yellow marble space, with a lavish staircase at one end, was the size of a football pitch. There were clusters of tables and chairs here and there, but not too many. It was lit by wall-mounted chandeliers and standard lamps which sent golden hues up to the ceiling, a glorious collection of Greek frescoes by the French muralist Louis Pierre Rigal.

The room, when I eventually got to it, had two beds and was actually more of a suite. I ran a bath and prepared to soak. I had managed a very short and unsatisfactory shower on the Zephyr and, since then, I hadn't really felt properly clean. I lay back and contemplated my mission thus far. I was one Inverness down with four to go. I had travelled 4,000 miles across the USA and was about to embark upon a much shorter journey to my next one. I licked my lips in anticipation and, with my big toe, I drizzled in more hot water.

From Inverness Illinois, on the outskirts of Chicago, my route would then take me due south, running parallel to the Mississippi, to Memphis and beyond. Then I would head west to Alabama, and finally to Florida. Even after the second Inverness, I still wouldn't be half way through the mission. I would have many thousands of miles yet to go.

Adequately bathed and barbed, I trotted down to the lobby and out onto the street to find a sizzling sirloin. I passed Thai restaurants, Chinese and others. Tonight, I felt the need for prime rib beef, the type you get from the hapless creatures the Zephyr had passed in countless fields along the way. I also felt like a nightcap but quickly abandoned any notion of trawling round the pubs of downtown Chicago. Why bother, when there was such a welcoming hotel to return to?

There were a lot of suits sitting at the bar drinking cocktails when I got back. I was lucky to find an empty stool, and I joined them. I wasn't feeling much like company and I couldn't be bothered with their insipid conversation. I was suddenly very tired, although I had no reason to be, given I had done nothing for three full days.

Ann appeared at my side, as if from nowhere. Americans are so forward. With hardly an introduction, she was telling me her life story. She lived in Syracuse in upstate New York and was an avid fan of New York's football team.

'I can pay for my apartment and my car and I can eat. But that's about it. The rest of my money goes on the Giants,' she explained. I knew what she was talking about. Too many people in Scotland are similarly obsessed with their teams, Celtic and Rangers mainly. Bill Shankly once said something which is quoted so often it has become part of Scottish legend. I used to empathise with it but, the older I get, the more I realise his statement is a sad indictment of Scotland and Scottish people.

'Football,' he said, 'isn't a matter of life and death. It's far more important than that.'

It's a great line, but too many people in Scotland are still living in Shankly's time when it comes to football. He was from the tiny mining community of Glenbuck in Ayrshire, where the pit was the only source of work for men, and where life was hard and football was an escape. In the 1930s Shankly left for England and became a legend. He was a player first with Carlisle, then Preston North End. As a coach, he learned his trade with minor clubs, like Grimsby and Workington before moving to Liverpool. There, in the 'swinging sixties', with the Mersey Beat booming around, he built a team which would sweep all before it. He was a short, gruffly spoken man. But his exterior hid a genuine, kindly person who was a socialist to his dying day, and his desire to win was legendary.

I can claim a rather tenuous link to the man. In twenty-five years as a TV reporter in Scotland, I have done two stories about him. One was an auction at Christie's in Glasgow of footballing memorabilia, including Shankly's football boots. I did a piece to camera, holding them and marvelling at touching a little piece of history. They were black, unlike the football boots of today, and had some yellow trim. In the 1970s the trim and the logo were immaterial. What mattered to the men who wore them was that they took a good shine, were clean and were serviceable. Today, of course, the logo is everything.

A year or so later, I was sent by STV to Glenbuck to cover the building there of a memorial to Shankly, which had been paid for by Liverpool fans. When I arrived I was saddened to see that the village no longer existed. When the pit was closed, the place became a ghost town. With no work, people just drifted away. All that was left was a large disc of concrete where the pit head had been, and the vague outlines on the ground of where the school and houses had stood. Back in the newsroom I did some research into my story and quickly learned that this tiny community, where Shankly had come from, where the Glenbuck Cherry-pickers was the local team, and where he first believed that football was more important than life or death, had raised fifty men who would become professional footballers. Thirteen of them went on to play for Scotland.

I flew to London the next day on an army job. There is no point in being on an aircraft if I can't see out and, as usual, I had booked a window seat. I pressed my nose against the glass and peered below as we flew over what I recognised as the houses and pit buildings of Glenbuck. From the air I got a better view of the football ground where the Cherrypickers had played, the scrap of grass among the shale and the coaldust where men, dirty from long dark days at the coalface, had run around gulping fresh air into their lungs and squinting in the daylight.

Then I saw, just a mile or so away, something I hadn't seen from the ground the day before. Between the village and the motorway, nestled in the hills, was a windfarm. The huge white rotors turned gently in the breeze, hundreds of feet above the seams of black gold they had replaced.

Ann and I swapped stories about our sports. Then the conversation got more maudlin when, over several gins and tonic, we discussed our careers. I told her what I did, and that periodically I had to interview people about deaths in their family. She nodded approvingly. 'I'm the person who tells you if you've got AIDS', she said.

I made my way upstairs and undressed on autopilot. I trotted to the football pitch-sized bed, thanking my lucky stars that I had taken half an hour to remove the cushions and throws before I went out for the evening. Then I opened the crisp white sheets and slid into their coolness. I must have been more tired than I realised because I slept long and deep and woke well after 10am, having dreamt about the next Inverness.

*   *   *

Things never stop in the media. Even in the mid-1980s, I was at the centre of a fast-moving industry and one in which I was burning to progress. One afternoon, David Johnston phoned me out of the blue and changed my life. He didn't go into detail, but Radio Forth had parted company with Vic Wood and the Sports Editor's job was mine, if I wanted it. This was a real break.

Reluctantly, I said goodbye to Miss Barron and thanked her profusely for all she had done for me. I told her where I was going to work but it didn't register. Unless it was BBC Radio Four, she wasn't interested. She was very polite throughout, however, and wished me well. The paper had been financially successful for years, and big newspaper groups across the UK had courted her, making attractive cash offers for the business. But she was desperate to hang onto the *Courier*, which had been handed down to her by her father Evan Barron and passed down to him by her grandfather James Barron. So she held out.

The *Courier* had spare office space to let, and the *Glasgow Herald*'s Inverness bureau was based there. The correspondent was a journalist called Stuart Lindsay, and he and Miss Barron became great friends. There were shrieks of horror across the UK newspaper industry when she eventually sold the business to him for a fraction of what larger companies were offering. Miss Barron retired, and died not long afterwards.

Even then, basic word processing software meant that a kid could put the paper together with a few clicks of a mouse. Today, the same child could do it with a swipe of an iPhone app. The *Courier* was overtaken by new technology and, not before time, the printers' house of cards came tumbling down.

But I had other fish to fry because I was on my way back to Edinburgh to take charge of Radio Forth's entire sports output, and would be the youngest sports editor in the UK commercial radio network. I was twenty-one years old.

It was a great job and I threw myself into it. I had daily dealings with Hearts and Hibs and other local clubs for my lunchtime and evening sportsdesks, and every Saturday I would produce and present the three-hour-long afternoon sports programme.

But the two Edinburgh clubs were pale shadows of their former selves, and Hearts would not repeat the glories of the previous season. After the 1986 World Cup, Rangers had appointed Graeme Souness as player-manager, and the Ibrox revolution followed. He signed a swathe of English players, many of whom had starred, as he had, in those Mexico finals. Rangers now had an enviable squad, and the focus of football attention was in the west of Scotland.

Radio Tay, our sister station in Dundee, had a reporter called Eddie Mair, who had a deliciously dry sense of humour and would go on to great things, but no permanent sports staff. So David Johnston would dispatch me to do the business there as well. This coincided with an unprecedented run in the UEFA Cup by Dundee United, who reached the Final. I had swapped the Highland League for the Scottish Premier League, and then I swapped that for European football. I would tootle down to St Andrews the day before each cup tie and interview the managers of United's opponents, who always stayed at the Old Course Hotel.

The UEFA Cup Final would be the biggest game of my life. I seemed to spend days in my car commuting between Edinburgh and Dundee for those games, but the adrenaline kept me going. The first leg was in Gothenburg, scene of Aberdeen's Cup Winners Cup triumph four years previously and the hosts ran out 1-0 winners. But that didn't daunt United because, with a full house at Tannadice in the return, the tie was wide open, and you'd have to say the Scots were stick-on favourites.

Matchday dawned, and I was in Dundee early to pick up as much colour as I could. I remember noticing that the Swedish fans enjoyed a beer as much as did the Scottish fans, and by lunchtime everyone was well inebriated. There was not a hint of trouble, and both sets of fans drank and danced away as the minutes counted down to kick-off. That was as happy as the United supporters got that day, however. Their favourites lost an early goal and despite a fantastic strike by John Clark, it wasn't enough.

Two things stick in my mind about that campaign. Radio Tay's studios were across the road from Tannadice, and the United players parked their cars there on matchdays. I got a few interviews in that car park, the nearest to my office I've ever used my tape recorder. It was also a lot easier than going through United's Jim McLean, a man who, although always perfectly polite and decent to me, I was keen not to antagonise.

David Johnston had given me this hideous bulky electrical gadget called a Motorola. It was a heavy, grey plastic thing with an aerial and a keypad and, if you pressed the keys and held it to your ear, you could speak to somebody miles away. I felt conspicuous even holding it, far less keeping it in its ghastly shoulder holster, and decided I would only use it *in extremis*. I well remember the moment when I plucked up the courage to switch it on. An hour before kick-off, after making sure nobody could see me, I made my first call on a mobile phone.

The UEFA Cup Final marked the end of the football season, but the big events kept coming. The Commonwealth Pool in Edinburgh hosted an international swimming competition, and I met and interviewed David Wilkie, a hero of my childhood, who had won Olympic Gold and Silver at the Montreal Olympics in 1976 and Commonwealth Gold and Silver in the 1974 games in Christchurch. I was more bowled over by meeting him than by the footballers I spoke to on my daily beat.

Before Andy Murray was born, there was already a healthy tennis scene in Scotland, and the natural amphitheatre at Craiglockhart hosted a major new Scottish Open event during my tenure at Forth. This was only moderately exciting until it transpired that Ivan Lendl, much later Murray's coach, would be playing, as would Argentinian star Gabriela Sabatini. Lendl was gruff and unaccommodating and my only memory of him was standing beside him at the urinal in the Craiglockhart sports center after a press conference. Gabriela was far more memorable. She was a tennis-playing prodigy and, at the age of seventeen, already a beautiful woman.

As is so often the case in Scottish sport, the weather played a huge part, and matches were delayed for hours. In the end, the weekend tournament was so disrupted by rain that it had to be concluded on the Monday. While we were waiting for the skies to clear, I got chatting with BBC commentator Derek Rae who told me some interesting news. Derek joined the business after sending to the BBC demo tapes of match commentaries he had done as a schoolboy while watching matches on the TV in his living room with the volume turned off. They took him on while he was still a teenager, and he became their main matchday commentator and an excellent one, to boot.

He told me the BBC were impressed with me, and were about to offer me a job on their flagship 'Sportsound' programme. I'd had lunch in Edinburgh with Charles Runcie, then the head of BBC Scotland Sport, shortly before I'd joined Radio Forth and, although he quizzed me intently, he had made no overtures. I loved my job at Forth and didn't want to leave. But the BBC was a national broadcaster, and 'Sportsound' was a standard we all tried to emulate. I floated back to my flat that night and pondered the situation.

The next big story was the golf Open, which was being held that year at Muirfield, near Gullane. This was very much on my patch and, although

I couldn't give a hoot about golf, I was very excited. I was distracted by the prospect of a phone call from Charles Runcie, a spot on 'Sportsound' and a move to Glasgow. The phone call I received shortly afterwards did change my life, but it didn't come from the BBC. My mother phoned me at work one evening to tell me that my father was dying.

*   *   *

The name Algonquin is applied to many things in today's USA. One, and the one in which I was interested right then, is a road in the suburbs of Chicago. Like many thoroughfares in America it seems unending, and it passes through several different townships and has a numbering system that John Napier, the Scotsman who discovered logarithms and after whom my old college was named, would struggle to fathom. Number one starts at each end and works inwards, but beware. It also starts in the middle and works outwards. And this depends on which town you are in. 18654 Algonquin (and some roads in the USA have more than 18654 houses) in Arlington Heights is a million miles away from 18654 Algonquin in Mount Prospect or 18654 Algonquin in Des Plains.

I have come a cropper because of this system several times down the years during many visits to the USA. If the smart aleck who discovered logarithms couldn't work out the US system of numbering buildings on long streets, what chance had I?

I drove up and down Algonquin's length, looking for the offices of the *Chicago Daily Herald*. I had an appointment with Sara Faiwell, the reporter who covered Inverness, Illinois. I hate being late. Even the mobile telephone wouldn't help me in this case. It is simple enough to phone home, but to phone from a UK mobile to a landline number in the USA requires all sorts of codes and prefixes. But I'd much rather be early than on time. And I'd much rather be dead than late.

Algonquin derives from the name of the native people who populated America long before Europeans settled there and ruined it for them. I am sure they were happy enough without the internet, gunpowder, aeroplanes, pornography and disease. Algonquin comes from the Maliseet word meaning 'they are our allies'. Maliseet is another tribe with another language. The Algonquins are closely related to other native peoples, the Odawa and the Ojibwe. Together, they form the larger Anicinape group.

Nowadays, Algonquin pretty well covers the grouping of native Americans who used to live, and some who still do, in a patch of continental America stretching from Virginia in the east to the Rocky

Mountains in the west, and up to Canada. Today most Algonquins live in Quebec, forming a grouping of around 11,000 people, speaking their own language along with French.

Whatever, I was getting fed up with driving one way, then the other along the interminable Algonquin road, looking for a newspaper office. At one end of Algonquin stands the global headquarters of Motorola. Not surprisingly, the security guard in his cabin eyed me warily when I turned up in the Chevy, map spread out over the wheel.

'Never heard of it, sir,' he drawled. 'But it's on Algonquin,' I protested, trying hard not to let the panic sound in my voice. 'There's a lot on Algonquin,' he said, lifting the barrier to allow me to do a U-turn inside his precious campus. I sped off again.

The road is like many of its kind in the USA. It is flanked by gas stations and fast food outlets. Every now and then, on little side roads that parallel the main carriageway, there are blocks of shops offering services like nail painting and mailboxes. But the overwhelming service providers are those offering food. I pulled into a gas station to ask for directions for the umpteenth time.

I then realised I was going the wrong way.

'No,' said the latest counsellor, with a camp flap of the wrist. 'You're looking for Arlington Heights. This is Hoffman Estates. It's a ways away.' 'How much of a ways away?' I asked, again glancing at my watch. 'Oh, a ways. There's a McDonalds marking the boundaries between the two towns. Good luck.'

His valedictory message made me feel like a bomber pilot about to embark upon a solo daylight mission over enemy territory. I took off again along Algonquin, scanning the sidewalks for McDonalds. There were, of course, hundreds. Finally, hidden behind a guitar shop well off Algonquin and down a narrow, dark lane, sat the office block containing the *Chicago Daily Herald*. Sara had told me on the phone when I'd made our appointment that it was easily seen from the road. What she really meant was that it was easily seen from the freeway, which I was not, of course, on.

I reached reception as the minute hand touched the top of the hour: our appointed meeting time. In the lobby, like some kind of sentry from a bygone age, was an ancient linotype machine, like the ones at the *Inverness Courier*. Sara came down to meet me. She was in her mid-twenties, petite, attractive and quiet. The newsroom was anything but quiet when we got up there. There is something so atmospheric about a daily newspaper office and this one was bustling away.

The desks were all high-sided booths, in the American fashion, with room for a PC and a phone, and that was about it. People were busying themselves getting the next day's paper away. I looked around for the Lou Grant character, or the bespectacled political correspondent with horn-rimmed glasses and a bow tie. Both must have been out. I was conscious that Sara was probably busy with her own story. The last thing she wanted to become involved with was my Invernesses. I promised her I would be brief. She smiled.

'I've been a reporter for five years and worked here for three years, the last eighteen months covering Inverness. It's a very quiet town. It's a school district and there is a municipal government there, but that is about it. There's a population of 7,000 people there with around eighty companies in one business park. You could drive through it, and many do, and not know there is any commerce there. That is, except Motorola.'

I asked her about the big stories, the issues which vex the 7,000. We were now in the boardroom and sitting at the top of the long table. It doesn't sound like many editorial conferences spend much time arguing the toss about what goes on in Inverness.

'There are one or two,' she said. 'There was a big campaign to have a proper war memorial there just last year. The town's decision not to have a Fourth of July fireworks display is proving quite controversial, and coyote attacks on small dogs is becoming an issue again.'

Actually, on reflection, when I was a boy reporter on the *Inverness Courier*, I would have been more than happy with presenting any one of those stories to Miss Barron. The war memorial became more of an issue when a local soldier was killed in Iraq. The fireworks were cancelled because somebody was injured at the last display, and more coyote attacks are being reported.

'On humans?' I asked, hoping my reporter's schadenfreude did not sound too obvious. That would be a story – coyote bites man. 'No, it's the small lapdog-type of pet which gets targeted,' she said 'Houses in Inverness aren't allowed to have fences.'

'So, coyote bites dog then,' I added.

The *Herald* is a family-owned daily paper with a circulation of 150,000. It has sixteen different editions, often with five different front pages, which cover the Chicago suburbs. The publishers live in Inverness. Sara grew up in Buffalo Grove near Inverness and went to journalism college in Iowa.

She did internships at different papers before, like me, she decided to start her career on her home town paper and, like me, she went straight there the moment she left college.

'Enjoy your visit,' she said, as she showed me out. 'Inverness is a wealthy community. It's known for the size of the lots and all the houses are a million dollars plus each. It's beautiful. The heater of the indoor swimming pool in one of the houses went up in flames a year or so ago and took the house with it. That was a huge story.'

The traffic on the freeway from Algonquin to Inverness was atrocious, so I came off at the first exit and drove parallel to it on a minor road. This not only made the journey much quicker, it also saved me an eighty-five cents toll, so it was a result all round. The going was so good off the freeway that I took a strategic decision to carry on out into the leafy suburbs and do a quick recce of the second Inverness, ahead of my visit in the morning. It was one thing being late for a meeting with the local paper's reporter, but it was quite another being late for a meeting with the Mayor.

I found it quite easily and memorised the route for the next day. But when I got there and walked around the town hall, I couldn't believe it. I thought there must have been some mistake. This couldn't be it. I checked the map, I checked the plaque on the door and then I checked the map again. This was it, all right. Scratching my head and thinking this may not have been such a good decision after all, I jumped back into the Chevy and headed back towards my motel. The hotel the night before in downtown Chicago had provided a hot bath and a good old night on the beer among real people. But that luxury suite had been replaced tonight by another unspeakable motel. This latest berth was on Dundee Road in a typically spartan and rather cold establishment. But it was clean and cheap and afforded a shower and a TV, which was all I needed. As I checked in that morning, the manager had asked me if I had any weapons.

'No,' I replied.

'Do you want one?' he said.

Actually that was a wee joke, but you get the picture. After my meeting with Sara, and my recce to the Inverness town hall, I crashed out on the bed, suddenly very tired.

I switched off the light. Tomorrow was going to be a big day, Inverness number two and a meeting with the Mayor. In a missile silo.

*   *   *

My father, Donald Edwards, was born in 1924 and started a career in the railway, which was interrupted by Hitler. In 1942, aged eighteen, he had been called up and joined the RAF.

He was a bright boy and, after he'd sailed through the intelligence tests, the RAF realised they had made something of a find. He was put onto a Morse operator's course and trained to be a WOP/AG or wireless operator/air gunner. He was looking forward to becoming aircrew because it meant he would get flight pay and wear wings on the breast of his uniform, which was very attractive to the opposite sex.

But the War put the kybosh on his plans. The Royal Navy was short of telegraphists and approached the RAF for some of theirs. He transferred from light to dark blue and, instead of flying, went to sea. Had this not happened, I would not be here today. The life expectancy of air gunners was short, and he would have stood a good chance of being killed in action, probably within months.

As a child, when I asked him what ship he had been on in the War, he would invariable reply 'hardship'. This was meant to be a joke, but I know there was more than a little truth in this. He served on several vessels, most notably HMS Wivern, a V&W Class destroyer which escorted convoys during the battle of the Atlantic. He was torpedoed and mined and suffered some particularly traumatic experiences. His tales could transport me there in an instant. He would be bobbing around in mid-Atlantic, aware that U-boats were prowling beneath the nearby waves. How a man could sleep at night in that knowledge escapes me. I salute him.

Like many men of his time, my father was a heavy drinker and smoker. There is no doubt in my mind that those ever-present dangers at sea played a part in his eventual ill health. He developed a taste for rum and plain cigarettes in the Navy and, by the time he stopped smoking and drinking in the 1970s, the damage had already been done.

I raced home from Edinburgh to see him and it was obvious that he was failing, but he never once complained. I knew what had to be done so I phoned David Johnston and told him I was resigning. He was disappointed, but understood. The next phone call I made was to Mike Hurry. We met for a pint that night and I explained the situation to him. My luck was obviously holding because when he drained his glass he told me that one of the news reporters at MFR had just quit to join the BBC.

My last job at Radio Forth was to cover the 1987 Open Golf Championship at Muirfield. I stood on the eighteenth green as Nick Faldo holed out to lift the claret jug, and I took my place behind Harry Carpenter of the BBC and ITN's Mark Austin to interview him. That Sunday evening I returned to my little flat off Leith Walk, packed my entire world into my car and drove through the night to Inverness. I started at MFR at nine the next morning and made the best of it. Six weeks later, my father died.

This was, of course, a great shock, and my mother and I took time to readjust. I've always been very close to her and, after my father passed away, I took on more and more of the family duties. I've always gone out of my way to look out for her, and shortly after he died, I took her away on holiday to the United States. We both fell in love with the country on that first visit and we've returned every year since.

I adapted to being a news reporter and began to thrive, quickly realising MFR was a great place to work. I much enjoyed it and, although I missed my father desperately, I look back on this time with great fondness. By now my mother was a nursing tutor and we got on just fine together.

It felt odd working at MFR and not being there on a Saturday afternoon. It meant my weekends were free for the first time since I was sixteen, and I could once again go and watch Caley. I could even go away for the weekend and not be bound by the sporting card. I also resumed my own footballing career, although Alex Ferguson never called.

On early shift, the 5am starts didn't phase me. I was well used to them after all those sports bulletins I presented. I'd also worked shifts in the railway as a student. To this day I'm grateful for the fact that I'm a morning person. But nothing could have prepared me for the early shift on 6 July, 1988.

I was first into the studios every day. That morning, despite the early hour, I instantly knew something was wrong. From the car park I could hear the newsdesk phones ringing non-stop, which was unusual at that time of day. The two teleprinters by the door were chattering away, but the machines were empty and the contents of their two massive rolls of paper had been strewn across the office. They were black with type. I walked several metres inside the building to get to the start of the roll. When I started to read, I couldn't believe my eyes.

'Two hundred men feared killed in North Sea after Piper Alpha explosion.'

As a morning person, I was hopeless at staying up late. and on early shifts I went to bed, usually after checking the headlines on the 'Nine o'Clock News'. Piper Alpha exploded around an hour later, and without mobile phone or pager, I didn't know anything about it until the next morning. It was a dreadful story and the biggest I had ever worked on. Technically, the accident site was on our patch and many of those involved lived nearby. When the men who died were named, I was dispatched to their homes to try to get interviews.

In the trade this is known as 'death knocks', and reporters are often blase about them. I still do them today and I don't enjoy them at all because I hate intruding on people's grief, although they sometimes yield great results. Knocking on the door of those Piper Alpha victims' families was my first experience of this, and it was to be a lasting one. I was also sent to RAF Kinloss where I interviewed the crew of the Nimrod which circled the blazing stub of the oil rig, coordinating the rescue mission. But it wasn't until I saw the TV pictures of the aftermath that night that I realised quite how serious it had been.

It's hard to imagine how that story could have been beaten, in a journalistic sense, but shortly before Christmas that year it was. On 21 December, Pan-Am Flight 103 was blown out of the sky over Lockerbie, killing 270 people on board and on the ground.

These tragedies apart, MFR had a bright and breezy news agenda, and we covered the colour and character of a culturally and geographically diverse area of Scotland. I used to rail against Aberdeeen-based Grampian being the TV station for Inverness because the two places had nothing in common. The same argument could have been applied to the MFR broadcast area, because people in John O'Groats had little in common with people in Buckie. But somehow it worked.

The head of sales was a bright, funny man called Rod Webster who, as well as being able to sell ice cream to the Eskimos, was hugely creative when it came to producing adverts and programmes. The station controller was a smart guy called Brian Anderson, who had a wealth of experience in the business, and these two men taught me so much about radio. My partner in crime on Saturday sports shifts was another veteran called Jeff Jones, who began his career on Radio Caroline, a trawler broadcasting illegally from the North Sea. Two other presenters – Tich McCooey and Gary MacLean – became for decades the voices of the station. Tich did the breakfast show and Gary then took over. For banter and music they were exceptional, and the listening figures proved it.

Alan Saunby had long since gone to STV, and Mike Hurry had taken over as head of news. He was a fine journalist and I learned more from him than anyone else. He was calm, cool and collected, especially under fire. I've never known anyone like him. Even when I messed up, his bollockings were sober and precise. He would show me where I went wrong and why. He did it in such a way that I never repeated my mistake.

Isabel Fraser had gone to Grampian TV to be the first Inverness correspondent, and the MFR newsdesk was very different from the one I had seen first as a sixteen-year-old schoolboy. She had been replaced by a wizened hack called Bob King who had worked in newspapers and radio for years. He had taken the first call to the BBC newsroom in London from a passer-by who had witnessed the Aberfan tragedy, when a slag heap of mine waste slid into the village, enveloping a primary school and killing 116 children and twenty-eight adults.

Bob was a great guy, but had been damaged down the decades by alcohol and stress. I learned many different lessons from him. While Mike had been subtle, Bob was a bruiser. He was an intelligent man who had studied divinity and spoke Greek and Latin, but you'd never have known it from some of his outbursts and the way he doggedly pursued stories. I know that a lot of his toughness rubbed onto me, and I am grateful to him for that.

Another journalist on that newsdesk was a bundle of energy called Iain Wilson. We were great pals but fought like cat and dog. I saw the Saturday sports programme as my baby, but he was now in charge and I suppose I was oversensitive about how he did things. He wasn't too confident behind the microphone and pronounced 'Southwark', 'SOUTH-work', rather than 'Suthirk', and 'midwifery', 'MidWIFEry', rather than 'midwiffery'. When I noticed he'd had trouble pronouncing the name 'MacInerney', and had written it out phonetically on his script as 'Mac and Henry', I ribbed him mercilessly about English not being his first language. He took it in good part, and gave as good as he got. The first ring of our bell on the day my father died revealed Iain Wilson on the doorstep.

Long before Children in Need and other media charity appeals, MFR ran a weekend dedicated to an on-air charity auction. Companies would offer, for example, a weekend's ski-ing lessons, and listeners would phone in and bid for them. Over the years this raised a lot of money for good causes

I can't remember how this came about, but somebody offered a sizeable sum of money if I would read the news underwater. I happily said yes, imagining a nice warm swimming pool somewhere. However, before I knew it, a North Sea oil diving firm became involved, and I was earmarked to read a bulletin from the murky depths of Invergordon harbour.

This was more difficult than you'd imagine. I couldn't have cared less about the challenges of broadcasting live underwater because I was more interested in how I was going to survive. I drove to Invergordon that day, feeling like I was *en route* to my own execution. When I arrived I found that Donnie Aird, the man who made MFR work on a technical level, had fashioned a mic which would be cabled up through the elastic ankle piece of my drysuit and into my helmet, without letting in the North Sea. I could have kissed him. The problem wasn't the mic or the helmet. The problem was the drysuit.

Even the smallest garment they had was miles too big for me and, when I stepped off the harbour into the water, I bobbed around on the surface because there was so much air inside it. They pulled me in by my lifeline and lashed all sorts of weights to my harness, including a sledge-hammer, but I still wouldn't sink. Suddenly, way out in the middle of the harbour, I felt the safety diver grab me and thrust my arm in the air. He yanked open my elasticated cuff and give me the biggest bearhug of my life, forcing the air out with a comedy rubbery farting noise. I sank like a stone. Thankfully, my helmet was equipped with a powerful headtorch which cut through the gloom and I was able to read my script which had been waterproofed in plastic and screwed to a specially weighted steel clipboard.

When I surfaced I was elated, and not because I'd just raised a sizeable amount for charity – I'd survived!. My joy was short-lived when the safety diver asked if I'd noticed the conger eel which lived in the harbour and had apparently taken a hungry interest in me. 'I chased it off,' he said. 'We're old pals.'

*   *   *

Sara had been right about the houses in Inverness. There was little more to Inverness than a large residential area, a supermarket, a fire station and a town hall. And the global HQ of Motorola. I had a half an hour to kill before I met the Mayor at his missile silo, so I drove around Inverness taking in the views.

Most of the houses were detached and large. Most had a double garage, some had a quadruple. They were all of relatively recent construction, and had been built in the modern American style, but they all tried very hard to look like something else: French or Italian, perhaps. All had sweeping drives and/or vast swathes of front lawn. Some had stone staircases leading to ornate front doors, and a few had delicate topiary surrounding the property. Others had been built around trees which were much older than the houses.

I drove up and down admiring the views. These houses were special, but I didn't know enough about the American property market to understand how special. Sara had been absolutely bang-on, though. These houses would have cost well in excess of a million dollars. They belonged to big-money businessmen and businesswomen like the family which owned that chain of newspapers, or executives who worked in downtown Chicago and could easily afford the hour-long commute here and back every weekday.

As I drove off to my meeting with the Mayor, I began to realise that there was something missing. Lovely as the houses were, immaculate though the gardens were, tranquil and inviting though the atmosphere was, it lacked something. I had pulled the Chevy out onto the main drag again and had nearly reached the missile silos before I worked out what was missing. I had driven around the place for precisely half an hour and I hadn't seen a single car, far less a human being.

However, my goal had been achieved. I had reached the town hall before the Mayor. I stood there, surveying the view. There were four cylindrical stone missile silos, each well over 100 feet high and topped with slate-covered cones. At ground level, joining all four, was a small Dutch-barn-shaped cottage building. Beside the town hall, very subtle and tasteful, was the war memorial which Sara had mentioned.

It wasn't quite a Presidential motorcade, but Mayor John A (Jack) Tatooles and his team swept into the car park with military precision. This perhaps should not have been a surprise, as Jack had been a Marine and had served two tours of duty in Vietnam. I would learn very quickly that Jack was a professional politician and an impressive one at that. Never one to miss an opportunity, he had contacted Sara, and she and a photographer had come along: to do a story on me!

'Michael, my mission here,' he said, gripping my hand in his vice-like fingers and slapping me on the back with a cruise missile, 'is to stop your trip right here and persuade you to stay. I have been to some of the other Invernesses in the US but this one is the real McCoy.'

I found it awfully easy to like Jack. He was sixty-five-years-old, tall and handsome in an all-American way. He looked fit and tanned, and there were very few flecks of grey in his dark locks. There was definitely something of the movie star about him, and he bore more than a passing resemblance to Robert Mitchum. He had a coterie of aides and we all trooped into the cottage.

We turned right into one of the silos, where Mayor Jack had his office. He sat at his desk and he bade me take the chair opposite. He watched me surveying the peculiar, circular room and clocked the puzzled look on my face. 'Nobody can put me in a corner,' he said. We both laugh. I was beginning to like Mayor Jack a lot.

I had come to interview him but, after a few minutes in his company, I realised that he was the one asking all the questions. I felt very much on the spot, and had to think quickly when I answered, because, of course, there was a journalist in the room. There is no such thing as 'off the record'.

Jack was elected in 1996 and was the longest-serving mayor of Inverness. He had not missed a Council meeting in his career. Clearly, politics was close to his heart and he was quick to quiz me about the government both of Scotland and the one true Inverness. When I mentioned the subject of independence, I saw a look of distaste on his tanned, Hollywood features. Of course, he was a staunch Republican and I would learn later that he had been involved in Senator John McCain's bid to become President. The SNP's independence campaign would not be on his list of favourites.

Jack served with the United States Marine Corps in Vietnam between 1965 and 1967. When he was demobbed, he went to law school. He then became an aide to the attorney general for Illinois, before working as a state prosecutor. He had been in private practice ever since and was still an attorney in Inverness.

'The bulk of my work is keeping people safe. So we focus on things like police and fire and building control. We take care of our residents. We handle construction and housing regulations and, of course, keep the streets clear of snow in the winter and clean in the summer.'

The Mayor promised to stand me lunch and, after showing me round the silos, we walked outside. The silos were, of course, not for missiles but for grain, and had lain empty for years. They had been built in 1900. In the 1980s some bright spark suggested that, if they weren't going to be used for storing grain, they should be used for something useful. If not, they should be torn down. It was something of a brainwave but I have to say they are the strangest public offices I have seen anywhere.

We walked round to the war memorial and stood solemnly there for a few moments. Mayor Jack was rightly very proud of it. It was newly built, simple, elegant and fitting. It had sections for the Army, Navy, Marines and Air Force, and was recently dedicated in the name of Corporal Peter J Giannopolous of the United States Marine Corps, from Inverness, Illinois, who was killed in action in the Iraqi town of Fallujah in November 2004.

Jack suddenly thrust his fist out to me and dropped an empty brass shell casing into my hand. 'That is one of the rounds fired by the honour party the day we dedicated the memorial to Peter. I'd like you to have it.'

I thanked him profusely. I felt privileged. I just wish the British public valued our servicemen and women as much as do the Americans.

*   *   *

Out on stories, I began to pay close attention to what Isabel Fraser and her Grampian TV crew were doing. I watched closely how they filmed things and worked closely as a team. Then I'd watch the cut story on the news at night and saw how it all worked. The bureau cameraman was a hilarious Mancunian called Steve Horrocks who went out of his way to show me how his kit worked, how he would set the iris for exposure, and what he had to do to compose a shot or choose a background for an interview.

In radio, I knew about sound effects and background noise and using music as part of my reports, but working with light and pictures was new to me. I was fascinated by it. My father had been an award-winning amateur photographer and made a bit of money on the side selling pictures to the Inverness papers, although he never once showed me around a camera. However, some of his skills must have been passed down genetically, because I love photography and became quite proficient. Given all this, I realised that I wanted to work in television and began planning how I could engineer a move.

Although I was not a fan, I started to apply for jobs at Grampian TV because it was the local station. I received many polite letters of thanks but no interviews. Around the same time I had an interview and screen test for a BBC TV job also in Aberdeen, but no offer. I settled down to wait. However my next move was not forward to television, but back to newspapers.

My tastes have never been sybaritic. I'm not interested in cars, I don't have expensive hobbies and I don't spend lavishly on clothes. I am careful with money, I joke about parsimony, but I am not a miser. The biggest outlay I have is on airline tickets, as I love travelling. But money has never motivated me. However, when I received a phone call offering me a job as the North sports editor of the *Press and Journal*, the Aberdeen-based broadsheet which covered most of Scotland, I was sorely tempted.

The job itself was not particularly challenging, or so I thought, but what made me gulp, blink and pinch myself was the salary. I was being offered double what I was earning at MFR. I was twenty-three years old and still living at home. With this kind of pay rise I could easily afford to buy myself a flat in Inverness and get on the property ladder at the same time as furthering my career.

Bill McAllister was the *P&J*'s Inverness bureau chief and a well-known personality in the town. He had been a journalist for years and was also a Labour councilor. He made me the offer over a coffee in Inverness one afternoon and I signed the contract there and then, the only time in my life I have let money make a decision for me. I threw in one condition, and that was that I was able to do match reports for Iain Wilson's Saturday sports programme on MFR. Bill could hardly say no, because he did exactly the same for the BBC.

I joined the paper just in time for the Highland League sides' annual foray into the Scottish Cup, and I travelled far and wide. It was really enjoyable at first. Every Saturday I would go to the game of the day and work on a 'Sunday for Monday' piece. This involved speaking to the players and coaches afterwards and digging around for a story. Several problems cropped up around this time.

The first was that I had taken over from an experienced journalist called David Love, who had held the position for years before me. David was a great Caley man and a good pal. He knew the scene inside out and had far better contacts than I had. An opportunity had arisen in Inverness for a freelance to service the national papers which had withdrawn their own bureaux men on cost grounds. David had spotted this gap in the market and left the *P&J* to fill it.

Two of the markets he serviced were the *Sunday Mail* and the *Sunday Post*, both of whom carried his columns. He would invariably attend the same match as me, and had interviewed the same personalities. The problem for me was that my 'Sunday for Monday' would appear as his 'Saturday for Sunday.' Being scooped like this was irritating, to say the least. It was made worse by the fact that, while David had been at the *P&J*, he had no competition. After I had taken over from him, he became my competition.

David and his brother Jim were journalistic stalwarts in Inverness. Jim would be the editor of the *Inverness Courier* twenty years later and offer

me a weekly column about life as a big-city TV reporter through the eyes
of an Inverness boy. The ink had barely dried on my first dispatch, when
he died, tragically young. David's freelance career had a meteoric rise,
and he started a news agency in Inverness which blossoms to this day.
However, my career dipped shortly after I joined the *P&J*.

At Radio Forth I had daily dealings with the top men of the day in
Scottish football, and had never heard a cross word. Even when things got
tough and there were difficult questions which a reporter had to ask, they
were answered properly and politely by these men, although normally
ridden with the usual clichés.

But the personalities with whom I now had to deal were very different.
Highland League managers, possibly because they weren't full-time professionals, were prickly in the extreme. Worse than the managers were
the chairmen and committee men. They would lift the phone and shout
at me for the slightest thing. It got to the stage where I would dread going
to Keith or Buckie or Huntly, because the minute I flashed my press card
to cross the threshold, I would be accosted by a blazer who would nip my
head about the paper's coverage.

Worst of all was Alan McRae, then the chairman of Cove Rangers, who
would phone me at all hours to harangue me, demanding better coverage
for his club than, say, Rothes or Brora Rangers. At the time he was involved
in a campaign to get Cove into the Scottish League and believed they
were more deserving of the headlines. I said that headlines were dictated
by newsworthiness, regardless of the club. I thought he had little chance
of getting top-flight status, given that the city already had Aberdeen FC
in the League and had a huge support. Nearly thirty years, on Alan is
President of the SFA and still courting controversy. Cove Rangers are still
in the Highland League.

One man with whom I had daily dealings without any problems
whatsoever was Steve Paterson, the Elgin City player-manager. He was
building a great team which went on to win many honours. He was a
pleasure to deal with, and I could call him at any time of the day or night.
I would often sit with him in the Borough Briggs dressing room after a
game and chew the fat. He went on to be Inverness Caledonian Thistle's
manager, and was in charge of the team the night they soundly beat
Celtic in Glasgow in the famous 'Supercaleygoballisticcelticareatrocious'
Scottish Cup tie. I was delighted for him.

I wasn't even disappointed when he left to become manager at
Aberdeen, because I thought he was a great guy and deserved all the

success in the world. It wasn't until his departure from Pittodrie, after a much publicised drinking session which caused him to be sacked after missing a league game, that I learned about all the problems he'd been having with drink and gambling. I had never noticed any alcohol-related issues during our dealings. It was sad.

My time at the *P&J* was very lucrative but deeply unhappy. I tried to make the best of it and slowly I began to come onto my game. At the beginning of the next football season, I had just started to look at estate agents' schedules for flats in Inverness when the decision about my future was taken for me. Somebody at Aberdeen Journals HQ removed a notice-board belonging to the National Union of Journalists.

At the same time, staff were called in one by one to have their contracts renegotiated, something that would ordinarily have happened collectively. The father of the chapel was called to a meeting with the managing director, and he was told that the company no longer recognised the union. A ballot for industrial action followed and, before long, 120 journalists in Aberdeen, Elgin and Inverness were on strike.

In Britain in the 1980s, the unions were being challenged and defeated by management around the country. The NUJ wasn't a particularly militant union, but the strike grew nasty. Initially, I didn't think the dispute would last more than a few days. A year later we were still on the picket line.

While I hadn't particularly enjoyed my time at the paper, I had been keen to carry on and make the best of it, with a view to getting into television as a sports reporter. Eventually, the editor hired somebody to do my job and I knew my career at the paper was over.

There was a strong campaign involving pretty well every non-Tory politician in Scotland, among them Alex Salmond and Donald Dewar, to persuade both sides to resolve the dispute and get everybody back to work. Throughout the year-long strike the paper was published every day, despite many contributors, readers and advertisers withdrawing their support. But, because the editor had to resort to hiring staff who wouldn't otherwise have got over the front door of the paper, the *P&J* was a pale shadow of its former self.

The editor, Harry Roulston, appeared in the dock of the High Court in Inverness charged with contempt of court, after one of the strike-breakers got the story badly wrong while covering a murder trial. The accused's defence counsel, Donald Finlay QC, described the error as the most disgraceful piece of journalism he had ever encountered. We felt vindicated by this because the paper's regular court correspondent, an outstanding reporter called Neil MacPhail who was standing on a picket line, would never have made such a basic error.

I was young and carefree. Unlike many of my colleagues, I didn't have a wife or a family to support. The dispute hurt me, but at the end of the day I had much less to lose than many others who had taken to the picket lines. We shared sunshine, snow and shadow and enjoyed camaraderie, but we all lost. The paper was damaged immeasurably by the strike, and 120 of us had spent a year on the streets.

Twelve months on, some of us went back to the *P&J* with the slate wiped clean. Others, like Ron MacKenna and I, felt that we could not. He went to the *Glasgow Evening Times* to become the local government correspondent, and the city chambers would be his beat. The strike sickened me, and I'd had my fill of blazers, pickets and Thatcher. I saw an advert for a vacancy at the world service of the Swiss Broadcasting Corporation in Bern, and I applied.

I knew it was the real deal when they flew me down to London for an interview at the Swiss embassy near Marble Arch. The interview went well but the news test was really hard. Thankfully, I had maintained my old habits during the strike and was still an avid radio bulletin listener, TV news viewer and devourer of the papers. I passed with flying colours. I was asked to translate a passage from French into English, and luckily there was still enough of my favourite other language in the deep recesses of my brain to enable me to breeze it. I made a mental note to thank my mother again when I got home for all those childhood French holidays.

As I left, Elspeth Danzeisen, who would be my boss, took out a bundle of £50 notes the size of a house brick, and peeled off the top inch. Pressing it into my hand, she thanked me for coming. I assured her that the pleasure was all mine.

*   *   *

I jumped into the Chevy and followed the Mayoral motorcade. We passed more houses but even now, a day on from my first drive round Inverness, there was still nobody to be seen.

I followed the convoy into the impressive Inverness golf club grounds and pulled straight up at the door. A young man in a tunic handed me a ticket and urged me to leave the vehicle. This was valet parking, and I suddenly realised I was somewhere a lot posher than any golf club in the one true Inverness.

Clearly, Jack was no ordinary member. Everybody greeted him deferentially. I was wearing a beige cord jacket, dark blue chinos, a checked shirt and deck shoes. I cursed myself for not bringing a tie. He was wearing a black sports jacket, black polo shirt and black trousers. I wondered if golf's 'man in black' himself, Gary Player, had been an influence.

The clubhouse was an attractive building, inside and out. It was unusually tranquil and elegant for something American. Portraits of previous captains adorned the wall, alongside landscapes of prominent holes at St Andrews, as you would expect. It exuded the reassuring calmness and tranquility which comes with great wealth.

We were shown through to the dining room and sat at Mayor Jack's usual table. I was faced by a fairway-sized linen napkin, what seemed to be a dozen knives and forks and half a dozen glasses. And this was just for lunch. Our table was beside the window, and the view out onto the course was easily the best in the building. The manicured fairways rolled away into the distance.

'Do you like golf, Michael?' he asked. I wondered why he calls me by my full name, and I wondered if I should have told him what I really thought about golf and golf clubs. However, I felt so comfortable here that I didn't. It wouldn't really have been good form to have said that, if I was ever elected to be the First Minister of Scotland, I would eradicate golf, level all clubhouses and turn the courses into public parks.

I told him the truth – well part of it – that I was quite a good golfer when I was a teenager, and spent as much time as I could on the municipal course in the one true Inverness. Membership of Kingsmills, the private course, was well beyond my family's means, and not even something I would have considered. After an incident when my then girlfriend was ejected from Kingsmills because her belt had a tiny strip of denim on it, golf became a taboo subject for me. It would be first on my target list after I had assumed the mantle of First Minister.

'I want to twin this club with the Kingsmills club in your Inverness,' said Jack. 'I want to start a mini Ryder Cup and play for it every other year. What do you think of that idea?'

I found myself staring in silence at the dozen knives and forks before me.

'This town was founded by a member of the McIntosh clan, Arthur McIntosh, who came from your Inverness in 1929. He came here because it reminded him of home and decided to name it so. He started off living in the north shore of suburban Chicago then moved here.

'We are very fortunate to have that link. I am looking forward to a lasting relationship with the town and a competitive relationship with the golf club.'

We ordered, and the longer I was inside, the more I liked this place, despite my usual revulsion for golf clubs and the rather delicate nature of our conversation. It was pleasant and understated. I felt completely at home. The menu was a treat, and the dishes were not over the top in complexity or cost. I ordered one of my staples when in the US: a club sandwich and a glass of half-fat milk.

I was right: Gary Player was a part of Mayor Jack's life. He and the man in black were friends. Close friends, as it turned out. 'At the Open at Muirfield in 1987, Gary and I had lunch with Jack Nicklaus, Henry Cotton and Arnold Palmer. We had a lovely time.'

I told him about working for Radio Forth and being on the green when Faldo won the claret jug that day. But I reckoned if he managed to have a table with guests like those at it, he wouldn't want to hear my tales of brushes with the celebrities.

'Do you know Greigy?' he asked.

I wasn't sure who he meant and scoured my scant knowledge of the world of golf. 'Greg Norman?' I ventured, another luminary I interviewed at Muirfield in 1987. He was defending the title he won the year before at Turnberry.

'No, "Greigy", John Greig of Rangers. He's a very good friend of mine. I know him and Alistair Johnstone of the ING international banking group very well.' Johnstone was the chairman of Rangers, briefly, before the club collapsed.

I gulped. It was mightily impressive that an American would know the Rangers legend. Football as we know it in Scotland doesn't figure very highly in America, even today when the USA has one of the top national teams in the world. Gary Player may have been big in the world of golf, but John Greig easily matched his status in the world of football, in Scotland at any rate.

'When we were at Muirfield in 87, Greigy took me to Gullane and showed me the sand dunes where the Rangers players used to train.' I smiled. When I was a youngster, I vividly remembered the TV pictures of the squad being beasted up and down in full training kit. It did wonders for stamina, but I'm not sure what it did for morale.

'We stayed at a castle a few miles away from the course and I have never been so cold in all my life. I think that's why you Scots have such funny accents, because your lips are frozen together!

'Greigy took me to this pub near the castle and we saw some kids playing soccer in the car park. He said, "watch this", and went outside to kick a ball around with them. I didn't know his standing at the time, but I sure did afterwards. The game stopped and the kids just looked at each other and said "God, it's John Greig". It was the equivalent of me bumping into Babe Ruth.'

After lunch, Jack and I took a little stroll out of the dining room, along a corridor, and through an anonymous door into the gentlemen's lounge. This was a slightly more raucous place than the dining room, but I felt no less at home. There was a pool table, and gaggles of men were sitting around playing cards or chatting. On one side of the room was perched a large and well-stocked bar. I walked with Jack as he worked the room, shaking hands and slapping backs. He was a pro.

'My challenge here is to keep the bucolic nature of Inverness intact,' he said, between tables. I looked ahead and everybody knew he was coming to see them. Their pleasure was obvious. I was in the company of a local hero. He was a real character who said the right things to the right people and worked hard to keep the area exclusive. It may also have been because residents in Inverness paid the lowest tax rate in the greater Chicago area and had done so for the past twelve years.

'Everything is growing up around us so it's a constant challenge. It's a sign of the times and we are surrounded by commerce and development. Apart from a couple of offices there's nothing commercial in Inverness. This is a residential neighbourhood and we want to keep it that way. I'm here because I love this town. This is where I live and raised my family and I want to protect it,' he said.

As he worked the room, I hit Mayor Jack with a hypothesis. He stopped and listened.

'A big Swiss pharmaceutical comes to you and says "we want to build here and give the area 1,000 jobs". Hypothetically speaking, what if that was to happen?' 'I'll give you the real answer to the hypothetical question – no.'

He showed me to the door, and the valet parking attendant went off to get the Chevy. We shook hands and said our farewells.

'You asked me about Vietnam,' he said, gripping my hand longer than a normal handshake. 'Well, I've done my research about you and I know that you too have seen combat. I'd like to thank you for your service and wish you well for your trip.'

CHAPTER THREE

Inverness, Mississippi

Where the Mississippi rolls down to the sea,
And lovers find the place they like to be.
How many times before this song was ending,
Love and understanding, everywhere around.
Mississippi, I'll remember you.

Pussycat

Having thoroughly enjoyed my time with Mayor Tatooles, I didn't hit the road, Jack, immediately after we parted. Instead, I drove the Chevy around Inverness for a while longer in my quest to find a human being.

The light was fading and I needed to head south shortly but, as I took one last look around, I found that I still couldn't see any people. I assumed they were either inside their houses, at work, or at the golf club with Jack.

It took an hour to get out of metropolitan Chicago and hit I-55 South, the main route to my next Inverness. I dropped down onto Algonquin again but, as soon as I saw the toll signs on the freeway, I came off and rejoined the parallel, unclassified and free route. I eventually hit the 55, which runs from Chicago to New Orleans via St Louis and Memphis, a few bucks to the good after the tollbooths. It's always the small victories ...

The day was slipping away to the west when I finally put rubber on that main road. And as I steered through the flat, featureless wheat plains, I couldn't help but think it was a pretty dull route and probably best travelled in the dark.

I had done my map recce that morning before checking out of the unspeakable motel, and had formed a mental timeline for the day. I had estimated that, all being well, I should make St Louis that night, rest there, and then keep heading south the next day. I had never been to St Louis before. After I had left St Louis, I concluded that not spending much time there had probably been a good idea.

The only notable thing about the journey was stopping for gas near the bridge over the Mississippi, close to the one I had crossed two days previously on the Zephyr. Service stations in the USA can be like hypermarkets where you can buy pretty well anything. As I proferred my credit card, I noticed a stainless steel briefcase for sale at $12.

A bargain is only a bargain if you need it, or so I'm told. I didn't really need this, but it looked great and was dead cheap. I bought it, and filled it with notebooks, pamphlets and newspaper cuttings from my trip. It was by my side from then until I returned to the one true Inverness.

Today, it is open on the desk in my study as I write this. I take it to work now and then if I'm working on a special project. One colleague let slip that she always thinks it's full of contraband. Another asked if I was an extra in a movie about the Colombian drug cartels. Every time I use it, I think of St Louis.

I can't say I was hooked by one sign I drove past on my way into town. It told me that Jefferson Barracks National Cemetery was three miles away, Ulyssess S Grant's farm five miles away, and the Busch stadium ten miles away. St Louis also hosted the Museum of the Dog. With sights like those, who wouldn't be back?

Having re-crossed the mighty river, I headed into town. I drove past the Gateway Arch, built in the 1960s and the tallest man-made monument in the USA, as I headed for my unspeakable motel. The Arch was pleasant to look at, and later I learned that it was created by Eero Saarinen, the Finnish architect who designed Dulles airport in Washington DC, one of my favourite buildings in the US. The Gateway Arch stands down by the Mississippi, as a monument to the westward expansion of the country.

The freeway cuts through the centre of the city and, on the way to the unspeakable motel, I saw the grandstands and elevated scoreboards of the Busch Stadium. Later, I drove past the massive Anheuser Busch brewery, where the clouds of steam and the heavy, hoppy smell took me back to the 1980s and my days in Edinburgh.

The smell and the memories of my student life brought on quite a thirst. My mouth was dry and I felt really tired. I glanced at my watch and realised I'd been driving for more than five hours. Maps can be deceptive, and the United States is an enormous country. I found the motel, and was delighted to see there were two restaurants within walking distance. So I checked in but didn't go to my room. Instead, I parked the Chevy outside and walked stiffly across to the first.

I sat at a window table and opened my new briefcase. Looking round to see if anyone was watching me use my new bit of kit, I spread out my maps and notebooks and began plotting my activities for the next day. I couldn't afford to spend much time in St Louis, and would have to keep heading south. I guestimated that, instead of loitering in what appeared on the face of it to be a pretty dull place, I could use any spare time driving alongside the Mississippi.

Now that I had stopped driving and my concentration levels had dropped, I was getting sleepy. I was also choking for that beer. Or possibly two. The waitress came over, and I ordered another of my US staples: the biggest rack of ribs they had. And, of course, a beer. Given I was in St Louis, a stone's throw from the Anheuser Busch brewery where they made it, I would have a Budweiser.

'I'm sorry, but we're dry,' said the waitress. She obviously registered the look of panic on my face. I must also have made a move to clear away all my wares, prior to bolting for the door and the adjoining establishment.

'Next door's dry, too,' she added, walking off to the kitchen with my order. 'Local bylaw.'

My frustrating evening didn't end there. I could have driven to the nearest service station, bought a six-pack of said local brew and taken it back to my room, but I was just too tired. I had a booked a non-smoking room but, when I entered, it reeked like pubs did in the old days. I just wanted to sleep but I couldn't face going to bed in this room.

I toddled round to reception, but because it was so late the door had been bolted shut. I had to engage with the nightshift through a security window. I felt rather exposed and was glad I'd stashed the briefcase in the car.

The woman working behind the counter was in good humour. 'Smell this one,' she drawled, handing me the keycard, 'and if you like it, it's yours.'

*   *   *

The trade union movement had one last swipe at me before I left for Switzerland. My flight from Heathrow to Zurich was delayed by a French Air Traffic Controllers' strike. The captain ordered the tug to push us back a couple of feet from the gate, so that technically we had departed and were no longer bound by UK duty laws. In a lovely touch, he ordered the cabin crew to break out the champagne. I didn't feel I had anything to celebrate because the day had been rather a melancholy one. I felt that I was leaving Scotland, and indeed the UK, for a self-imposed exile. I'd had my fill of everything and just wanted to keep my head down for a while.

I've never been one for drowning my sorrows, and I never drink alcohol during daylight hours. I can recall the bitter sweet taste of the champagne to this day, and remember how I spent that flight contemplating my navel.

My career, indeed my life, had been one successful break after another. I had started in this business while still a fifteen-year-old schoolboy and had become one of the best-known names in the game. But I had foolishly taken a job because of the salary rather than for the job itself, and I had fallen flat on my face.

My overwhelming feeling was of bitterness and anger: not directed at Bill McAllister, because he thought he was giving me another break, nor at the NUJ, because nobody twisted my arm to go on strike. I was angry with myself. I was determined to make the most of Switzerland and bounce back stronger and, more importantly, smarter. I had another glass of champagne after take-off, and I felt much better when I saw the Alps in the distance.

Zurich airport is built around a railway station, and within minutes of landing I was on a train to Bern, my home for the next three years. I took a taxi to the Swiss Broadcasting Corporation HQ and met a Swiss journalist called Martin Feller, a dear friend to this day, who gave me an envelope which contained reams of documentation and a set of keys. The keys were to an apartment which had been rented for me, and the documentation concerned my status as a 'gastarbeiter', or guest worker.

The next day I went to the Fremdenpolizei, the police department dealing with foreign workers, where I had a chest x-ray to prove I didn't have TB. Then, in a consummate display of Swiss efficiency, I was paraded down a line of desks where I answered questions about this, that and the other. At the end of the process, after confirming I was neither a refugee nor bent on anarchy or terrorism, I left with a Swiss Ausweis, confirming I had the right to work in Switzerland and, with pages of Germanic Fremdenpolizei stamps in my passport, confirming that I had the right to be there.

Bern struck me as a pretty but sleepy little gingerbread village, and I expected fairy-tale characters at every turn. The 'aldstadt' or 'old town' was my favourite, with its 'lauben': covered arcades on each side of the streets. It's delightful in the summer, when the cobbled lanes are lined with flower boxes and the bustle of passers-by is accompanied by the gentle trickle of fresh water in elaborate stone fountains from which livestock once drank. It's even more picturesque in the winter when snow has fallen, the light is down and the temperature is very low.

The old town was built on a spit of land surrounded by the River Aare. Because its source is the glaciers of the Bernese Oberland, the water is a pleasing turquoise colour but is shockingly cold. Having swum in Loch Ness and the North Sea as a boy, I thought I knew what cold water was all about, but the Aare was, if possible, even colder.

While I loved the quaintness of the town, the Swiss took some getting used to. Martin knew what was what, as did his university friend Urs Geiser who would become my big pal on nightshifts. There was another Bernese journalist called Beat Witschi, who had a very un-Swiss fashion sense and who dressed in flamboyant, colourful clothes. These lads had two things in common. They had all studied in Scotland and they spoke English with broad Scottish accents. Fuck me, Beat could even play the bagpipes! I loved them, and they were very good to me.

But, in general terms, the Swiss were a pretty stuffy and staid lot. To be fair to my three amigos, they enjoyed a good joke against themselves but they had travelled and knew how others viewed them. Switzerland was a land of contrasts and, while I saw an open and permissive attitude towards drugs and prostitution, there was hell to pay in your apartment block if you made a noise after 10pm. And so it proved when I had a flat-warming party. I invited all my new chums and neighbours, and we drank late into the night. But the couple upstairs left at 10pm, and phoned at 11pm to complain about the noise.

On my way to work one morning on my first week, I dropped my rubbish bags at the front door of the block just as an old lady was passing. She unleashed a verbal assault against me in Swiss German, which I didn't understand. I smiled at her and walked off to get the tram to work. When I de-bussed at the other end, I joined a group of people waiting to cross the road. The red man seemed to be taking an inordinate length of time and, having carefully checked to see that there was no traffic approaching from either direction, I stepped out. Accompanied by lots of tuts and several 'oy, oy, oys', I reached the other side. Martin, Urs and Beat shook their heads quietly and explained that jaywalking was virtually a capital offence in Switzerland. My day was to get even worse.

That night I returned to find that the binbags had been emptied on my doorstep. I was flabbergasted. The Hauswart, or concierge, knew where to deposit them because he had slit them open and found an envelope bearing my name. He had also posted a curt note through the letterbox to tell me my crime had been putting the rubbish out a day early, and that this was my punishment.

He was a horrible little ferret and the kind of guy you could well imagine as a KGB informer back in the days. He always lurked around the place like a bad smell, and I was sure he was up to no good. Decades later, I switched on the TV news halfway through a bulletin to hear about a man who had imprisoned his family in the cellar for years. The pictures showed a Germanic-looking housing block, and I immediately thought that Ferret had been rumbled. But I was surprised and a little disappointed to learn that the story was about Josef Fritzl in Austria and not the Ferret in my flat in Bern.

He shouted at me, again in Swiss German, when I next saw him on the stairs after the binbag incident. I wanted to punch his lights out, but he was an older man and I didn't feel it was right. However, on evenings I came home drunk, I would let the air out of the tyres of his bike or piss on his flowerbeds. Again, it's the small victories.

He had a little cubbyhole in the basement, next to a cellar which contained our nuclear shelters. I'd heard so much about these that I couldn't wait to have one. Swiss law, I wasn't surprised to learn, demanded that you kept a month's worth of canned food and water in these shelters in case Moscow or Washington pushed the button. I incurred Ferret's wrath, and the wrath of many neighbours, when I crammed my shelter with my skis, bike and crates of beer. When Ferret bitched about this, I feigned linguistic ignorance, even though, after three years I had picked up enough Swiss German to know full well what the wee scrote was on about.

The dialect spoken in the capital is, not unreasonably, known as Bern-Deutsch and bears no relationship that I ever discovered to High German. It's an unusual tongue, and comprises lots of hacking and spitting noises. I always thought it was more phlegmish than Flemish. Three useless things about me you don't know: I can't shave unless I'm stark naked, I can play the William Tell Overture on my cheeks with my fingers, and I can speak Swiss German. I've never found any practical application for the last two.

The job was fascinating, although not taxing. I worked for Swiss Radio International, the world service of the Swiss Broadcasting Corporation. There were umpteen different language services, and each had its own staff, studios and programmes. There were journalists there from all over the world, and each had different stories to tell.

In that newsroom I soon realised that I was a Ford Escort in a news world of Jaguars and Bentleys. And, while I could write a news story standing upside down, I understood that whatever skills I possessed were pretty rough and ready, and that they would require significant polishing before I tried to get back into the UK job market. I was a streetwise, foot-in-the-door reporter. My colleagues were proper journalists who could speak several languages and who all had degrees.

My salary made the *P&J*'s look miserly and, even though the cost of living in Switzerland was not cheap, my modest lifestyle permitted me to salt away a sizeable sum every month. I made up my mind that when I returned to the UK I would do two things: use my nest egg to buy a property and study for a degree. While in Switzerland I also dusted off the manuscript of a novel I had started shortly after my father died, and I resumed work on it.

The stories on which we worked at Swiss Radio International were lengthy and complex. We covered serious global issues about politics, economics and foreign affairs. I hadn't been there for more than a week when Iraq invaded Kuwait. This was a dramatic story which kept us going for months. A year later 'the gang of eight', hardline communists opposed to President Gorbachev's policies of *perestroika* and *glasnost*, tried to overthrow him while he was on holiday in the Crimea. I'd never before written news stories about a war or a coup. Interesting times.

But the best bit about Bern was leaving the place. Because Switzerland was so centrally-placed, and having a Swiss bank account with a telephone number paycheck going into it every month, I was able to travel far and wide. Berlin was a favourite destination before I had a girlfriend in Florence who would meet me for the weekend there or somewhere conveniently equidistant, such as Milan, Turin or Venice. It was all too perfect.

I spent weeks in Vienna reading Graham Greene and going to classical music concerts, desperate to lose the dilettante tag. I flew to Helsinki for a few days and, when I became bored, I took a train to Turku where I boarded a ferry for Stockholm. When I eventually got bored there, I returned to Bern. When I went to Iceland I felt totally dislocated and alien after I flew from Geneva to Glasgow, and I spent the afternoon walking around the shops on Sauchiehall Street while waiting for the connecting Icelandair flight to Reykjavik.

I went on a trip across Russia on the Trans-Siberian Express and fended off overtures from half a dozen women, who wrote to me afterwards saying they knew Boris our sleeping car attendant. We were told before our trip that all the sleeping car attendants were KGB agents.

I was flattered by their letters and the moderately pornographic photographs they contained, but I couldn't help them in any way. Today, I wish I'd strung them along a bit, and had generated better pornography by pretending I worked at Faslane. True to form, old Boris kept in touch by letter for a while, but he dropped me when he realised I had no secrets to sell.

The train took several days to travel between Moscow and Irkutsk and it was an enjoyable experience, if not as luxurious as the Zephyr. In the bar of the Irkutsk hotel, I began chatting to a party of students from East Germany and became pals with one of the girls. The next night, she suggested we go for a walk, which seemed silly to me as the temperature was minus 20C. But she knew her way around the city. She took me to a bar frequented by locals, where we drank cheap vodka late into the night, away from the claustrophobic atmosphere of our hotel which was alive with KGB minders keeping an eye on straying foreigners.

We were almost certainly followed wherever we went that night although, being a novice, I couldn't spot our tail. Hotels occupied by western tourists were routinely surveyed in those days. Knowing that some shifty KGB man secretly filmed us with a hidden camera in her room later that night, and that the video tape of a plump, pink Scotsman's moves might exist in a KGB archive somewhere, still gives me nightmares.

Claudie was a beautiful girl with long dark hair and mesmeric green eyes. She was studying Russian in Moscow and was due to return there two days hence. I would also be in the capital then *en route* back to Switzerland and, not having mobile phones in those days, we made plans to meet up.

In case of delays, which were all too common when you flew on Aeroflot, we agreed to wait outside Lenin's mausoleum on Red Square every hour between 3pm and 8pm until we met. I felt like a character in the John Le Carré novel I was reading. When she raced across Red Square and hurled herself into my arms that afternoon, the picture was complete.

She wasn't allowed to bring guests into her university dorm, so we went back to my hotel near the Kremlin and ran upstairs to my room, where I ordered champagne and caviar prior to picking up where we'd left off in Siberia. By now I felt more like James Bond. It was wonderful.

In the days before emails and text messages, we engaged in the old-fashioned practice of writing letters to each other. It wasn't easy for her to get a visa to come to Switzerland, so I made plans to go to East Germany. We arranged to meet in Berlin at the start of her Easter holidays and, after a few romantic days there, she would take me back to Jena to stay with her family. I couldn't wait. My romantic fantasy was heightened one afternoon when a man in a blue uniform with a post horn on his peaked cap turned up at my flat in Bern with an envelope for me. Puzzled, I signed the form on his clipboard and thanked him, before opening the only telegram I have ever received in my life. It was from Claudie in Moscow to tell me what flight she'd be on.

By now I was an old Berlin hand, and I stood at Schonefeld airport like a local waiting for a prodigal's return. For once, Aeroflot's Moscow flight was on time, and the arrivals door opened to reveal Claudie looking even more beautiful than I remembered. She ran across the concourse towards me with her arms open wide, but she sprinted past me and threw herself into the embrace of a man standing a few yards behind me.

'Mike, I'd like you to meet my boyfriend Max,' she said, having prised herself out of his arms after what seemed like an hour later.

I slept alone that night in the five-star hotel suite I'd booked in West Berlin, and drank the bottle of champagne I'd ordered to be iced and waiting for our return, while disinterestedly watching a Bundesliga match on TV. Love's young dream were shacked up in a B&B somewhere. When I think back, I should have just bugged out of the situation but, bizarrely, I joined them again on the train to Jena the next morning. We had a compartment to ourselves, and I sat squirming while Claudie and Max devoured each other.

Jena was a place my father had often talked about throughout my childhood. As a keen photographer, he told me that East German cameras were the best in the world. He said there was something about the way the Carl Zeiss factory in Jena ground glass that made their lenses perfect. I found his eulogies odd, because the optics of periscopes on the U-boats, which tried to kill him daily during the War, were made by Carl Zeiss in Jena. He was dismissive of Japanese cameras, and always said he preferred his battered old East German Werra, with its Jena-ground Tessar lens, to a Nikon. Maybe that's why I decided to stick it out with Romeo and Juliet: to pay some kind of homage to my dad in their home town.

Her parents were old-fashioned Germans and very fine people. They made me welcome, despite the fact that materially they didn't have much at all. They had lived through World War Two and the Cold War, and were now desperate to enjoy the new Germany. I spent a lot of time with Claudie's delightful grandmother who was in her nineties and who spoke movingly about both World Wars. It was a humbling experience, and I was often close to tears in her company. I had a litre bottle of Johnnie Walker in my battered old rucksack and, when I gave it to Claudie's father, he reacted as though I'd given him a cheque for a million dollars.

The next day he asked me if I'd like to go to Dresden, and I almost bit his hand off. We three chaps spent a fabulous morning exploring this Saxon jewel, still shattered by the allied firebomb raids of 1945, before he and Max suddenly decided that it was time to go. Something was clearly afoot but I didn't know what. Despite being an unreconstituted Scotsman, I wanted to see more of the beautiful Meissen porcelain on show in the Dresden City Museum, but my pleas fell on deaf ears. As we headed back to the car I heard the sirens.

'Neo-Nazis are coming,' said Max. 'Today is Hitler's birthday. We must leave.'

'But I'd like to see that,' I said.

Both men looked at me as though I had two heads. We trotted back to the car. Soon I would see all I needed to, as escaping traffic was halted to allow the police to bring out dogs and even water cannon to try to quell a full-scale riot. I sensed that both men were deeply ashamed that I was seeing this. My pronouncement that, as I was a journalist, unpleasant things were to be confronted and not ignored, was dismissed out of hand.

The next day was my birthday, and I endured another excruciating train journey back to Berlin with John and Yoko, thankfully minus hangover. We got an S-Bahn train to Potsdam where I was to meet Max's parents before I would finally be released from my ordeal. I was greeted at their trim suburban bungalow by a lovely couple who presented me with a rose as a birthday gift. They spoke excellent English and, like Claudie's parents, were desperate to enjoy a future without the Berlin Wall.

Max's father had been in the Luftwaffe, and had been taken prisoner in France not long after the War started. He said he loved Scotland, because he had been sent to a POW camp there and worked on a farm for the duration.

'Perhaps you will know the place,' he said proudly. I was expecting a big town or city, like Dundee or Perth, with an agricultural hinterland. 'No, no,' he said. 'Ecclefechan!' I couldn't help but laugh. It felt so incongruous that he knew a name like that.

Like Claudie's parents, they were lovely people who had endured so much. It was obvious how similar they were to my own family, and that they and their forebears would have endured the same wartime agonies of deprivation, despair and death, and of waving off sons to war not knowing if they would return.

My father never hated Germany or the Germans. He eulogised about German cameras, and we had Audis and Volkswagens down the years. He said that the German sailors who tried to kill him were exactly the same as he was: conscripted to do a job they didn't want. One of his many War stories was about the German Negers, or manned torpedoes, which attacked his convoy. He said that Wivern's sonar had picked up the Germans' trace, and had launched depth charges which blew to pieces the sailors straddling the weapons. When their body parts were recovered and lain on Wivern's deck, he saw that they had been teenage boys exactly the same as him.

He was never bitter about the attempted attacks by these men. He knew that they faced virtual suicide missions every time they were deployed, as they had to drive their torpedoes towards allied shipping using nothing more sophisticated than a watch and a compass. After they had selected the targets and set the weapons running, the German pilots also faced a long and dangerous swim back to their mother ship.

On our first family holiday in Tunisia, when I was a little boy, we became friendly with a German couple named Berger. He was old enough to have been in the War and, despite language issues, he got on very well with my dad. I would blithely sketch away on a notebook while the grown-ups chatted. To my father's horror, he noticed that I had just completed the elegant lines of a Spitfire doing a victory roll with a Messerschmitt aflame, plunging earthward in the background. Surreptitiously, he took the book from me while Herr Berger danced with my mother. He told me soberly that, had they seen the sketch, it would have deeply offended the Germans, so from then on I was to stick to drawing the Apollo astronauts and their Saturn V rockets, without exception.

My father hated the 'two world wars and one world cup' type of nationalism. He was sentient about the War. He knew better than any of us that the only difference between our family and the Bergers, Max's parents and Claudie's parents, had been a mad bastard called Adolf Hitler.

We got the S-Bahn back to Berlin's Zoo Station where I said goodbye to Ryan O'Neal and Ali MacGraw. It was hugs and kisses all round, before Max announced that he and Claudie were to be married and would I be a special guest at the wedding? I thanked them profusely for their company and their parents' hospitality, and jumped on a train to Switzerland. I never saw either of them again, but I still have Claudie's telegram somewhere.

I returned to Bern and resumed my storywriting about the UN security council, the ICRC and the Uruguay round of talks at GATT, the General Agreement on Tariffs and Trade. This was an international body which fixed the global price of millions of things, from shoelaces to car tyres and, although its dealings were boring to the point of rendering you catatonic, they were crucially important.

Saddam Hussein retreated, ignominiously defeated, from Kuwait, yet still clung to power in Iraq while his conquerors George Bush and Margaret Thatcher were voted out of office. I became interested in Africa, as we covered the troubles flaring in Liberia and Rwanda. Then, as the former Yugoslavia fragmented following the collapse of the Iron Curtain, Slovenia announced its secession, sparking a lengthy and bloody Balkan civil war, only an hour and a half's flight from London.

The generous leave entitlement and excellent salary meant I was seldom in Bern on a day off. If I had two days off or more, I would leave Switzerland altogether, even if I just popped over the border into France or Italy. I read voraciously and I was writing a novel. I wasn't interested in sunbathing, nor am I to this day, but was happy instead to sit in a hotel room with a balcony overlooking lakes, seas or mountains, and enjoy the peace.

In the winter I skied and became quite accomplished. I nearly killed myself a dozen times but escaped with only cuts and bruises. Upon my return to Scotland, STV sent me on a ski-ing story in Glencoe not long after I had started. I lasted twenty minutes before I wiped out, rupturing my cruciate ligaments. I had to have my left knee rebuilt and gladly hung up my skis to concentrate on my football career. Sir Alex Ferguson still didn't call.

For as long as I can remember, my mother had said that, when she retired from nursing, she would head off somewhere like Africa or India to help children who had been affected by war, famine or drought. As a boy, I can remember sickening TV pictures of children in God-forsaken parts of the world, their bellies swollen by hunger and my mother saying that she was going to help them one day. I don't believe that my father or I thought she was serious. But shortly after she retired, she did it.

She answered an ad in the paper, and travelled down to London to meet ex-Beatle George Harrison and his wife Olivia who were setting up a charity called Romanian Angels to help AIDS orphans. My mum wasn't interested in the Beatles and, in that stoic way of Scottish nurses, seemed underwhelmed by meeting George, except to say he had been exceptionally charming. However she adored Olivia. I was flabbergasted when, at the age of sixty-three, my mum signed up to travel to Romania to work in the orphanages.

AIDS came to Romania in the 1980s and blood stocks quickly became infected. The country's health problems had been hidden by the Ceausescu regime but, when he was deposed and executed, his despotic legacy was there for all the world to see.

Women who required blood transfusion in pregnancy quickly became infected, as did their babies. Once the regime had fallen, and western cameras were allowed to film what Ceausescu hadn't wanted anybody to see, the scale of the problem became apparent. Images of gaunt, wide-eyed children locked up in overcrowded, filthy hospitals filled the world's news pages and TV screens.

Whatever your feelings about the Beatles, the Harrisons were to be commended for their philanthropy. And they didn't simply assuage any guilt by writing a large cheque, believing they'd thereby done their bit. They set up a mechanism to ensure that their money had a practical application. It was to the massive port city of Constanta, where AIDS had first entered Romania, that my mother went.

Switzerland's proximity to Romania meant visiting would be a dawdle, or so I thought. The main religions in Romania are Orthodox Christianity and Roman Catholicism and, given the number of Romanians working in Switzerland as 'gastarbeiters', there was no surprise that Zurich airport was packed with them in the run-up to Easter that year. Instead of coming straight back to Switzerland from Constanta, I planned a special trip. Burning a hole in my pocket was that amazing thing called an Inter-rail ticket! For a very low flat fee it provided you with unlimited rail travel across the European network. I have blithely ripped the arse out of these tickets on many previous occasions, and had enjoyed journeys which cost in total far more than the face value of the ticket. My plan was to visit my mother but, instead of returning to Switzerland, I would head off from Bucharest and explore more of Eastern Europe.

I had to purchase a visa to enter the country when I arrived at Bucharest airport, and the swarthy sunglasses-wearing clerk behind the barred window wouldn't entertain the bundle of Romanian Leu I tried to use, demanding instead a crisp $20 bill, As I turned round, I noticed that suddenly the whole immigration hall seemed to be full of sunglasses-wearing officials, some uniformed, some not. Many people were wearing sheepskin-lined denim jackets, and everybody seemed to be smoking.

As the doors opened to the arrivals area, I was nearly knocked over by the noise and cloud of cigarette smoke. There was a rush of humanity towards me, because I was clearly the only Western European man anybody had seen for ages. I was inundated with locals trying to rent me a car or sell me jewellery. Then a tiny woman threw herself into my arms and my face was full of familiar-smelling hair. Her arms were locked round my neck, and my ears were filled with that beautiful Inverness accent.

'How ya doeen?' asked my mother.

'Yer seeing it,' I replied.

For a woman in her sixties, my mother showed extraordinary courage. She battled her way through the throng of people and out to the front of the airport, where she haggled with a taxi driver to take us into town. There are few things more terrifying than my mother in full sail, bargaining with some poor unfortunate soul over a price.

He dropped us at a hotel which he said was where westerners stayed. After checking in, we walked around central Bucharest. Ceaucescu had not long been executed and democracy had arrived but it was still a chaotic, confused place, with piles of rubble and filth everywhere.

We dined well in the hotel for a few dollars, and retired early because we had to catch a 6am train to Constanta. The whole thing was similar to the Soviet Russia I was used to and, sure enough, the lights had hardly gone out when there was a knock at the door. I ignored it. Another knock followed shortly before sunrise, and I ignored that too. But the phone calls were harder to ignore. In my experience of Moscow and Leningrad, these were made by people who had seen you check in and wanted to try to sell you stuff in exchange for your hard currency. Like the official at airport immigration, they had no interest in the local script. They wanted US dollars.

But the first phone call was from the newsdesk at the *Daily Express* in London, asking if I knew whether or not Annie Lennox was staying at the hotel. I explained that I was a Scottish journalist on holiday and, should I encounter the Aberdonian songstress at breakfast, I'd phone in with a quote. The night editor offered me £500 for any pictures I could get to them, but I saw no sign of her.

Despite the early hour, Bucharest central railway station was thronged with people, not all of whom were travelling. Like the airport, there seemed to be too many people just lounging around wearing aviator sunglasses and watching what was going on. Again, everybody was smoking. It was a menacing place to be, and I wished I hadn't had on the expensive leather jacket I always wore when travelling.

The train to Constanta was like no other I'd ever been on. Each compartment was furnished with six upholstered armchairs which were bolted to the floor through thick carpets. The locomotive was brightly painted in reds, blues and whites, and was spotlessly clean. But the journey was much like any in Eastern Europe back then: dull and drab.

Constanta was a busy port, and the cranes were visible as the train approached. My mother shared a flat with six remarkable women from the UK, all nurses of varying ages and experience. I was humbled to be in their company. From my battered old rucksack I withdrew two litres of duty-free gin, which was greeted with almost feverish glee. We drank into the early hours and I listened in silence to their stories.

In my experience, nurses are a pretty tough bunch. As a child, I never got much sympathy from my mother if I was ill, and I only went near a doctor if I had a limb hanging off. These women had experienced all sorts of things during their careers, but what they were encountering here in Constanta was something none had come across before.

The children, from newborns to toddlers, had been abandoned by their parents because they were HIV positive or had been orphaned by AIDS. Until the Harrisons had become involved, the children had been shut up in grim hospital wards and forgotten. But, even with only the most basic medical care, the nurses were able to bring much comfort to them. They were bathed every day, dressed in clean clothes and given a cocktail of drugs to try to slow down the onset of AIDS. Most importantly of all, the children were offered unconditional love for the first time in their lives.

My mother took me to the wards where she and her friends worked. I'm afraid I don't have the words to describe the experience. I have seen some hideous things at home and abroad, and in war and peace, and now in my fifties I'm afraid the memory of that hospital and those children still makes me weep.

My mother had clearly aged and had lost a lot of weight living in dreadful surroundings, but she was making the best of a bad situation. However, no matter how hard I tried to entice her back to Switzerland with me, she was adamant that she still had a job to do in Constanta and refused point blank to leave. In the end, after a forty-year career in the NHS and nursing her parents and my father through terminal illnesses, she returned to Constanta the next year for a second six-month stint with the Harrisons. My God, she was tough.

For about three years after her time in Romania, every so often I would get an unusual phone call from her. This was long before caller display but I knew who was ringing and why, because the call started with a few seconds of silence as she composed herself, regained for a moment her Scottish nurse's stoicism, and told me that yet another of her babies had died of AIDS.

After a tearful goodbye, I boarded the armchair express back to Bucharest, looking forward to the next leg of my journey. But, if anything, the main station there seemed even busier and more threatening than it had been a few days earlier. People would walk up to me and fondle the soft leather of my jacket, chatting away to each other about its quality and ignoring me totally.

My eyes lifted to the departures board, and my heart jumped when I saw a particular name. Excitedly, imagining quaffing an ice cold gin and tonic as the Romanian scenery slipped past my compartment window, I joined the lengthy queue for the solitary ticket office clerk. When I reached him, I waved my Inter-rail pass and asked for a reservation on that night's Orient Express to Paris.

He examined the ticket then slid it back to me between the bars of the window and simply said 'No.'

I repeated 'Orient Express, Paris' in French, and pointed up to the board. He couldn't have failed to understand what I wanted.

'No,' he repeated.

'What do you mean "no"? Why not?' I wailed. No reply.

Digging into my pocket I withdrew my bundle of Leu, a 100 Swiss franc note, my remaining $20 bill and a Clydesdale Bank fiver which my mother had found in her handbag and had given to me that morning. He just sneered.

My last resort was to pull out my American Express card, which I kept for emergencies. I flashed it at him. His response was to beckon to the man behind me to come forward to the window. I was astonished. There was nothing I could do. The queue was now even longer, and there was no way I was going to be able to stand in it again, for however long it took, only to be met with the same response. My romantic notion of a trip to Paris on the Orient Express had disappeared.

The Orient Express on the departures board was obviously not the luxury train of old, upon which passengers were either wined and dined to the highest level or murdered in a snowstorm. That train had ceased to run to Bucharest in 1962 but had since travelled many other routes serving other exotic destinations.

Time for Plan B. It was midday. Going anywhere by train was no longer an option because my ticket was seemingly not acceptable to Romanian railways. Neither was my cash, far less my credit. I mulled it over for a moment or two before going outside and jumping into a taxi.

'How much to the airport?' I asked the driver, noting his aviators and denim/sheepskin combo. The only US currency I had was the $20 dollar bill, and I would rather have walked to the airport than give him that. I showed him the Scottish fiver, which, for some reason, he took gratefully.

The airport departures area was thronged with more smoking, badly-dressed people, but I didn't care about the chaotic post-revolution scenes because I was about to do something I had never done before and have never done since. Tarom was the Romanian national airline, and I walked up to the ticket desk and cleared my throat.

'A single ticket on the next plane please,' I said, proudly.

The attractive dark-haired girl behind the bars wore a pained expression.

'Where would you like to go?' she asked. Clearly, she had never had a customer like me before.

'Anywhere,' I said grandly, shrugging my shoulders. My plan was to get the hell out of Dodge and pick up a train from wherever onwards using my Inter-rail ticket. I had no idea where I wanted to go. All I knew was that I had two weeks leave, and that I was happy just to mooch around Europe until it was time to return to Bern. However, the girl disarmed me totally when she said that the next plane out of Bucharest was bound for New York. Pleasing as it would have been to go to the Big Apple, that wasn't any use to me.

'Ah,' I said. 'Well the one after that.'

'That goes to Brussels,' she said.

'Perfect,' I replied and whipped out my Amex card. This was good news. I'd been to Brussels many times and I knew I could get a train from there to virtually anywhere in Europe. But again my railway reverie was short-lived.

'We don't take credit cards,' she said coldly. 'US dollars only. Cash.'

'How much is the ticket?' I asked.

'How much do you want to pay?' she replied quietly, after a pregnant pause.

I was dumbfounded. There was clearly some scam going on, and everyone was on the make. It was worse than Moscow had been during the Cold War. My natural parsimony and aversion to being ripped off was balanced by my desire to get the hell out. I showed her my 100 Swiss franc note, then worth about £40, and the $20 bill, but she screwed up her nose, shook her head angrily and turned her attention to the man behind me in the queue.

I was truly, royally, wholly, deeply fucked.

Nobody accepted American Express and I didn't have enough cash to buy either a train ticket or a plane ticket. Not caring where I went that day, as long as it was out of Romania, might possibly not have been helping matters. Perhaps a plan would have helped. This was before the advent of Switch cards and Romania had no cash machines, so I had no way of getting my hands on any money.

I was pretty hacked off. I had a Swiss bank account with thousands in it, and the credit card which was supposed to get me out of problems anywhere in the world. But neither was any use. The railway was closed to me and I couldn't fly out. I didn't know what to do. I walked off, not knowing where in the world I was going.

Suddenly I felt a tap on my shoulder. I turned to see the Tarom girl again. She thrust a hand-written airline ticket into my paw.

'We'll take the Swiss francs for the ticket,' she said, 'but the $20 is for me. My commission, you understand.'

I handed over both notes on the spot. My flight out of Bucharest had cost me about £50. I went to the *bureau de change* and attempted to change my tattered but unspent bundle of Leu into US dollars. I was now starving and knew the airport restaurant would only accept hard currency from a westerner. But the post-revolution rate of exchange meant that the same quantity of Romanian script I had purchased on my arrival for $200 would get me only $20 in return. I whispered under my breath that the clerk should go and fuck himself. I wasn't that hungry. I still have the Leu somewhere.

I boarded an ageing Tarom airliner an hour or so later. I noticed it was a BAC One-Eleven, a common sight in the UK especially around Inverness's Dalcross airport in the 1970s. I was so sick of Bucharest that I couldn't have cared less had I left on a Sherman tank pulled by unicorns.

From Zaventem airport I got the train into Brussels, and I was delighted when my Swiss bank card was accepted in a cash machine. I was solvent again. My plan was to stay the night here and get a train onwards in the morning. I had already made up my mind that I would be travelling west. I'd had enough of the east.

But I changed my mind to north when I saw the overnight train to Copenhagen on the Gare Du Nord departures board. I'd never been to Scandinavia and I realised that this was a perfect opportunity. I dived into the ticket office and booked a couchette, a cheap bunk in a six-berth compartment. Fortified by the prospect of waking up in Denmark, I wandered down to the Grand Place, treated myself to a large steak, then settled down to wait in a pub with a beer and Frederick Forsyth for company.

But when the long train pulled in to the station, my heart sank and I feared that my deeply difficult day of travel was far from over. I checked my ticket to make sure that I was waiting at the correct place on the correct platform for the correct coach on the correct train. I was, yet the coach which squealed to a halt in front of me was a shining blue and gold, first class wagon-lits. The door hissed open and an immaculately uniformed steward trotted down onto the deserted platform.

'Monsieur Edwards?' he asked, smiling. He didn't seem fazed by my several days of stubble, tattered Levi 501s, scuffed Timberland boots and that leather jacket.

I smiled back, and told him that I was the passenger he was expecting, but added that there had clearly been some error, because I had booked a second class couchette costing only a few francs and was scheduled to spend the night with five farting Belgians.

'There is no error, Monsieur,' he said. 'Second class is full tonight and you've been given a complimentary upgrade. Welcome aboard. A nightcap from the bar?'

My plans to travel on the Orient Express that night had been dashed, yet my journey would eventually surpass the fantasy. I lay back in my impossibly comfortable cabin, between crisp white sheets and sipped an ice cold gin and tonic. I slept deeply, as I only can on a train, and woke just once: not, of course, at Mossend, but with the feeling that somehow the train was on a ship and we were at sea.

*   *   *

It was a leisurely four-hour drive along the 300 miles from St Louis to Memphis: the birthplace of the blues. I scanned the atlas again over scrambled eggs and rye toast at the dry restaurant where I had dinner the night before, and cast an eye over the Mississippi's course as it meandered south to the sea.

What I was looking for was a spot, or preferably a stretch, where the road paralleled it, and along which I could drive the Chevy, gazing wistfully at arguably the most famous river on the planet. But I-55 comes close to St Louis in the boredom stakes and, apart from flat fields and the occasional small town, there is nothing really to recommend it and certainly no sight of the Mississippi.

The musical city on the river wasn't my final destination. It wasn't even really my next destination. I was heading for Inverness, Mississippi, 150 miles further south. I faced another two and a half hours on this boring road, so I was going to make sure that I made the most of every moment in Memphis.

The name conjures up all sorts of mystical and romantic notions. Memphis was the ancient capital of Egypt, and only gave its name to the US city in 1819. But, many centuries before, it was a hub of Egyptian commerce and religion, occupying a strategically important position at the mouth of the Nile delta.

As a youngster, I was more interested in ancient Egypt than I was in Elvis Presley, but I appreciated the fact that, while I was not a fan of him or his music, millions of people were. As a boy with a good nose for news, I remember very well the night in the summer of 1977 when the King died. I was shocked, not because I was a fan but because I realised just how enormous was the news story.

Elvis was born in Tupelo, Mississippi around 100 miles from Memphis, and moved there with his family when he was thirteen years old. He made his first recording at Sun Records when he was still a teenager, and he was spotted by Colonel Tom Parker a year later. The rest is history. In this day and age we have many more megastars whose often meagre abilities are magnified by fatuous TV talent shows and the internet, but Elvis was probably the first artist to attain that status.

I racked my brains to think of any Elvis song I had heard and that I moderately liked. 'Hound Dog' and 'Suspicious Minds' were, in my view, overplayed. I heard them but I wasn't listening to them, if you follow. 'Jailhouse Rock' was the same. What made matters worse was his awful rendition of 'Love Me Tender', a song I may have quite liked had he not spoiled it totally by bursting into laughter half way through. To this day I can't believe it was released as a single, and even more unbelievable is that Terry Wogan played it. As I drove through Memphis, I came to the conclusion that Elvis's 'In the Ghetto' might be the only song I wouldn't turn off and might even hum later on.

That said, it would be remiss of me to come to Memphis and not visit Graceland, the home of the King of Rock and Roll. With a song in my heart, if not on my lips, I drove off I-55 and headed down Elvis Presley Boulevard to the colonial-style house built in 1939 and which is the second most-visited house in the US. There are no prizes for guessing which is the first.

In some ways, Graceland is similar to Southfork ranch in Dallas, where the TV series of the same name was set and filmed in the 1970s. It is almost a fantasy, a dreamlike place which, although of course real, has such an aura about it that the visitor feels dislocated from reality. I'd visited Southfork several times but this was my first time at Graceland. I did feel like I was on a film set, though, and it was surreal to parade through the King's house. Like Southfork, it is much smaller than you imagine (it must be something to do with TV camera lenses, which I should know about, but don't), and I felt distinctly odd and uncomfortable.

The house's architecture is described as 'colonial revival' and, once inside the white colonnaded entrance which perfectly sets off the light gray limestone frontage, you get an idea of the man. Kind of. Two giant gaudily-coloured peacocks set in stained glass form a doorway into the music room from the living room. The former houses a grand piano and an ancient TV set: in the latter, at five metres in length, is the longest sofa I've ever seen. Yet the rooms are not big, and this house is not a place which drips wealth, as one might expect, or even atmosphere.

The kitchen is much like any other American kitchen, and is quaintly fitted out in the décor of the day, with impossibly large microwaves and fridges. Two rooms stand out as interesting, and gave me an idea of what motivated Elvis. The basement is where he sat and watched three TVs at the same time. His record collection is along another wall, and the room is turned out in a garish yellow and brown formica look, with a carpet so yellow that it gave me a headache. Pleasingly, there was a well-appointed bar in the corner.

But it was the jungle room which I enjoyed the most. The shaggy green carpet, which resembles a lawn, and the dark wood and stone walls are a mere sideshow to the waterfall in the corner. The couches are upholstered with fur. It is splendidly eccentric and, while I wouldn't have anything like it in my house, it was a pleasure to see it. In 1976, a year before he died, he had this room converted into a recording studio, and it was here that he laid down his last two albums, one aptly titled 'From Elvis Presley Boulevard, Memphis Tennessee'.

A lengthy corridor is flanked by platinum and gold discs, framed and on the walls. At the end is a room where one can view some of Presley's more outlandish outfits, such as his bejewelled white, caped jumpsuits. On a stand beside a mannequin, and of most interest to me, is a piece of music history: the King's Guild acoustic guitar. Lisa Marie's wedding dress is there, too, but I was more interested in the Guild.

Parts of the house are totally off limits, and I can understand why. The bathroom where Elvis died is not part of the public tour. After years of drug abuse, he collapsed there on 16 August 1977. He was rushed to hospital but could not be revived. An autopsy found fourteen different substances in his body, ten in significant quantities. His cause of death was recorded as a heart attack, with polypharmacy a factor.

His music, however, endures. His voice was, without question, powerful, and charisma oozed from his every early performance. He rode the new phenomenon called television, and very quickly 'Elvis the Pelvis' became a superstar. By the time he crossed my radar in the 1970s, his career had slumped and been relaunched. But he still wasn't my kind of thing at all.

When I saw him for the first time on TV, he was already unwell and addicted to prescription drugs. He was slurring and overweight, and his sweating face atop those grotesque high-collared jumpsuits made me cringe. When he died, I knew it was a major moment in cultural history but I felt no sense of loss. Maybe, at twelve years of age, I was simply too young. I was more moved by the death of Frank Sinatra.

The gardens are special. Out the back are stables and a squash court. Elvis loved horses and martial arts and, despite his ill-health, was an accomplished squash player. Behind the pool is the meditation garden where Presley used to sit and contemplate, and where he and his immediate family are buried.

Around 80,000 fans lined the route of his cortege from Graceland to Forest Hill cemetery in Memphis. In a tragic moment that day, a car crashed into a group of them outside the house, killing two people. There was a further twist when grave robbers attempted to steal his body, and he and his mother were hurriedly exhumed and re-buried back at Graceland.

Today, the graves are still a popular tourist destination, and thousands of fans make the pilgrimage every year. In that tranquil way you get in the South, the gardens are hushed and sombre. Between a small circular pool with gentle fountains spraying and a semi-circular wall inlaid with stained glass windows, lie four graves. They belong to Presley's parents, Vernon and Gladys, his grandmother Minnie Mae and, of course, himself. There is also a stone in memory of Jesse Garon, his unborn twin brother.

Presley's grave is a mass of candles, flowers and cards left by adoring fans. Even today, forty years after his death, some of the inscriptions are incredibly moving. Many of the cards and flowers are left not in memory of Elvis, but of fans of his. One I saw read simply: 'Dad, you were his biggest fan and you loved coming here. I now think of you being here together.'

At the foot of Presley's stone, beneath the inscription, is a small motif of the three letters, TCB, and a lightning bolt. This is a reference to the private code Presley and his staff shared about life together: taking care of business in a flash.

The heavens opened in that slow, Southern way as I left Graceland. The trees exuded an earthy smell, and the tarmac steamed as rainwater lashed steadily onto it. It was mild and humid and lovely. Walking to the car park I passed a compound which houses Elvis's cars and planes. My eye was immediately drawn to his pink Cadillac and his giant Convair four-engined jet airliner, named Lisa-Marie after his daughter, which he used to travel the world. Alongside it is a smaller Lockheed executive jet. Also on show are yet more jumpsuits, capes and gold discs.

But I had had my fill of the King, and wanted to spend the rest of the day enjoying the legacy of another American cultural hero, whose bequest to humanity was far greater than Elvis Presley's.

*   *   *

After the visit to my mother in Romania, I returned to Bern determined to further my career. If I was going to realise my ambition, I would have to leave the lucrative Swiss existence before I became lazy and over-comfortable. I had to find a way back to Scotland and a job in TV.

In those days the *Guardian* newspaper had a media section on a Monday, and I would make a beeline to the international newsagent at the Hauptbahnhof in Bern to buy my copy. I'd then scan the situations vacant column to see if there was anything worth my while applying for.

A few weeks later I flew back to Inverness and spent some time at home. I'd phoned up Andy Stenton, an old pal who was then the head of news at Northsound Radio in Aberdeen, and arranged to go and see him for lunch and a blether. He always had his ear to the ground and would know where there were any jobs going. I'd previously discussed working for him at Northsound, but going back to local radio was the last thing I wanted to do. Also, Aberdeen was full of bad memories for me because of the strike, so it really was the nuclear option.

It was a Monday morning, and I bought a copy of the *Guardian* at Inverness station bookstall before jumping on the train to Aberdeen. It was the best 50p I've ever spent, because screaming out at me was an advert for journalists at STV in Glasgow.

We'd barely left Inverness station, but I wanted to pull the communication cord and jump off. It was all I could do not to leave the train at Nairn and catch the next one back. Aberdeen was the last place on the planet I wanted to go that day, and I owe Andy Stenton an apology because, throughout our conversation at lunchtime, my mind was locked on my application for a job at STV.

For the remaining few days of my break in Inverness I was like a cat on a hot tin roof. I couldn't settle. I went for long walks along the Caledonian Canal banks, and worked out how I would word my CV and application, and I rehearsed my answers should I be fortunate enough to get an interview. I flew back to Switzerland transfixed. After poring over the CV and letter of application for days, I finally popped the envelope in the post. I'm not religious, but I've never prayed so hard in my life. The next few days were agonising.

My reverie was shattered on the tram to work the next Monday when I saw in the *Guardian* that Aberdeen-based Grampian TV were also looking for reporters. I locked myself away in my flat in Bern and carefully crafted a second letter of application. I slipped it into the post, and sat back to wait. With two applications on the go, I'd never have a better chance.

The next event on my horizon was a two-week trip around the Civil War sites in the US, but I was so wrapped up in the possibility of working in television in Scotland that I could hardly focus. Ordinarily, I'd be devouring guidebooks and plotting my route on maps. However, on this occasion I could not have cared less. I'd been in Switzerland for three years, and I knew that I was losing ground on my contemporaries back home. I still felt this gnawing angst that people were getting good jobs in television while I was disappearing in a sinecure.

When the stiff white envelope bearing the STV frank on it arrived, I sat staring at it for ages on the kitchen table before I dared open it. I screamed with delight when I eventually read that they were offering me an interview on the morning before I was due to fly to the USA. This was obviously the real deal. This was a serious TV company. They sent me an open return air ticket between Switzerland and Glasgow which, even in those days, would have cost hundreds of pounds. I was beside myself with excitement. Of the two, I was expecting Grampian to offer me an interview. I couldn't believe STV were interested in me, but they obviously were.

With my US bags packed and ready to go, I flew to London and then Glasgow and presented myself at STV's Cowcaddens studios. It was long before the days of Twitter and online news services, so at the airport I bought all the Scottish papers and ploughed through them on the bus into town.

I knew I was potentially entering the lion's den with a big city TV station when I saw the front page splash on the *Glasgow Evening Times*. The headline read 'Executed', and the text told how Glasgow gangsters Bobby Glover and Joe Hanlon had been shot dead, reportedly in their anuses, and their bodies dumped in a car in the city. The story further revealed that the vehicle containing the corpses had been parked facing the route to be taken later that day by the cortege of another Glasgow gangster, shot dead the week before, allegedly by the two men. The picture was pretty graphic. I gulped.

But the STV interview was much more convivial than I'd imagined it would be. It started with a screen test in a proper TV studio with lights, make up, the lot. I had an earpiece inserted and I read from the autocue. I'd been in radio long enough to have developed my broadcasting voice and, while I was confident I sounded the part, the issue was whether or not I looked the part.

Towards the end of the bulletin, I heard the director's voice in my earpiece telling me the next package wasn't ready and I had to fill for thirty seconds. This was clearly a stunt to see how I would react. My mind was racing, but I tried not to show it and I used the remaining time to ad lib about the latest ongoings in the Glasgow underworld: all information I'd gleaned from reading the papers on the bus. When I unhooked my tie mic and unplugged my earpiece, I stood up and felt the back of my shirt completely sodden with sweat. It must have been the lights, I told myself.

I then had an interview with Blair Jenkins, who was the Director of Programmes at STV. He was an Elgin boy and an ex-reporter at the *Aberdeen Evening Express*, the sister paper of the *Press and Journal*. We spent a merry thirty minutes or so discussing Highland League football, the *P&J* strike and our mutual friends in various newsrooms across the country. I was impressed by him: he was a very clever man. But we barely discussed anything that I thought was relevant to the vacancy.

The studios weren't what you would call tidy. They were strewn with newspapers, notebooks and video tapes of various formats. They were obviously busy people here, and this reinforced my view that STV was the real deal. As I jumped on the plane back to Switzerland that evening, I had the same feeling I had when I left Moray Firth Radio as a work experience schoolboy all those years ago. This is where I wanted to be.

I changed planes at Heathrow and connected with the Swissair flight for Geneva. I was drained when I got back to my flat in Bern that night, not least by the excitement of the day but also by all the travelling and the prospect of flying back to London again the next morning and then onto New York, before connecting to Atlanta to begin my Civil War trip. But I was wide awake and buzzing with excitement when I got home to see the stiff white envelope bearing the Grampian TV frank on the hall floor. Surely not.

Grampian were offering me an interview a week hence at their Queens Cross studios in Aberdeen. This was more good news, but the time and date were no use because I'd be in the USA. I phoned from Heathrow the next morning to ask politely if it was possible to change the appointment. The person to whom I spoke couldn't make that decision, and asked me to call back. I did this from JFK without success, then again from Atlanta, before I got the answer I'd been dreading. They were sorry, but the slot I'd been allocated was the only one available.

The question I kept asking myself as I drove around Georgia was 'how badly did I want to work for Grampian?' I thought I'd done well at the STV interview but I also felt I was more likely to get a job with Grampian, for no other reason than that I grew up in the broadcast area and knew well the places and the people in the news. STV was a much bigger station which handled bigger issues. Their stories were about meaty subjects, politically and socially. There was a lot of crime, as I now knew. However, Grampian was a smaller concern with a totally different and much softer news agenda, covering the oil industry and agriculture primarily. I would love to have worked for STV but I was more likely to get a job at Grampian, and to keep it.

I knew there was no argument. I would take the hit and abandon my trip, because my career in TV was more important. The night before the interview, with more than a week of my holiday remaining, I drove to the airport at Jacksonville in Florida, returned my hire car and booked a flight to Aberdeen via JFK, Manchester and Glasgow. I handed my credit card over to the girl at the ticket desk and told her I didn't want to know how much it cost. She laughed as I signed the invoice with my eyes closed.

It was at Aberdeen airport that my problems began. The flight from JFK to Manchester had been very late and I only just made my connections. I was more jet-lagged than I'd ever been in my life, and arrived at the carousel at Aberdeen airport feeling lousy and looking awful. Things were about to get worse. While I had made it, my luggage hadn't. I'd had the foresight to bring a suit with me on my trip, but it was in my battered old Samsonite somewhere over the Atlantic. I had an hour to get to my interview. I told myself that the world didn't owe me a living and that, if I wanted this job and a career in TV, then I just had to get on with it.

I hailed a taxi into town and got the driver to drop me at a barber's. But it was packed and, with time running out, I ran around until I found a woman's hairdressers where I asked the girl to wash my hair and give me a wee trim. I then ran into Burton's and bought socks and undercrackers, a suit, shirt and tie, before diving into Boots for a razor, shaving cream, toothbrush and toothpaste. I raced along to the only place I could think of to get ready: the toilets at Aberdeen railway station.

The place stank. The floor was awash with urine and there was nowhere to hang anything. I stripped to the waist and had a wash and a shave and then got changed into my new outfit. Men came and went from the toilet all the time, most giving me strange looks. Then, with my travelling clothes (the ubiquitous Timberland boots, faded Levi 501s and leather jacket) crammed into the Burton's bag, I hailed another taxi to the Grampian TV studios at Queen's Cross. I made it with moments to spare.

The news editor was a lovely man called Al Gracie, whom I'd met before. We got on very well during the interview, but I can't say I took to the woman from HR. While he was happy to talk news, she was very aloof and seemed to be wrapped up in trivialities and dreamed up the most improbable scenarios to see how I'd react. I wanted to tell her that I'd been in enough newsrooms to know that things didn't happen that way, but I decided against it.

I didn't tell them of my nightmare journey, that the flight had cost a king's ransom, that I'd cut short my holiday, that I'd had to buy clothes for the interview, and that I'd had to ablute in public in the station toilet. We parted on excellent terms, and I felt that in the circumstances I'd done fairly well. I jumped on the train to Inverness and spent the remainder of my leave at home. I was shattered that night and realised that getting my foot in the door in TV would be harder than anything I'd ever done before. But I felt I'd done exactly the right thing by abandoning my holiday early. I had two very hot irons in the fire.

Grampian said they wanted to fill the vacancy quickly so, as arranged, I phoned HR shortly before I returned to Switzerland. I'd had time to reflect on the interview in the intervening days and, when I looked at it in isolation and not in the context of the journey to get there, I thought I'd done enough to get the job. I was twenty-eight, the perfect age. I was a local boy, I'd worked in radio and newspapers in the region and I'd also done my stint at Radio Forth and, of course, in a world service newsroom in Switzerland. I'd worked in news and sport at home and abroad and I had a really good CV. I felt really confident.

But the HR woman told me that, while they'd enjoyed meeting me and hoped I thought the interview had been worthwhile, I wasn't what they were looking for.

I was devastated.

I tried to forget the lengths I'd gone to simply to get to the interview, and to concentrate instead on the facts. I stopped myself from thinking back to the negative views I held of Grampian as a kid: that I felt it marginalised the Highlands, where I grew up. I told myself that had I really believed that, I wouldn't have wanted to work there. Instead, I focused on the reality that, no matter how good I thought I was, they clearly didn't share my view. Despite my experience, despite where I grew up, they didn't fancy me at all. Was it because I'd been on the *P&J* strike and might be a union agitator? Was it because I didn't have a degree? At the end of the day, I realised that I simply wasn't good enough.

I enjoyed a last quiet day at home in Inverness before flying back to Switzerland. On the plane to Zurich I formulated a plan. It was shortly before Christmas and I'd volunteered to work over the holidays to allow those colleagues with families to take time off. I told myself I'd enjoy the festivities as much as I could given my work schedule, but in the new year I'd buckle down and make a concerted effort to get a job in TV back home.

Going back to college or university to study for four years was out of the question. People were taking my opportunities in TV and I had to stay in the industry. I decided to contact the Open University and study for a degree by correspondence. I had plenty of leave and spare time in Switzerland, and figured it was do-able. A degree would possibly make the difference.

By now, I'd abandoned the idea that I had been successful with STV and, with both Scottish options now closed to me, I thought that perhaps I should try further afield. I considered Anglia TV or Border TV and thought that, with a degree, I might be in with a shout. I'd done newspapers, I'd done radio and I'd had enough. I wanted to be a TV reporter. By the time the flight touched down, my resolve had returned.

When I got back to my flat late that night, after a mentally and physically exhausting two weeks on the road, there was another stiff white envelope on the mat waiting for me.

It contained a letter from STV telling me I'd got the job.

* * *

I turned out of the Graceland car park and stayed on Elvis Presley Boulevard until it became Bellevue. Then I hung a left onto Vance, then Mulberry, then past houses, car showrooms and diners until I reached the National Civil Rights museum at the Lorraine Motel.

It's more of a US historic and cultural symbol than it is a museum, and it's like no other museum you'll visit anywhere else. The Lorraine, marked by an Art Deco sign, was one of those archetypal American motels where you could park your car pretty well at the door of your room. A complete section has been walled off, and left much as it was on that day in April 1968 when Martin Luther King Jr was assassinated here.

Parked at the door beneath King's room are two American cars from the 1960s. Both are white. One is a '59 Dodge Royale, with green fins protruding, Batmobile-style, from above the rear lights. The other is a '68 Cadillac. They are replicas of the vehicles that were parked in those spots on the day of the assassination.

The most striking part of the museum is Room 306, King's bedroom. The curators left it the way it was, and its simplicity is deeply moving. King always stayed here. He usually shared with his friend and fellow Civil Rights campaigner Ralph Abernathy, and Room 306 had become known as the King-Abernathy suite by the hotel's owner, Walter Bailey. It is typical of a low-budget US motel room, with two double beds and a small bathroom in the back. Outside the bathroom, and in view from the door, is a small sink. Opposite the two beds stands a dresser, on top of which sits a TV.

What made it live for me was the fact that King's bed is unmade, because he'd been feeling unwell and had lain on it prior to going outside onto the balcony. Between the two beds is a stool, on top of which is a

tray of food and an ashtray with cigarette ends in it. On one bed is a copy
of the *Memphis Press Scimitar* dated 4 April 1968. I was captivated. The
unspeakable motels I use in the US are more or less identical, but this one
was redolent with history and atmosphere.

The last moments of King's life were spent on the open balcony outside
the room. He had spoken to people in the car park below, and finally to
the musician Ben Branch. King had asked him to play 'Take my Hand,
Precious Lord' at an event which both were scheduled to attend in
Memphis that night. His last words were 'play it real pretty'.

Then he was shot. A single bullet smashed his face and travelled down
his spine, causing irreparable damage before it lodged in his collarbone.
He immediately collapsed, surrounded by his aides, among them
Abernathy and Jesse Jackson. Despite emergency surgery at St Joseph's
Hospital in Memphis, the great man died later that evening.

When I was a child, possibly the first thing that caught my attention
about King was the remarkable speech he had made the day before his
assassination at the Mason Temple in Memphis, home to the world's
biggest African-American Pentecostal church. The speech was touching,
moving and powerful, as his oratory usually was. But there was something
else, something prescient. Even as a youngster, I was touched by the way
he seemed to know his fate and was resigned to it.

'And then I got to Memphis. And some began to say what would happen
to me from some of our sick white brothers? Well, I don't know what will
happen now. We've got some difficult days ahead, but it doesn't matter to
me because I've been to the mountain top. I would like to live a long life.
But I'm not concerned about that. I just want to do God's will. And He's
allowed me to go up to the mountain and I've looked over and I've seen
the promised land. I may not get there with you. But I want you to know
that we as a people, will get to the promised land. So I'm happy, tonight.
I'm not worried about anything. I'm not fearing any man.'

The line 'I may not get there with you' haunts me to this day.

His assassin was James Earl Ray, a petty criminal and failed porn movie
director, who had served in the US Army at the end of World War Two.
Ray was openly racist, and after the assassination he had planned to flee
to Rhodesia which had just announced a unlilateral declaration of independence from the UK and which was being run by a white minority
government. It was said that he murdered King because he wanted to be
a notorious criminal.

Ray used the bathroom of the boarding house at 422 South Main Street, opposite the Lorraine, to stalk King and to fire the fatal shot. The range is less than 100 metres. Police ballistics experts thought that, in order to fire the fatal shot from that range and at that elevation through a window which was only open a few centimetres, Ray was probably standing in the bath when he squeezed the trigger.

The bathroom is encased behind the same protective glass as Room 306. But you are still standing in the room where occurred one of the most significant moments of the twentieth century, an event which snuffed out the life of a great man who led a crusading movement to ultimate victory.

Ray ran from the boarding house, dropping nearby a bag containing the rifle and his binoculars. He flew to London, and was arrested at Heathrow Airport after his false passport was noticed at immigration. From there, he was extradited back to the USA. He admitted the assassination, knowing that had he denied it, gone to trial and been found guilty, he would have been sent to the electric chair. He was sentenced to ninety-nine years in jail, and had a year added after he escaped in 1977. He died from hepatitis in prison in 1998 aged seventy, protesting his innocence after having recanted his confession.

The assassination caused a global shockwave, the impact of which was felt for years afterwards. More immediately, Loree Bailey, the wife of the owner of the Lorraine Motel, suffered a stroke moments after the gunshot, and collapsed. She died four days later. An autopsy on King catalogued the horrific damage Ray's bullet had caused, and also noted that King's heart was similar to that of a sixty-year-old man, such was the strain of leading the Civil Rights campaign.

One of the main exhibits at the museum is a display comprising a yellow refuse lorry, with various pieces of rubbish strewn across the floor. Standing next to it are mannequins with placards around their necks proclaiming 'I am a man'. They are being herded around by mannequin National Guardsmen. It was this sanitation workers dispute which had brought King to Memphis. His flight from Atlanta had been delayed by a bomb scare, but Ray knew why King was in Memphis, he knew when he was coming and, of course, he knew where he would be.

I find it hard to imagine what it must have been like being a black person at that time. Being told to sit up the back of the bus because the good seats down the front were reserved for whites. Not being permitted to sit at the counter in restaurants because those seats were for whites only. Worst of all, your children being sent to different schools simply because of the colour of their skin. And in my lifetime.

Yes, such apartheid existed in South Africa in the early years of my life, but this was happening to black people in the supposedly modern USA, Britain's greatest ally, at a time when they were putting men on the moon and the Beatles were coming up with 'Love Me Do' and Elvis with 'Love Me Tender'. I have never experienced such discrimination. It's abhorrent to me.

Idols come and go, rock stars, footballers: whatever.

But Martin Luther King is my enduring hero.

* * *

Forgive me for reverting to another football analogy, but having been rejected by Grampian and getting a job at STV made me think along the following lines. I saw a parallel with a player with Inverness Caley Thistle who had a proven pedigree in the Scottish Premier League and was ready for a big transfer. He had gone for trials with Arsenal and had been told he wasn't good enough for them, but had been signed by Barcelona instead. That's how I felt, and I headed back to Scotland with a spring in my step.

But I had one more travel nightmare to endure on the way home. I said farewell to Bern and jumped on a train, never imagining for a moment that I would spend ten busy years working in television before I returned. I had promised myself a final few days of relaxation in Paris before I started on the most challenging part of my career.

Most of my kit was boxed up and left in the nuclear shelter of my flat for later collection. I travelled back to Scotland carrying two suitcases and a rucksack on my back. The cases contained every item of clothing I possessed, including my only suit, and the rucksack held every sock and shoe I owned. After mooching around the city of light for nearly a week, I headed back to Scotland the day before I was due to start at STV.

This was long before the Channel Tunnel had opened, and it gave me the greatest of pleasure to jump on a train for Calais at the Gare du Nord. I dumped my cases on the rack in the vestibule of the coach, keeping the rucksack at my side because I had in it my wallet and passport. Shortly before departure, a group of schoolchildren boarded and I moved to the next coach for some peace and quiet. I threw myself into my seat and watched as France slid by.

The rest of the journey was spent in quiet contemplation until we arrived in Calais and I walked to the back of the coach, only to see the

French countryside through the glass panels in the rear door. Where was the coach containing my luggage?

Of course! I should have remembered. I'd made the journey often enough to know that the train splits at Amiens, with half of the coaches going to Calais and the other half to Boulogne. The following morning, I was due to start the job of my life at STV. I was in Calais, while every article of clothing I possessed, including my suit, was in two cases which were somewhere in the vicinity of Boulogne harbour. I still had the rucksack, so at least I wouldn't be stuck for shoes and socks. But this was scant consolation. I looked down at my scuffed Timberland boots, faded Levi 501 jeans, scruffy fleece and battered leather jacket, and swore fulsomely. I couldn't believe I'd been so stupid.

I sprinted off the train and found a SNCF official dozing behind a barred window. I persuaded him to lift the phone to his counterpart at Boulogne. Yes, the carriage cleaners there had found my two cases, and they had been locked up in lost property. I heaved a huge sigh of relief and thanked him profusely. Goodness only knew when I'd be able to collect them, however. I sprinted for the ferry and, seconds after I boarded, the gangplank was raised.

From Dover I took the train to London, and another to Glasgow, where Ron MacKenna met me. I'm not a tall man and, although Ron and I are of similar height, he is much stockier than I am. He offered to lend me a suit but it enveloped me. He and his wife Debbie made me very welcome, and I crashed on their sofa until I got more permanent accommodation. That first night I was hardly able to sleep with excitement.

The next morning, instead of thinking about my new job in journalism – a future of battling for the truth against the enemies of fact – I was outside Marks and Spencer in time for the shutters going up so I could buy a suit, shirt and tie and get to STV on time. I was OK for socks and shoes.

My first day in the newsroom at Cowcaddens passed in a blur. It started in an impressive fashion, with a meeting which involved the entire news staff and which went through the previous night's programme with a fine-toothed comb. It was discussed in intimate detail: what had gone well and what hadn't. Everybody was involved, from producers to reporters to technical staff, and no blushes were spared. I realised within a few minutes that I had been right in my assessment of STV. It was the real deal.

Everybody was given a copy of a confidential document called a news schedule, which consisted of three or four sheets of A4 paper outlining the diary stories of the day and the resources available to cover them. But the best stories – the stories reporters dig up for themselves – were not on the schedule, and I was desperate to start. I thought I knew the business. I certainly knew what a story was, and I had quite a pedigree in news and sport in newspapers and radio. In Switzerland I'd spent some time shadowing the staff at the CNN studio in Bern and had sat in on some edits. But I very quickly realised that I knew nothing about television news, so I sat down, shut up, watched and listened.

Alan Saunby had joined STV from Moray Firth Radio and was the business correspondent. I learned much from him. He was always busy because, at this time, many of Scotland's traditional heavy industries were slowly but steadily shutting down. He would spend the day out on a story, and burst into the newsroom with a few minutes to go before we went on air. He'd sprint into the editing suites in a flurry of videotapes and newspaper cuttings, and I realised that little had changed since we'd last met at Moray Firth Radio all those years before.

Then, more often than not, he'd race back out again to do a live outside broadcast at a factory which had just received the bad news that it was closing with the loss of hundreds of jobs. He is the hardest-working man I've ever known and a cracking reporter. He's the kind of person who can hold a conversation on any subject under the sun. His hobby was travelling, and there are few places he hasn't been. Already fluent in French, German, Spanish and Italian, as a treat to himself he learned conversational Chinese and Japanese prior to visiting the Far East.

For the most part, I shadowed people in the newsroom and, on occasion, I was allowed out on a job with a reporter. I'd sit in the back of the crew car and spoke when I was spoken to. I quickly learned that television news is not like any other kind of journalism. It is complex, increasingly so, and much of what you do is governed by technology.

In those days you would jump in the car, usually a Volvo estate, which was always driven by the cameraman. The sound engineer would sit in the passenger seat, behind him sat the lighting man, and the reporter sat behind the driver. The reporter, in those last days of union activism, was the least important member of the crew and often ridiculed, despite the fact that he was responsible for the finished product.

To deliver that, after he had left his three colleagues in the Volvo, the reporter went into an edit suite and worked with another team mate, the film editor. This was all new to me. In newspapers I occasionally went out on a story with a photographer, but in radio it was just me and my tape recorder. I think it's called a steep learning curve.

Reporters would go out on a job with a pocketful of change and would spend ages looking for callboxes to phone the desk or their contacts. Mobile phones fitted with cameras and internet browsers were then a thing of fantasy. Forgive me if I get out my pipe and slippers, but reporters today don't know how lucky they are. And what happens when the wi-fi fails, guys?

It was months before I was allowed out on a story without an established reporter there to hold my hand, and it was a big story. I can't claim it was a story I'd dug up or because the desk thought I'd do it well. Everyone else had been assigned elsewhere when it broke, and I was the reporter nearest the door.

A mother had killed herself and her two children by running a hosepipe from the exhaust into their car in woods near Blanefield on the outskirts of Glasgow. We raced to the scene. I'd knocked on doors on stories more out of hope than expectation before, but I'd never done it with a camera crew in tow. Coincidentally, the first door I hit was at the cottage belonging to the farmer who, that morning, had made the grim discovery. Not only did he take us straight to the scene, but he also gave us a very strong interview.

He'd smashed the side window to try to rescue the occupants of the car, and the broken glass was still scattered among the pine needles. I did my first piece to camera there, and it was awful. But it didn't matter. I'd gone there on the off-chance and had returned with the goods.

It was all backslaps and 'well done' when I got back to the newsroom. It went far better than I ever could have imagined, and my stock went up several notches. But, when I got the train home that night with the praise still ringing in my ears, I was hit by a sudden and profound melancholy as I remembered that my triumph was based on the tragic deaths of children. I was chilled. Children. Human beings. This was the career I had chosen, this was the job I wanted. STV was the real deal, I was right. But what a life I was starting.

Since that first report, I have covered many tragedies, accidents and murders and have reported on deaths by the thousand. I always try to keep focused on the story until the deadline, and think of the human cost afterwards. It is never lost on me.

Days after I touched down in Glasgow I contacted the Open University and enrolled as a student. I was certain that having a degree would do me far more long-term good than it would harm. I signed up to four years of study for a degree in American history, and I would come home from work every night shattered. But, instead of flaking out on the sofa watching the Champions League, I got my head into the books. When I wasn't working or studying for my degree, I was battering away at my novel. It was an interesting time, without question.

Everybody told me to go and live in the West End of Glasgow, so I started the process by securing a bedsit in Wilton Street from where I could begin flat-hunting. I could also easily get to work by jumping on the subway to Cowcaddens. However, I quickly began to loathe the area, a feeling I hold to this day. I was fed up of its putatively Bohemian label, I disliked the cachet which Ashton Lane held for no reason I ever understood, and I was fed up to the back teeth of bumping into people who worked at BBC Scotland, then headquartered on Queen Margaret Drive. Even students began to irritate me. I remembered how hard I had worked at Napier. Students here apparently didn't study at all. To listen to them, you'd think they were at the Sorbonne.

It grew very tedious hearing people bang on about the West End atmosphere or arranging to meet me for a beer in 'The Chip.' As far as I was concerned, the area was full of workshy wankers, pseuds and poseurs and I detested it. If you see me there today, I'm there for work and not by choice. If you see me there today and I'm not on a job, I've obviously lost my mind. So stick me on a bus heading south, will you?

So I never enjoyed my time in the West End, and I quickly realised that I could get far more bang for my buck property-wise south of the Clyde. I bought a big two-bedroomed flat in Shawlands for a fraction of the price which a one-bedroomed property would have cost me in Hyndland.

The estate agent was banging on about gas central heating and the common close, but the key selling point for me was the little box room off the main bedroom which the previous owners had used as a nursery. It said to me the word 'study' and, although it was nothing like Frans Evenhuis's exquisite studio in Hollywood, it was to be my mancave. It was tiny, but I squeezed a desk and a filing cabinet in there, as well as a blotter, a reading lamp and eventually a computer.

Having expressed an interest in the military, the desk assigned me to work on any stories which this involved, including coverage of the fatal crashes of an RAF Hercules in Perthshire and then, a year, later the infamous Chinook disaster on the Mull of Kintyre. The latter accident claimed the lives of senior police, military and intelligence figures who were *en route* from Belfast to a special meeting at Fort George near Inverness. Slowly and steadily I was gaining experience, and the desk was learning to trust me with increasingly complex and important stories.

You never forget the momentous events in your life.

I've been fortunate to have had several such moments. This one happened one Sunday afternoon during an edition of 'Scotsport', presented by my pal Jim White. Although the commercials have paid my mortgage for quarter of a century, I usually pay them scant attention. Ad breaks are usually a cue to pop on the kettle or visit the loo, but on this occasion I was rooted to the sofa. The ad exhorted me to join the Territorial Army.

I had often considered this in my youth, but career and family circumstances had prevented me. Now here I was, established at STV, working on a novel, a property owner, and well into my OU degree. Was this the time?

I memorised the phone number on the ad and raced through to the hall. Before Jim came back on with part two of 'Scotsport', I had made the call. The man to whom I spoke told me he'd put an information pack in the post that evening. More importantly, he told me the upper age limit for joining was thirty. I had just celebrated my twenty-ninth birthday. It was a case of now or never.

The military had always fascinated me. I had built on my basic knowledge by reading the right things and watching the right documentaries. My father's stories were still foremost in my mind. And I loved the great war books and the memorable films.

The information pack arrived, and I devoured every word. I phoned the number on one of the pamphlets and I was directed to my local Army Careers Office, who booked me in for an interview.

The STV early shift started at 4.30am, but I was bright-eyed and bushy-tailed when, shortly after lunchtime, I ambled into the office of Colonel Robert Watson at Walcheren Barracks. That meeting changed my life. Very soon I would never amble anywhere again, and certainly not into anyone's office. I wore my standard M&S suit, a shirt and tie from Next, and black shoes which had not seen brush and polish for some time. Robert greeted me in a tweed suit, a shirt with a slightly frayed collar, a Royal Scots tie, and brown brogues which had been polished and bulled to within an inch of their life. He had a fob watch which dropped on a leather thong from his buttonhole into his handkerchief pocket. His clothes were old but of excellent quality.

Robert was around sixty years old. He had a delightful lisp and what I would quickly learn were 'bugger's handles': long wispy whiskers around his cheekbones. I took to him immediately, and we chatted long into the afternoon about why I wanted to join the TA. I have met many men like Robert throughout my Army career, and they always give me a sense that they're rather foggy old buffers, but underneath they are all sharp as tacks. He read me in an instant.

He looked me up and down, saw my clothes, saw my build, saw me. He had already read my CV and knew precisely what I was all about. He listened to my carefully prepared speech about wanting to serve my country, about doing a job that was different and which made a difference, about wanting to follow my grandfather and father into service, and about craving adventure. After coffee and biscuits, we shook hands and parted. He recommended me for officer selection.

A taxi back into town would have been too expensive, and normally I would have waited for a bus. Instead, despite the 3am alarm call that morning, I walked all the way, my heart pounding with excitement and my head full of ridiculous Wellington-esque romance. I was striding forward at the head of my men, leading them into hell under enemy fire and safely out the other side, in time to go home for tea and medals.

I didn't know it then. but within a decade I would see war twice. I'd come under fire from Iraqi Scud missiles, carrying who knew what ghastly substances in their warheads, and I'd narrowly escape a baying mob, determined to tear me apart in Afghanistan. Of course, I knew there was an element of danger in joining the TA and there was every chance I might get called up. The Balkans war was ongoing and Saddam Hussein was still in power in Iraq. But, like many young people, I was determined to do my bit. It would all be over by Christmas, I told myself, and, of course, nothing bad could ever happen to me.

A week later I had an accident in Glencoe while working on a ski-ing story for STV. I didn't know it at the time but I'd torn my cruciate ligaments and would require a major operation, a week in hospital and months of rehab. That delayed my commissioning into the army but I wasn't going to let it stop me.

On the wall of my study was pinned a piece of A4 paper which I still have somewhere. It listed my goals, and nothing was going to get in my way.

It read: 'COMMISSION, KNEE, DEGREE, NOVEL.'

A year after I joined STV I was taken to one side by the news editor and asked how good my French was and if I had a valid passport. I was intrigued. He told me the fiftieth anniversary of D-Day was coming up, Clinton, Mitterrand *et al* were going to Normandy for the commemorations, and I was being sent to cover it. This was all too good to be true. It was the first of many overseas trips at STV and what a way to start!

We had special accreditation to get into the various locations where the VIPs were meeting the veterans, but cameraman Steve Kydd and I were missing the one vital pass we required to get close to Clinton. We were working with the ITN crew, who were also without passes, and their reporter was Colin Baker, a man I had long admired. He was the journalist who once recorded a piece to camera outside the Old Bailey which was more famous for the bit that wasn't broadcast. It went like this:

'Colin Baker, ITN at the Old Bailey (*four-second pause*) soaked, with cold feet and an aching heart, married, several children, pissed off, really dreadfully pissed off.'

I was in awe of him, not for that piece to camera, but because he was an incredibly talented reporter. In the few hours we were together, I was like a sponge. But, without the correct passes, neither ITN nor STV were getting a story that day.

When his producer informed Baker of our joint predicament, he scoffed and grabbed the keys of the people carrier we were sharing. The US Secret Service and the French Gendarmes weren't going to stop him. He took us on a circuitous route around the Normandy countryside, trogging across fields and speeding through farms. At one farm, a flock of hens scattered out of our way and a pile of baskets collapsed, just like they always seem to do in films. Suddenly we could see the sea, and the beach at Arromanches was below us. We were inside the cordon without the passes.

'I used to come here on holiday when I was a kid,' he said, throwing the keys to the producer. Then we trotted off to see Bill Clinton.

* * *

I had spent the day in Memphis visiting dead American heroes, and I didn't have time for Beale Street, the two-mile-long avenue widely regarded as the home of the blues since people like BB King, Muddy Waters and Louis Armstrong started playing there. I had visited before and, while I quite like blues music, I'm not a huge fan of the way important places around the world become commercialised tourist traps. Anyway, it was time to jump back onto I-55 and head south from Tennessee into Mississippi and to Inverness number three.

There is something peaceful and pleasant about driving in the American South on a Sunday when the weather is not good. You couldn't describe it as cold, but it was certainly cool. Clouds were gathering, and there was thunder in the post as I gunned the Chevy onto the freeway and sat back for a long drive. Happily, the road was quiet.

I deliberately hadn't bought any Elvis CDs at Graceland, although I had considered purchasing a CD of Martin Luther King's speeches at the Lorraine Motel. I headed off in relaxed fashion with Tom Petty's aptly-titled 'Southern Accents' album playing gently instead. It was a moment to take stock.

My new silver briefcase, which lay on the passenger seat of the Chevy, contained a notebook full of scribbles about my journey. It had been an interesting few days since I'd got off the Zephyr and, looking back, it felt that being with big Bob on the train had been a long time ago, almost in another era.

I flicked the CD forward to the album's title track. Tom's tobacco-crusted vocal chords fitted the mood and place perfectly as I accelerated out of Memphis. For me, this was better than Beale Street. I wasn't tired but I certainly felt relaxed and reflective, and the 150-mile journey south was no hardship. Indeed, I was looking forward to it. The Chevy was comfortable, the music was warm, and all was well in my world.

*   *   *

'How much court reporting have you done?' asked the news editor. I was not all that long in the STV door, and I could sense that this was an opportunity which would be offered to somebody else if I gave the wrong answer. An hour later I found myself at the High Court in Glasgow.

The North Court's Victorian oak panelling is today all too familiar to me, but at the time it was novel and redolent with drama and history. The first case I covered there for STV was a fatal accident inquiry into the death of a baby who had, instead of oxygen, compressed air fed into his hospital incubator.

A few weeks later, I graduated onto another FAI (Fatal Accident Inquiry), which was investigating the death of a recluse who derived satisfaction from making hoax 999 calls. But the last time he did it, he assaulted the female police officer who came to the door of his high-rise flat to investigate. Her male colleague wrestled him off her, and the trio tumbled back into the living room where the hoax caller stumbled into an armchair. The chair tipped backwards, causing the heavy spherical glass shade of a standard lamp to fall on his head, killing him.

Every story I covered was a slice of life. I did the usual diary fodder pieces but soon found myself entrusted to cover crime and the courts.

Mhairi Julyan was a sixteen-year-old girl who had been abducted, raped and murdered just yards from her Kilmarnock home. The newsdesk despatched me to Ayrshire to report on the manhunt, and I delivered stories for the lunchtime and evening news every day, culminating in the testing of every man in the area after the killer left traces of his DNA at the crime scene. Gavin McGuire, a known sex offender with a record of brutal crimes, was quickly apprehended and put on trial. I was assigned to the North Court again for every day of the proceedings. The case against him was overwhelming, and he was found guilty.

This was my first taste of the barbarism that I was to encounter all too often in my daily working life. McGuire had been released from jail little more than a fortnight before he attacked Mhairi. He had a string of previous sexual offence convictions, and the Judge Lord Clyde described what had happened as 'an atrocity without mercy'. He jailed the killer for thirty years, and made it clear he thought McGuire should never be released.

For a boy from Inverness who had come to Glasgow via the douce streets of Bern, this was a wake-up call. Sadly, life in the big city was all too cheap and, from that trial forward, I would cover many more instances where life was taken, usually with unspeakable savagery and often on the most ridiculous premise.

When the producers of the STV crime drama 'Taggart' approached me to play a cameo role in the 100th episode, I was honoured and flattered. I learned my lines in the same way I learn my words for a piece to camera and, of course, the make-up and lights were nothing new to me. However, the producers may well have rejected the plot as too outlandish if someone had approached them with the most sensational story I have ever covered.

There is no such thing as a typical news day, and 21 September 2006 dawned with no apparent lead story. That morning, I was assigned to an interesting tale about a couple from Pakistan who were claiming asylum in a Glasgow church because they believed that, as Christians, their lives would be in danger if they returned home. They had been given a room in the chapel house of St Patrick's, in the Anderston area of Glasgow, while they worked out what they were going to do.

The priest answered my phone call, and he told me that we were welcome to come and interview him and the couple that morning. When my cameraman colleague and I arrived half an hour later, I was touched by the size and beauty of the church and the obvious charisma of Father Gerry Nugent. I was impressed by him from the outset. He was in his late fifties, highly intelligent and unlike any man of the cloth I'd ever met.

He showed us into the kitchen of the chapel house where I met Masih and Christine Raymond. I interviewed them both, then we all went back through to the church where we filmed some set-up shots and I did the interview with the priest. He was full of energy, and promised not to rest until the couple had been given permanent residence in Scotland. They could stay in the chapel house until then. As the cameraman and I were leaving, a pretty young girl in her early twenties stuck her head round the door for a matter of seconds before disappearing. I would find out later her name was Angelika Kluk.

Four days later, she was reported missing after she failed to turn up at her cleaning job in Glasgow. I joined dozens of other journalists at Stewart Street police station in Glasgow that day, where her sister Aneta give an emotional news conference. It was totally out of character for Angelika not to be in touch, she said. Her tears were heartbreaking. The news conference revealed that Angelika, a student of Scandinavian languages at the University of Gdansk, had also been living in a room in the chapel house at St Patrick's where she had also been taken under the wing of Father Nugent. At the same time, the church handyman, Pat McLaughlin, had disappeared. People began to put two and two together.

We jumped into the crew car and sped round to the church. There was already a police cordon in place, with the familiar blue and white tape stretched across the road. And so began another chilling episode in Glasgow's rich crime history.

Four days later, at around five-thirty in the afternoon, I received a phone call from a police contact telling me that the missing church handyman was not Pat McLaughlin but Peter Tobin, a registered sex offender with a history of dreadful crimes. Detectives were holding a news conference and we scrambled our satellite truck to police HQ on Pitt Street. I broke the story live at six o'clock

I raced round to St Patrick's, where minibuses full of police officers were arriving. They quickly dressed in white paper suits and disappeared inside. An hour later, I received another phone call from my contact to say the body of a young woman had been found in an underground chamber inside the church. By Monday, the handyman was in custody, having been arrested in London. It was a crime which shocked the nation.

Months later, Tobin went on trial at the High Court in Edinburgh for the rape and murder of Angelika, and I sat through every day of the six-week-long case. It was, without question, the most dramatic trial I have ever covered, with every witness providing testimony which grabbed the headlines and which produced audible gasps from the public gallery.

Tobin was defended by Donald Findlay QC, a master of the theatre of the courtroom. From every prosecution witness he drew facts and figures which cast doubt on his client's guilt, and which painted a shocking picture of a dysfunctional situation inside the church.

The first morning Tobin walked into court three at the High Court in Edinburgh, I was sitting in the press bench behind the dock and I found I couldn't look him in the eye. That day, we saw the horrific police scenes of crime video of poor little Angelika, naked and punctured by stab wounds, bundled up like a rag doll and discarded in a chamber beneath the confession box of St Patrick's. She'd been bound and gagged and battered with a lump of wood and raped around the time of her death. Every morning thereafter when Tobin tried to stare me out, I always held his eye.

The other witnesses spoke of an alcohol-fuelled sexual culture in the chapel house, where ecclesiastic vows and marital fidelities were ignored with abandon. Father Nugent spent days in the witness box, and Donald Findlay spared none of his blushes.

The priest admitted that he was an alcoholic and that he and Angelika had been involved in a sexual relationship. He also admitted earlier sexual improprieties with parishioners. Angelika was allowed to stay rent-free in the chapel house in return for cleaning duties, he said. It was clear that she also performed other favours for him.

Another witness, Martin Macaskill, a married man from Greenock, told the trial that he and Angelika had been involved in an extra-marital affair, had engaged in sexual intercourse in her room at St Patrick's, and that Father Nugent had known what was going on. The pair had met while she had been the nanny of a wealthy family holidaying in Edinburgh over the summer, and he had been the chauffeur driving them around Scotland. In her evidence, his wife agreed that she had been aware of the affair but had done nothing to stop it.

Angelika's diary was read to the jury. In it, the heartbreaking naivety and romanticism of a young woman was made public. Fate threw one of Britain's worst-ever sexual serial killers her way, into an already sickening set of circumstances and, as a consequence, she died a horrific death.

What happened was not, of course, her fault. It wasn't even Gerry Nugent's fault, sacrilegious, manipulative and abusive though his behaviour had been. Macaskill was just a weak man, flattered by the attention of a beautiful young woman and guilty only of betraying his wife.

The fault lay with Peter Tobin.

There were other twists. Tobin had become unwell after he'd fled to London and had collapsed in the street. He was taken to a hospital in Queen's Square where staff recognised him, because by then he was Britain's most wanted man and his picture was all over the media. So as not to provoke the suspect into again attempting to flee, a police officer dressed himself in a nurse's uniform and walked down the ward to arrest him.

After much jousting with Donald Findlay, Gerry Nugent wrapped himself up in so many untruths and half-truths that his testimony was full of holes, and he was convicted of contempt of court. But, although he had been guilty of a gross betrayal of his calling, had taken sexual advantage of a young woman in the chapel house, and had allowed a man he knew to be married to have sex with her there, he was not the killer.

After his evidence, Gerry Nugent was sacked from his parish by Glasgow's Archbishop Mario Conti and went into exile, but he didn't go very far. I tracked him down to a parish house in Ibrox, where I tried to interview him for a piece to be broadcast at the end of the trial. Cameraman Bobby Whitelaw and I watched the house for a time and, when we saw Father Nugent come home from the newsagent with a rolled-up tabloid newspaper under his arm, I waited for ten minutes before knocking on the door.

He gave me a warm welcome and ushered me inside, but he was nervous that I was secretly filming or recording him. I assured him that I wasn't, but only after I'd taken off my jacket and tie and unbuttoned and opened my shirt to reveal my bare breast *sans* device, would he speak to me. Clearly troubled and very hungover, Gerry told me little of use from a broadcasting point of view. He spoke of his regret about the whole thing, but would give me no quote other than that he sought forgiveness for his sins. He said the church had offered him a room in this new parish house and that, if he did a TV interview, the Archbishop would almost certainly throw him out. He died a few years later aged sixty-six and, as if to draw some kind of line under the whole affair, STV sent me to cover his funeral.

The law dictates that juries are not allowed to know an accused's previous convictions in case it prejudices their deliberations. At the time, nobody knew the extent of Tobin's record. It was only after his conviction for Angelika's murder that enquiries were launched into connections he may have had with other missing women. I had done many stories about Falkirk teenager Vicky Hamilton who disappeared in 1991. I never thought for a second that Tobin, who had once lived in Bathgate from where Vicky disappeared, had also killed her.

Closing speeches were heard on the Friday, and the jury would be sent out on the Monday. On the Friday night, cameraman Colin Matheson and I were on a plane to Poland. Our mission was to gather as much material as we could about Angelika for the big piece I would do at the end of the trial.

When we arrived in our hotel in Gdansk that night, I retired early and, from the sizeable Polish equivalent of the Yellow pages, copied into my notebook the addresses of every church in Gdansk. As you can imagine, there were many. Carrying a mountain of camera kit and a laminated A4-sized picture of Angelika, Colin and I wandered around Gdansk knocking on church doors and patiently explaining what we were about. Twenty-four hours after our arrival, and easily more than twenty churches down the list, we hit the jackpot.

Her priest, father Michael Mitka, remembered Angelika well, and gladly gave us an interview. He couldn't have been more helpful and we couldn't have been more relieved. The next day we spent at the university, where I had arranged to interview Angelika's classmates and professor.

As our taxi took us back into Gdansk, I noticed the unusually shaped dockyard cranes at what was once the Lenin shipyard, icons of the famous anti-Soviet Solidarity trade union movement of the early 1980s. I had an idea. We stopped briefly to allow Colin to get some shots of the cranes, and I chatted up our driver.

'Does Lech Walesa still live here?' I asked. The driver nodded in the affirmative.

'Do you know where?' he nodded again. 'Everybody in Gdansk knows where he lives,' he said.

'Take us,' I demanded. He looked at me as though I had two heads. I knew that I would have something of a world exclusive if Gdansk's most famous son talked on STV News about Gdansk's most famous daughter.

The driver took us to a heavily fortified villa overlooking the town. Walesa had led Solidarity during the dark days of Soviet Communism and whipped up such a movement of opposition to the Moscow-controlled puppet Polish government, that it eventually comprised ten million members. Solidarity became a political party and Walesa was elected President in 1990.

Two men came to a side door, their black leather jackets almost certainly concealing guns. Both had the wispy coil of tubing belonging to earpieces dangling down the back of their necks.

I made sure my hands were in view at all times as I introduced myself and asked if the former President was at home. One man replied that we'd missed Walesa by an hour or so and that he was en route to China. I was really disappointed.

Tobin was duly convicted, jailed for life and ordered to serve twenty-one years. He was later sentenced to thirty years for Vicky Hamilton's murder, in a trial I also covered at the High Court in Dundee. For the murder of Dinah McNicol in 1991, he was given a whole life sentence. The bodies of Vicky and Dinah were buried in the garden of Tobin's former house in Margate. In jail, he has boasted of up to fifty more killings.

My piece, broadcast at the conclusion of the legal process, was a great success. While the BBC had covered every day of the trial as I had, we had made the extra effort to go to Poland on no more than a fishing expedition and had come back with the prize, but they had stayed at home.

That programme was nominated for an RTS award and my colleagues and I flew to London for the glitzy ceremony at the Grosvenor Park Lane. We were pipped at the post by a piece on the Morecambe Bay cockling tragedy. I was disappointed, but I don't know how I would have felt had I triumphed from poor Angelika's misfortune.

I have no interest in boxing as a sport. But I must qualify that. Twice a week for a couple of years I had gone to the Glasgow boxing gym owned by former British, European and Commonwealth welterweight champion Gary Jacobs, and I'd loved it. I was never fitter. Everyone in the newsroom at STV knew I had boxing connections and, when it was announced that former world heavyweight champion Mike Tyson was coming to fight at Hampden Park, I was assigned to the story.

Not only was it a huge sports story but also a major news story. Women's groups argued that Tyson, as a convicted rapist, should not be allowed in to Scotland, where he was due to fight the relatively unknown Lou Savarese. Their objections were made on the day an ISO container was opened at Dover harbour, revealing the bodies of fifty-eight people who had suffocated while trying to enter the country illegally from mainland Europe. Campaigners said that, while desperate people were going to such lengths, a convicted rapist should not flout immigration rules and be allowed in for a sporting fixture.

UK laws at the time forbade anyone who had served a jail sentence of more than a year from coming to the UK, unless there were exceptional circumstances. Clearly, the 'exceptional circumstances' rule applied to Tyson, and he flew into Heathrow on Concorde before taking up residence at the Grosvenor.

STV despatched me to cover his press conference at the hotel, where we would also be given access to film his training. The Grosvenor was packed with boxing fans and journalists, and we media types were ushered through to the ballroom where a boxing ring had been set up for Tyson. He would take a few questions before he started his session.

Shortly before the 10am start time, a member of Tyson's team came in and told us that the event had been cancelled. You could have heard a pin drop. Apart from the expense STV had incurred apparently for nothing, it was so frustrating that I had got this close to him but would have to go home empty-handed. We all trooped back through to the restaurant, but I had lost my appetite.

I phoned the desk to break the bad news. Tyson's decision would leave a three-minute hole in that night's programme. I suggested that I should head out to Brixton, where Tyson had been so mobbed by fans on his previous UK visit that he'd had to take cover in a police station.

As I was speaking to the newsdesk, I'd wandered off into an area of the Grosvenor which ran parallel to the lobby. What I saw there caused my mouth to drop open in astonishment. I ran back into the lobby to grab the cameraman, and we raced back into the side passage where Mike Tyson, wearing a Scotland football top, was sitting with his manager, Shelly Finkel.

I looked over my shoulder to check that my colleague had the camera to his eye, and was recording furiously. The two men were about ten yards away. Tyson saw me and I held up my microphone. I gave him the 'any chance?' eyes and walked towards him. I managed only a few paces before two enormous black men in tracksuits emerged from nowhere and threw their arms out to block me.

'That's close enough,' said an American voice.

The pictures were just what I needed, and I thought we'd better get them back to STV for the lunchtime news. The cameraman and I trotted outside to hail a taxi to take our tape back to the ITN studios, from where it would be sent up the line to Glasgow. On the pavement I came face to face with Tyson. I grabbed my chance and thrust the microphone under his nose.

'Mike Edwards STV News, Mike. Are you looking forward to coming to Glasgow?

Tyson grabbed the badge on his Scotland top and thrust it towards me. I thought he was about to kiss it, which was all good and well, but what I needed was an interview.

'Look, look, look,' he said pointing to the detail of the badge. 'Can you read?'

'Yes,' I said.

'Alright!' was his response.

This was hardly an in-depth, sit-down interview with the world's most famous and controversial boxer, but he then rejoined his minders and he walked off up Park Lane, the cameraman and I walking alongside. I thrust the microphone under the linked arms of the security cordon and threw Tyson another question.

'Mike, do you have a message for your Scottish fans?'

He looked towards the camera and gave the thumbs-up. Then he made a peculiar whistling sound and turned to me.

'It's gonna be a piece of cake, a piece of cake.'

Now that I had his attention, I wasn't going to let go.

'Are you going to win?' I asked. My question was not about the bout with Savarese, nor boxing in general, but about the controversy surrounding his visit.

'Yessir, I'm gonna win,' he said.

Tyson then stepped away from me. Another coterie of bodyguards appeared, because by now the pavement was thick with fans and, belatedly, journalists. I'd got a scoop. Tyson didn't give an interview to anyone else.

Cameramen see things with different eyes. A few yards away from the front door, my colleague grabbed me and huckled me towards the head of the pack. Tyson was now over my shoulder walking towards the door, his Scotland top clearly visible.

'I'm rolling,' he said. 'Piece to camera! Go!'

There was no room for error. If I made a mistake, I could hardly go up to Tyson and say, 'Sorry Mike, but I've arsed that right up. Any chance you could walk down the road one more time so I can try it again?' This is why you don't see reporters doing pieces to camera at a ship launch.

Many times down the years people have asked what's my method for a piece to camera. The question confuses me and I have to ask them to elaborate. They mean 'method' as in 'method acting.' I invariably reply that my method is that it pays my mortgage.

Years before I started in television, I read a book called *Chickenhawk* about helicopter pilots in Vietnam. The author revealed something about aviation which I'd never considered. Regardless of what was the mission or destination, helicopter pilots always scanned the earth looking for a spot to land in an emergency: a field there, a road here, a football pitch somewhere else.

For some reason, this meaningless piece of trivia stuck in my mind and, ever since, if I'm walking around and pass a place or an event, I start thinking about the words I would use for a piece to camera. This habit has helped me to handle situations like the one I was now in with Tyson. Call it a 'method' or whatever.

Suddenly, 'It's a ghost town at lunchtime on a Sunday but, between nine and five, Monday to Friday, these streets are the beating heart of Scotland's financial sector', became, 'Mike Tyson will shortly leave London and move to Glasgow, where he'll put the final touches to his preparations for the big fight at Hampden. After calling off his planned news conference this morning, he's saying very little publicly today, insisting he'll do his talking in the ring instead.'

Those who know me will tell you that I'm never stuck for something to say. The point is that a TV reporter should be on top of everything that's happening nationally and locally, and prepared at all times to work on any story. Part and parcel of the story is the piece to camera, the where, the when and the what to say. Shrinking violets and non-news junkies need not apply.

Shortly after checking in to the Glasgow Hilton, Tyson then went to the Gallowgate and, from the roof of somebody's car, addressed crowds of his fans who had gathered outside. The car was damaged in the process, but I'm sure the owner never complained. Would you?

On the day of the fight, Hampden was packed with people who had paid up to £500 a ticket. The bell rang, and Tyson and Savarese weighed each other up for a few seconds before the fight started in earnest.

My boxing mentor Gary Jacobs had told me about the tactics involved in boxing. Ahead of one title fight at Madison Square Garden, he and his team had spent hours studying the opponent's form and watching his fights on video. They had a plan, which involved subtle changes of style from the start. However, at the bell the plan went out the window, and the bout descended into a slugging match where any thoughts of tactics evaporated.

And so it proved at Hampden. Tyson had Savarese on the floor within eight seconds. When the challenger got to his feet, Tyson then rained such a shower of blows on Savarese that referee John Coyle tried to stop the fight. But Tyson continued, and in the end his corner intervened, although not before Coyle himself ended up on the canvas trying to separate the boxers. The fight lasted thirty-eight seconds.

You'd think this would mean the end of an extraordinary moment in Scottish sporting history. However, immediately after the bout he told a TV interviewer that he wanted a tilt at the British world champion Lennox Lewis, adding he wanted to tear Lewis's heart out and eat his children.

This may well have been entertaining to his fans but it wasn't very edifying for the rest of us. In later years, Tyson said he'd been high on cocaine and marijuana throughout his time in Glasgow. This tallied with the way he'd behaved when we crossed paths in London, and also for his comments about Lennox Lewis.

However, what I could never have expected was his admission that, to pass his drug test after the Hampden fight, he'd used a rubber penis filled with someone else's urine to give a sample. 'Once you take your fake whizzer out and you start the urination process,' he said in his autobiography, 'the person doing the testing generally looks away. All you have to hope is that the urine in it came from a man and not a pregnant woman. That might be hard to explain.'

News reporters are seldom seen at sports events, unless there is a news angle to the story. I never fail to laugh at the enmity newspaper sports reporters have for broadcasters, news broadcasters especially. I think it stems from the fact that TV and radio break stories before newspapers are even printed, but the internet and social media has changed all that. Today, when I turn up at a sports news conference I barely get a civil word from the scribes. And when STV sent me to Florence for the Rangers UEFA Cup semi-final against Fiorentina in 2008, cameraman Neil McLaren and I were totally shunned.

On Tuesday 20 January 2009, I was sent by the desk to a news conference at Murray Park, the Rangers training ground. A similar warm reception awaited me from the ladies and gentlemen of the sporting press but, saying hello to them all and smiling broadly as I took my seat, I was determined to let them see how little their petty vendetta meant to me.

Disappointingly, many were clearly unable to use shorthand and, when the American midfielder Maurice Edu came into the room to be questioned at the news conference, they all reached forward and dropped their tape recorders onto the top table. I sat in the front row with my sharpened pencil ready to scribble my best teeline in my spiral reporter's notebook.

Edu's backside had barely touched his seat when I beat everybody to it and asked the first question. Every other journalist in the room turned and glared at me, outraged that I had breached some unwritten protocol or other, had spoken before them and had not demanded of him an answer about a groin strain or the merits of the 5-3-2 formation.

'Maurice, what's your reaction to the inauguration of President Obama in Washington this morning?' I asked.

You could have heard a pin drop before the eloquent young man answered. He told me about his pride at that moment, and how he had never dreamt that one day a black man would be the President of the United States. I could feel the eyes of the sports hacks drilling into the side of my head, but I don't think I could have cared less. After Edu had finished his genuine musings about the new era for the American people, I thanked him and turned, smiling to face my colleagues. When one of the tabloid hacks asked the groin strain question, I put my pencil in my pocket and closed my notebook. I had a better story.

The news/sport ley lines have crossed many times down my quarter century at STV. I was at Glasgow airport the morning Fergus McCann arrived in Scotland to save Celtic. He gave his views to the waiting hordes of newsmen but. as the cameraman and I afterwards returned to the car park, we were delighted to notice that the Celtic official who had come to collect McCann had parked his vehicle next to ours. Our camera rolled again and Fergus gave us an interview all to ourselves.

McCann had come and gone by the time the club enjoyed its greatest triumph since Lisbon. *En route* to the 2003 UEFA Cup Final in Seville, the team notched up a remarkable victory over a very good Liverpool side at Celtic Park. During the game, Liverpool's Senegalese striker El

Hadji Diouf careered off the pitch and ended up teetering into a section of Celtic fans. As he extricated himself, he turned and spat into the crowd.

Scotland went crazy, and the might of the footballing and legal world fell on Diouf. UEFA banned him for two games and Liverpool fined him two weeks' wages. He was also charged with assault, and appeared before Glasgow Sheriff Court. From the start he maintained his innocence but, just as the trial was due to begin, he changed his plea and was fined £5,000 by the Sheriff.

I was there to cover the trial and, when Diouf left the court, I was one of many reporters who thrust a microphone under his nose to get his reaction. He said nothing as he walked off to his waiting limousine. I thought I'd try a different tack and threw him a couple of questions in French, his native language. I figured I might get lucky as I had with Mike Tyson, but Diouf just smiled at me and walked on.

With no interview from Diouf, I decided I'd try to voxpop his lawyer, the Glasgow solicitor Joe Beltrami. The defence Diouf had mounted via big Joe was an unusual one. The footballer claimed one of the supporters had clapped him on the back of the head as he extricated himself from the crowd. He said this was the worst possible insult in Senegal, where such an action was deemed to be reminscent of a gangmaster counting slaves as they boarded ships to America. He said his automatic reaction had been to turn and spit, which, he added, was not illegal in Senegal. UEFA agreed, and fined Celtic for their supporters' threatening behaviour.

Had Tyson and Diouf deigned to give me an interview, it would not have been an easy ride for them. Many people have misconceptions about the media and how it works, but professionals like Tyson and Diouf knew the system inside out and were well aware that, in their position, silence was the best option.

On numerous occasions I've phoned people up about stories and asked them for an interview, to be told that they have a dental appointment and won't have the time, and anyway there's nowhere to park our outside broadcast unit vehicles. It often takes a while for them to understand that it's just me and a guy with a camera, and it will take ten minutes.

Another favourite reponse from the potential interviewee is that he can't do it today but will be available tomorrow. It's hard sometimes not to be rude when you explain to them that tomorrow is the television equivalent of the newspaper that wraps a fish supper.

Generally, the media deals with professionals who know how and when to give an interview, and the benefits or otherwise of so doing.

However, sometimes total novices give the best interviews. It's just pot luck. The hardest interview to conduct is the 'death knock', and I've done too many of these. Sometimes you get threatened with physical violence or verbally abused, while on other occasions you get taken inside, given tea and scones and hear someone's life story.

I knocked on the door of one bereft family the morning after a mining accident at Coalburn in Lanarkshire, and the woman who had just lost her husband gave me a touching interview. 'Aye son,' she opened, 'I heard your footsteps on the path there and I thought that was my man coming home from the nightshift.'

After one death, I knocked on a door in a particularly rough *arondisse-ment* in Glasgow's East End and was ushered in by the man of the house. The cameraman waited in the car for my signal, and all looked well for an interview. The grieving man began to eulogise about his dead son and, as this was the kind of emotional tribute I was looking for, I was on the point of asking whether he minded if I got the cameraman in. But the father beat me to it.

'What rank are you anyway?' he asked.

I was confused. I asked what he meant.

'Well, are you a sergeant or an inspector?'

Then it dawned on me that he thought I was a detective. I introduced myself and explained what I wanted. My feet hardly touched the ground as he threw me out.

One Sunday I was sent to Methven in Perthshire where a car full of teenagers had ploughed into a vehicle coming the other way in the early hours. Showing off to his female passengers, the driver had overtaken another car on a blind summit resulting in a dreadful accident with five fatalities.

After getting shots of the scene and an interview with a traffic policeman, cameraman Danny Livingston and I needed some voxpops so we went to the local shop. Many people we tried to interview politely declined because they knew the victims, which was fair enough. Then a man drew up in a large 4x4. Dressed in tweeds and a bonnet, he began abusing us the moment his brogues hit the pavement.

'You people are scum, you're vultures, you're bloodsucking parasites. This community is grieving. Why don't you fuck off and leave us alone. Journalists? You're disgusting! Go and get a proper job!'

He disappeared into the shop and emerged a few moments later with, hypocritically, a huge bundle of newspapers under his arm.

The hardest place to get an interview was Royal Deeside in the aftermath of the death of Diana, Princess of Wales.

When the phone goes in the middle of the night, it's never good news, is it? That night, ITN had called the STV news editor in the early hours, and he was scrambling me to get up to Balmoral, where the Royal Family was holidaying, as quickly as possible. Cameraman Ross Armstrong and I were in the crew car twenty minutes later and on our way to Balmoral. I would spend a week there working on the story of a lifetime.

Because the Royal Family is so popular on Deeside, none of the locals would speak to me on camera throughout the duration of my visit. So unpopular were we, that shopkeepers would come out onto the pavement and ask us to move away from their premises as we tried to voxpop passers-by. The landlady at our Ballater B&B was barely civil to us, and the clients of the pubs where we drank at night fell silent when we walked in. Then they growled at us. Soon, the village was packed with journalists from all over the world as the most famous family on the planet came under intense scrutiny.

Prince Charles had gone to Paris to collect his estranged wife's body by the time I arrived at Balmoral, but we were there to see the Queen take Princes William and Harry to Crathie Kirk that Sunday morning. It was an outing which was to prove controversial, but not as controversial as her decision not to return to London.

Nowadays we are used to flowers, toys, candles and even football tops being laid at the scene of a tragedy. But, until Diana's death in 1997, this was a very un-British thing to do. Normally loyal subjects began questioning the Queen's decision, suggesting that the royals had misjudged public opinion, and should have left Balmoral and returned to Buckingham Palace immediately the news of the incident had broken.

I saw the Queen's sombre face as her car drove past me towards Aberdeen airport when she at last returned to London. Ross and I then believed that our job at Balmoral was over. I had reported live into every lunchtime and every evening news programme since my arrival and, although it had been fascinating, we were both exhausted. But another big story was brewing.

Hampden Park was being rebuilt, and Aberdeen's Pittodrie stadium was scheduled to host Scotland's vital World Cup qualifier against Belarus. But because the game would be played on the day of Diana's funeral, Rangers striker Ally McCoist asked not to be selected out of respect for the Princess. His Ibrox team mates Andy Goram and Gordon Durie were also said to be considering their position.

At the time, the Scottish Football Association was run by Jim Farry, a man who had the reputation of being unpleasant and unhelpful to the media. I'd met him a few times and I have to say he was always perfectly polite and fair to me. But during the week of Diana's death he ruffled many feathers by insisting that the game be played at the scheduled time, funeral or not.

The Scottish Secretary Donald Dewar demanded the game be postponed by twenty-four hours, but Farry was having none of it. In the end, with calls being made for Farry to be sacked, the game was re-scheduled for the Sunday. Had it gone ahead on the Saturday, it would have been the only sporting event to have taken place in Britain on what was regarded as a national day of mourning.

That Friday night I was reporting live from the Scotland team hotel in Aberdeen. I had managed to speak to national coach Craig Brown an hour or so before I was due to go on air. He agreed to join me live at the top of the programme but, as I stood in front of the camera with the title music blasting into my earpiece, there was no sign of him. We had a reporter live in London ready to talk about preparations for Diana's funeral, we had a reporter live in Edinburgh ready to talk about how Scotland would mark events, and I was live in Aberdeen ready to report on the controversy surrounding the game. But still no Craig Brown.

The first two did their stuff, and the presenter was halfway through his introduction to me when Craig appeared through the crowds and took his place by my side, just in time for me to say, 'well I'm joined now live by national coach Craig Brown'. I've always liked Craig, and that night he went up several notches in my estimation.

Diana's death came a year after Dunblane, the biggest story on which I've ever worked and also the most traumatic. But, while the horrors I experienced that day in March 1996 will stay with me forever, they obviously don't come close to the heartache felt by those directly involved.

The morning started as most news days did, quite slowly. The first reports came in around 10am, saying only that somebody had fired an air rifle at the school building. This in itself would have merited little more than a brief mention in the evening news. But somebody in our political unit then took a call from a contact in the Scottish Office who had been briefed by Central Scotland Police about the magnitude of the events.

My story that day was to go to a manor house near Beattock which was setting up a special project for problem teenagers. We had the radio on all the way down the M74, listening as the horror of what had happened in Dunblane unfolded. A gunman, carrying two automatic pistols, two .357 magnum revolvers and 750 rounds of ammunition had gone into the school. Sixteen children, all but one aged just five, had been shot dead in the gym, along with their teacher. The gunman, subsequently named as Thomas Hamilton, had then shot himself dead.

We got as far as Lesmahagow when the desk ordered an immediate about turn. We were to head straight to Dunblane, where my brief was to go to the ambulance station to interview the paramedics who had been first on the scene.

That night, and for several nights afterwards, the nightly news was broadcast live from the scene. It was only when I watched the programme from one of our outside broadcast unit vehicles that the enormity of what had happened struck me. I thought that tragic and violent events like this only ever happened in America. That the victims had been innocent little children made it all the more sickening. I couldn't believe it. The pictures of parents sprinting down the road towards the school in stark terror that morning are etched in my memory.

Journalistically, of course, it was a huge story, and one or two things about the coverage of the tragedy stick in my mind. The police held hourly news conferences in the Victoria Hall near Dunblane railway station, and I noticed that the woman sitting in front of me was Kate Adie. I was disgusted, and I wasn't the only one. She was widely regarded as a war correspondent, and I thought her appearance was wholly inappropriate. It wasn't her fault. I could imagine some desk jockey at the BBC newsroom in London despatching her because it was such a big story, totally missing the point.

One of the Dunblane parents was an executive at the *Daily Record* in Glasgow, and Chief Reporter Anna Smith went with him on the agonising journey to the school. While the police kept the media at the gate, they waved his car into the school grounds. She was the only journalist inside the cordon, and was there little more than an hour after the shootings. She stood beside parents who didn't yet know if their children were alive or dead. Her close-range account of events was the scoop of the year.

One STV cameraman working in Dunblane that day lived in Stirlingshire and knew a man who was a member of the local shooting club and who was crazy about guns. He figured his friend might know who had been responsible for the shootings at the school and would give us an interview if he did. He phoned his pal but there was no response, so he left a message on the answering machine. Then he went to the man's house but there was nobody home, so he dropped a note through the letterbox asking the man to call him. The friend's name was Thomas Hamilton.

Early the next morning I was sent to the Glasgow Hilton where Prime Minister John Major had stayed the night ahead of his visit to Dunblane. Major was being guarded by armed Special Branch officers, one of whom recognised me from the evening STV News. We chatted briefly, and he pointed me in the direction of the Number 10 press officers. We agreed that, since I was the only journalist there, I could 'doorstep' the Prime Minister as he left for Dunblane.

Our camera was already rolling as the police motorcycle outriders took up position beside the Jaguar which was parked at the front door of the hotel. Flanked by his bodyguard and private secretary, John Major stepped outside.

'Good morning Prime Minister, Mike Edwards STV News. Can I ask your reaction to the events in Dunblane?'

'Good morning Mike,' he replied before giving me a lengthy interview. Far from a quick doorstep question, Major seemed happy to chew the fat. But when I reached the subject of gun law reforms, he drew proceedings to a halt. Still, it wasn't a bad exclusive.

When I got back to the studios, everybody was crowded round the newsdesk, reading the contents of a brown envelope which had arrived in the morning mail. One letter, addressed to the news editor and written in Hamilton's neat hand, explained how he had felt slighted after being sacked by the Scouts for improprieties against young boys, how he knew he was being talked about in the community, and how he bore a grudge against Dunblane primary school. There were also copies of letters to the then Scottish Secretary Michael Forsyth, a local MP, and one to the Queen in her capacity as patron of the Scouts Association. The letters outlined his sick justification for carrying out his barbaric act. He had posted them on his way to the school.

A month or so after the tragedy, STV sent me to Dunblane on the day the gym was torn down. I remember that, when the growl of the demolition crane ended, the birdsong at the school was incredibly and symbolically loud.

The nightly news doesn't generally cover stories about events which go according to plan. That's not how it works. The opposite is the case, and

I've found myself covering instances of where things have gone disastrously wrong.

One day, I was following up on another story in Uddingston when the desk called me and sent me to the Maryhill area of Glasgow after reports of an explosion. When I got there the area looked like a war zone. The building had been destroyed and casualties were milling about with bloodied bandages on their heads. It was surreal. Around 100 people worked at Stockline Plastics. Many were inside going about their normal business that lunchtime when liquefied petroleum gas leaked from a tank and exploded, causing the building to collapse. Nine people were killed and thirty-three injured.

A couple of years previously, I had been inside the factory investigating allegations that the company had been involved in making illegal stun guns for sale. Now it was a smoking pile of rubble. With admirable fortitude, firefighters worked round the clock for days to free people trapped in the wreckage. They were backed up by colleagues from all over the UK. I remember driving up Maryhill Road and seeing fire engines parked there which had come from as far away as Kent and Cornwall.

There were other tragedies aplenty. I've worked on plane crashes, train crashes and too many car crashes to count. I covered the world's worst E-Coli outbreak which claimed more than twenty lives in Wishaw and the first UK deaths, a mother from Glasgow and her unborn baby, from bird flu. Some of the things I have seen are etched into my memory. I reported from the Red Road flats in Glasgow, where a Russian mother, father and adult son leapt to their deaths from the fifteenth floor after their application for asylum had been refused. In the grass outside the flat lay the deep indentation where the trio, roped together, had hit the ground.

Thinking I was seeing something from a disaster movie, I stood and looked on in disbelief at the wreckage of the Police Scotland helicopter on the roof of a Glasgow pub. Mystery still surrounds precisely why an experienced ex-military pilot apparently switched off the fuel pumps to the helicopter's two engines. Ten people died: seven in the busy pub, and the pilot and two police officers aboard the aircraft.

A year later, almost to the day, the driver of a bin lorry collapsed at the wheel as he drove along Glasgow's Queen Street, knocking down and killing six people, among them an elderly couple and their eighteen-year-old granddaughter. When I arrived at the scene, the lorry was still wedged into the wall at the entrance to Queen Street Station. The next day I had the task of knocking on the doors of the victims' families. They were all exceptionally polite but nobody would be interviewed. Months later, I covered the Fatal Accident Inquiry into the tragedy, and heard how driver Harry Clarke had a history of blackouts behind the wheel but had never reported it to his employers or the DVLA.

There was much speculation that criminal proceedings would follow the FAI, and during Clarke's evidence he answered dozens of questions about the accident with the words 'no comment,' in case he incriminated himself. The families of the victims were so disgusted that they walked out of the courtroom. In the end, the Crown controversially decided not to prosecute Clarke, and I was at the Court of Session in Edinburgh to see an attempt by the families to mount a private prosecution, which is rare in Scotland. I was also in court weeks later, when the three judges who heard the case gave their reasons for refusing the bid. The families, although dignified, were clearly heartbroken when they came outside to the waiting cameras.

Virtually every court case involves a tragedy. I covered two particularly sad cases at Kilmarnock Sheriff Court. The first involved a labourer on an Ayrshire building site who jumped into the cab of a roadroller and, although unqualified to do so, drove off. A few yards down the road he found himself unable to stop the machine and, after he lost control, he ran over and killed a child.

The second was another dreadful tragedy in which a Galston woman, Alison Hume, fell forty-five feet down a disused mineshaft while walking home across waste ground. Her family quickly found her and raised the alarm, but she lay hypothermic with broken bones for five hours while police, firefighters and mountain rescuers debated about how to get her out. Shortly after she was brought to the surface, she suffered a heart attack and died in an ambulance on the way to hospital. Again, the Crown chose not to prosecute. The family was devastated.

In these cases, in fact in pretty well all of them, the families of victims of crime or tragic accidents always act with commendable dignity, despite their bereavement. I can't take sides and I have to report events dispassionately, but some stories are breathtakingly sad, and my heart goes out to the victims and their families.

Of course, it wasn't all tragedy and disaster. There were also many moments of humour, even hilarity. Cameraman Neil McLaren was a magnet for funnies. The day he first used a satnav, he noted how the destination was marked by a chequered flag in the corner of the screen. He was staggered when he arrived at the house to find that the owner, possibly because he was a Formula One fan, had a chequered flag fluttering on top of a high pole in his garden.

An art lover, Neil tells of the time he went to the Rijksmuseum in Amsterdam to take in an exhibition of the work of the Dutch master, Rembrandt. He was sitting enjoying the Night Watch when a large American ambled in, scanned the room and left hurriedly, saying to his wife, 'No Rembrandts in here honey. They're all by some guy called "Van Rijn".'

Neil and I were about to interview a young mother one day and having set up the camera and lights, he started to test his microphone.

'One two, one two,' he said in the time-honoured fashion. The woman's youngster started tugging at her sleeve.

'Mummy, mummy,' she said urgently.

'Not now darling, mummy's busy,' came the reply.

'One two, one two,' said Neil again into his mic.

'Mummy, mummy,' said the wee cherub yet again.

'I've told you darling, mummy's busy, be quiet please.'

'One two, one two,' he proferred.

'Mummy, mummy,' said the girl, more urgently this time.

'What is it?' screamed the mum, obviously nervous about her interview.

'Mummy that man can't count up to three.'

Then there was the man I stopped while I was covering the story of a missing circus elephant near Glasgow. Time was passing and the desk was bellowing at me to deliver something for the lunchtime news. The man was digging in a trench near the place where the animal had last been spotted. I rolled out of the crew car, microphone in hand.

'Excuse me, Mike Edwards STV News. Have you seen an elephant?' He lowered his shovel, looked at me quizzically for a moment before he replied.

'Today?'

Somebody in showbusiness once said never work with children or animals, and there is truth in that. I've done the occasional piece to camera holding a baby or a puppy, but so much can go wrong that it's not really worth the risk. The one exception to this was Dolly the sheep. She was a superstar! She had been cloned by scientists at the Roslin Institute near Edinburgh, and was so used to being filmed that she would walk over to the cameras and pose.

I held her a couple of times for a piece to camera, and was surprised how easy she was to handle. What a pro! The rights and wrongs of cloning are for others, but I must say I was sad when I learned she had died. If only some of the people I have dealt with could have been so laid-back. As an aside, staff named her Dolly, after Dolly Parton, because she had been cloned from a mammary gland cell.

During one bout of particularly bad weather, STV sent me to cover the plight of families in the Clyde Valley who had been hit by power cuts after storms had blown trees down onto high tension wires in the area. It was a random task. We had a rough idea which houses had been left powerless, and it was down to me to knock on doors until I found somebody who could help us.

It is often part of my job to approach strangers and ask them to do things they ordinarily would rail against, like go on live national television. As you can imagine, some people are more cooperative than others. The third or fourth door elicited a family who had a toddler and a new baby, and they'd been without electricity for two days. It was a great example and thankfully, when mum realised her kids would be on TV that evening, even though she couldn't see the programme, she didn't take much cajoling.

My only problem was that it was late in the afternoon and heading back to Glasgow to edit was out of the question. We'd have to do it live. The scene was set. The family had lit loads of candles and there were a couple of torches on in the corner of the living room. Baby had just been bathed in water warmed on the gas stove and the room had a certain feel of the nativity about it.

Suddenly the satellite truck engineer came running in holding an extension cable. 'Mike! Mike, we've got a huge problem,' he said.

'I've had a leak in the generator fuel tank and I don't think we've got power to get the dish up. Ask the family to plug this in and we'll fire her up from the mains.'

I paused for a moment and smiled.

The penny suddenly dropped.

'Bastard,' he said quietly.

ASLEF had called a strike, and I was despatched to Glasgow's Queen Street Station to capture the commuter chaos for the evening news. Your average Glasgow train traveller was obviously well used to the problems, and had either made other travel arrangements or had taken the day off.

ScotRail allowed us onto the concourse to film the usual platforms devoid of trains and 'cancelled' signs on the departure boards.

It was like a scene from a disaster movie. The station was eerily silent and deserted, except for a solitary woman who sat on a bench in the middle of the concourse surrounded by her messages in half a dozen carrier bags, looking around her and wondering what she was missing.

The Red Road high flats in the Balornock area of Glasgow, the tallest in Europe when they'd been built in the 1960s, were due to be demolished: a story that meant rich pickings for us. There were those who were desperate to be re-housed, but others had grown up in the tower blocks and felt an obvious attachment to them. One drawback of my job is that you catch a few minutes sleep when you can, usually in the crew car on the way to or from a job, and you eat similarly.

Obviously, not everywhere is blessed with a supermarket where you have a choice. Too often, I have to eat out of petrol stations or burger vans. Don't get me wrong: some burger vans are very good. Others are not. The one in Balornock was OK, and I had just ordered a bacon roll on the morning of the demolition, when the proprietor engaged me in conversation.

'You're that reporter aren't you? There's one of you guys I can't stand. Is it you?'

*   *   *

Winona is known as 'the crossroads of Mississippi' because of its geographical location in the state and the convergence there of three highways. I swung off I-55 and headed west for the first and only time on my trip. Ten minutes later I was at my destination.

Inverness, Mississippi, is heralded by a large green-bordered grey sign, adorned with a large goose and the words 'where the songs of the Cypress meet our delta's green pastures'.

This was all rather nice and quaintly charming in that Southern way. But long before you reached the sign, from a healthy distance away, the town is announced by a silver, spaceship-like water tower, a massive metallic sphere atop a silver spike, with 'Inverness,' emblazoned in black. Cotton bales adorned the road leading in, and I stopped to pick up a few loose odds and ends so I could touch it in its raw state for the first time. By the time I reached the quiet little downtown area, there was no doubt I was in the Deep South because the tranquility was healing. I jumped out of the Chevy and walked around.

'In that slow southern style', lyrics from the Alannah Myles 1989 hit 'Black Velvet', rolled around inside my head as I wandered. I figured her record producer boyfriend, who wrote the song for her, must have been here at some point and was inspired by the place to pen that line. I found out later that the song had actually been written as a tribute to Elvis.

The buildings were low and the streets wide. A couple of cars rolled along, and a few souls went about their business. Storm clouds had passed and the sun was out again, although the oppressive southern heat was absent. After three hours in the Chevy, I needed a lift. Coffee and doughnuts, please.

There was a small restaurant across the road from the police station, and I drew in. A large white Ford Crown Victor police car sat outside, with 'a duty to protect – an honor to serve' emblazoned on the wing. I noticed that the headrest of the passenger seat had a pair of handcuffs attached to it. It made sense to do this, but I couldn't imagine there was too much crime here. I was hoping to ask a burly cop about his huckling tactics, but the restaurant was empty. I had an impending appointment, but there was time for caffeine and sugar as I reviewed some facts and figures.

The last census in Inverness Mississippi was in 2000, and it registered 1,153 people living here. That census gave the breakdown as 59% African-American and 39% white. However, in all the time I was there, I never saw a single black face. For every 100 females there, there were eighty-two males.

The Town Hall enjoys a fine address – East Grand Avenue – but it's a bit of a misnomer, as it shares the building, which was erected in 1972, with the library. Like everything else, it was very quiet. Mayor James E Weems showed me into his office, and we sat and chatted about life. What he told me reflects the words of 'Black Velvet' and the ambience you feel the moment you arrive in town. Jimmy was in his sixties, white-haired and fit from years as a soldier and farmer. He was nearing the end of his second term in office, and looking forward to retiring.

'There was always an agricultural economy here and Inverness once boasted the biggest cotton gin in the world. But it's a different place now,' he sniffed, wistfully. 'The economic downturn has hit even here. Bell Agricultural are still here. They make a lot of spraying equipment but times are hard. The biggest employer is the local hospice, which says a lot.'

The town is small and the buildings single-storey, apart from the water tower. The police station, the library and Jimmy's office are obviously community focal points. It may be small and slow, but people live here and raise families. They work and earn and spend. Memphis is too far to commute, but Indianola is not far away.

'People stopped growing cotton and turned to soya and corn,' he said. 'There's more of a return from those commodities now, so people have switched, which is a shame but it's understandable.'

His desk was wide and cluttered with paper and pens, but there was no computer or laptop. On the back wall was his certificate of office and a couple of plaques, beside a not-too-brilliantly-painted picture of a Mississippi paddle boat. I said nothing in case he had painted it, or it was a gift from a friend or one of his grandkids. There was also a small cartoon caricature of him fishing, drawn by what looked like a street artist. Black ballot boxes with broken seals lay beside an ancient filing cabinet against the side wall, indicating a recent election.

His workload was taken up not by big-ticket political issues, but by things which were a million miles from Washington DC, such as utilities and preparation for tornadoes. Inverness was virtually destroyed by a tornado in 1971. Most of the town's buildings were ripped apart and twenty-one people were killed. Understandably, tornadoes are a huge issue here.

'Inverness has just signed a big deal with a major telecommunications company to install fibre optic cabling for local phone, internet and TV usage. And I'm also working hard to have self-starting generators introduced, which kick in when bad weather causes a power outage.' I think he noticed me bridle a bit when he used the word 'outage' instead of cut. I'm not a fan of American English. 'The storms in the south have to be experienced to be believed', he said. Temperatures regularly reach 105 Fahrenheit.

Then he told me his biggest concern was a local park which was in the middle of an eighteen-month project of redevelopment. He said the US Fish and Wildlife Service would give Inverness a grant to cover the costs. But, before receiving this money, the town had to find the money to have the work done and present a paid invoice to the accountants at the Service's HQ. I could see how this would be a big local issue, but it's hardly gripping stuff. I can't imagine being a news reporter here.

Jimmy asked me about the one true Inverness, and we talked about my home for a while. Like most Americans, he was intrigued by the debate surrounding Scottish independence. The Civil War mentality has largely long gone from what was the secessionist South, and all the focus is on the union. Many Americans can't understand why some Scots would want to leave a union like ours.

'Inverness got its name from a woman named McInnis who came from your home town and settled here in 1899. The railroad was the big money spinner at the time and she invested heavily and made a packet. Like so many places in the USA, the town grew around the railroad. I've heard about the Loch Ness Monster. It's quite a story!'

All the talk about Mrs McInnis and the unusual spelling of her name got me thinking. The last thing I ever wanted was to make Jimmy feel uncomfortable, but I couldn't help but wonder if his name Weems came from the Scottish name 'Wemyss', and his forefathers changed it because they were fed up being called 'wemiss' by people. You couldn't blame them.

Feeling a little claustrophobic, after Jimmy and I parted I jumped back into the Chevy and headed out of town. I passed the Tidy Truck trailer washdown point, and kept going. Inverness traverses and is bordered on one side, by a meandering waterway called the Mound Bayou: what we in the one true Inverness would call a burn. I imagined it would be full of catfish, probably snakes, and possibly even an alligator or two, so I didn't linger.

Growing in many parts of the bayou were beautiful Bald Cypress trees, the trunks of which emerge from the water with a wide base, resembling the engines at the foot of a space rocket, before merging into an elegantly slender trunk. Each had a number of tidemarks due to the southern rains which vary the level of the bayou. This is what the South is all about. I was in the heart of the slow, southern style that Alannah sang about. It is very laid-back indeed.

On the other side of the bayou, houses appeared. Some had rowing boats lashed outside, because the waters come pretty close sometimes and householders leave their cars on the road and need the boats to reach their homes. Many of the houses were typically Southern, and had wide verandahs with swing seats on them. Others had pillars at the front and were similar to Graceland but smaller, although not by that much.

I passed the Olde Fannie café and then, perhaps not surprisingly, I drove along Pond Avenue which pretty well parallels the bayou. Thankfully, it was a fairly sedate waterway during my visit. The houses alongside it were beautiful, and I would hate to think of them being trashed when the rains came. This is how things are in the Deep South, a place about which so much is written and sung. Cotton grows here, slaves used to work the land here, and the Civil Rights movement was born here.

As I drove around, I could feel little connection with the TV series and films about the Deep South which I had seen as a kid and adult. Yes, the feeling was one of tranquility, but I experienced none of the atmosphere which I had expected. It was too quiet. I didn't get a sense of 'Mississippi Burning', far less 'In the Heat of the Night'.

That was it. Maybe it was because there was no heat? I was used to seeing dramas set here, with sweat dripping off the characters and fans twirling. But throughout my visit, while the welcome was warm, the temperature was decidedly not. It was overcast but not unpleasant. I made a mental note to come back here when it was 105 Fahrenheit, as Jimmy Weems had said.

I'd been invited to tea by another pillar of the local community, a former school teacher who'd heard about my visit and knew all about my journey. Just as my trip had hit the headlines in Illinois, it was the talk of the steamie here in Mississippi. Petite and pretty Charlotte Sibley would be filing a report on our meeting for the next edition of the Inverness newsletter. We sat on her verandah, although disappointingly she didn't have a double swing seat on which I had kind of set my heart. And when she said 'come for tea', what she really meant was 'come for iced tea'. It was lovely, but I was dying for a hot brew and a chocolate biscuit.

'I've lived here all my life,' she opened, 'but I have also travelled. I've even been to your home town and done the boat trip looking for the Loch Ness Monster!'

Like many Americans, Charlotte claimed Scottish ancestry, and she attempted to trace her roots while on a family holiday to Scotland in the 1990s. I tried not to flinch when she said 'Scotch' instead of 'Scottish'.

'I was very impressed with Inverness, Scotland, and I even learned to drink hot tea!'

We sat and chatted and, after a while, some neighbours popped by. Everybody here looked like characters out of central casting. The women wore leisure clothing, blouses with thin polo-necks beneath, and slacks and soft shoes. The men wore denim jeans and checked working shirts.

'The lifestyle here means we have been able to produce the cream of the crop of young people ready for the world. We all have a very strong Christian community and we do everything together,' said Charlotte. The neighbours nodded their heads in agreement.

She had a delicious southern accent, just like like Scarlett O'Hara in 'Gone with the Wind'. She talked about the waterway near her beautiful wooden board house and called it the 'bow.' I realise after a while that she was saying 'bayou.' I closed my eyes and willed her to say it again. Happily, she did so, time and time again.

'It is a wonderful place to grow up and raise your own children. I grew up here. It's a community which is very supportive of young families. It's dead calm here, unless there's something going on at the school or church then you can't get parked at all.'

I closed my eyes and let the peace wash over me. My daily life in a busy TV newsroom was a million miles away from this. But could I handle it for long? Probably not. Nice to visit. Fascinating place full of lovely, lovely people but, while the stress of my job means I crave peace and quiet, I thought I might go crazy here.

'Country living is the best to my mind,' said Lee Evans, a broad, strong man who was roughly my own age. His eyes were deep set and his hair cut militarily short. He told me he was a construction project manager with a $10 million company, and works all over the South.

'I can see how other people grow up and I'm happy we still have the same slow pace. It's a traditional family and church southern town – we still hunt and fish. I went to college at the University of Southern Mississippi at Hattiesburg, but I still stayed out in the country. The big city life is just not for me, there's too much hustle and bustle and crowds.'

Lee told me he was working in Gulfport which, as the name suggests, is a harbour town on the coast. Years after Hurricane Katrina, which was the third-worst storm in US history, there was still ongoing construction work and he was working on a major project.

'We're hundreds of miles away but we could feel the winds here. It was horrible that so many people didn't know what to do down there once she hit. There was an emergency plan but it wasn't big enough. It was based on Hurricane Camille in 1969, which lasted for four hours. Katrina lasted four times longer.'

As I was about to depart, I felt sad. The lifestyle here is not for me, but the place is beautiful and the people were genuine and kind. My hosts presented me with an Inverness T-shirt which bears the town's emblem: a busy amalgam of a catfish, a cotton boll and some wheat stems. I was very touched, and jumped into the Chevy with a heavy heart.

CHAPTER FOUR

Inverness, Alabama

Sweet Home Alabama
Where the skies are so blue.
Sweet home Alabama
Lord I'm coming home to you.

Lynyrd Skynyrd

I was now three Invernesses down, more than half-way across America, and becoming well used to the road. The Chevy was a comforting companion, offering me music when my mood dictated, and a warm or cool air flow as the outside temperature demanded.

As I ate up the miles, I could not help but think that the ground here is red and white, blood and bandages. This is the land of the Civil War and the Civil Rights movement. The rich earth has been fed by the blood of soldier and slave. The white is the cotton of the plantation, a continual reminder of the white man's domination over his black brother. And the white is also the robe and hood of the Ku Klux Klan, whose badge is a white cross with a drop of red blood in the centre.

I drove through Columbus, nicknamed 'possum town' by native Americans, the last big town on my route across Mississippi. During the Civil War, Columbus hosted an arsenal and a military hospital, and the former prompted the Union army to attempt its seizure. But the Confederates successfully defended it, thereby sparing the town's glorious ante-bellum homes from inevitable destruction in an attritional urban fight.

Many of the casualties from the battle of Shiloh came here, and the town's inhabitants mourned the deaths of men on both sides. The Civil War poem 'The Blue and the Grey' was written about Columbus, after Francis Miles Finch had seen the ladies of the town placing flowers on war graves, regardless of the provenance of the fallen.

Columbus would be worth a stop, if for no reasons other than that it hosts the largest toilet seat manufacturer in the world, and that it was the birthplace in 1911 of playwright Tennessee Williams. However, time was pressing and I wanted to reach the next Inverness before dark. I crossed the state line into Alabama just as the sun dipped below the horizon in the Chevy's mirror.

As might a child, I imagined ghosts emerging from the ether after I'd passed through. Ghosts from the Civil War, ghosts from the plantations, and ghosts from the Civil Rights movement. They'd be wearing the blue and grey of the two armies, or the cheap, thin, scant garments given to the slaves who worked the cotton fields, or the formal clothes of people demonstrating against blacks and whites being forced to use different washrooms.

In my mind's eye, the soldiers on both sides of the conflict wore their caps, each sporting the crossed-swords badge. They had those moustaches of the time, and perhaps clay pipes in their pockets beside a pouch of the tobacco from the very plantations over which they were fighting. The only badges sported by slaves were the scars of the scourge or of the manacles that bound them. The protestors bore different scars: on their heart and conscience.

Birmingham is the largest city in the state of Alabama, although not the capital. It takes its name from the city in the UK, and it came into existence in 1871 after the Civil War as a result of the conjoinment of the burgeoning steel industry and the expanding railway network.

The city was the only place on the planet where significant quantities of the three raw materials – coal, iron ore and limestone – required for the production of steel were readily available in close proximity to each other. Many of the early inhabitants were pioneers from the original Birmingham, and they had already learned the lessons of the Industrial Revolution. They came here to forge their fortunes in steel.

The defeated South realised that industrial manufacturing was the way ahead. Cheap, non-unionised labour from the plantations headed in their tens of thousands to Birmingham, seeking work in the furnaces rather than in the fields. The slaves were now free, but they still had to earn a living. Birmingham became part of an industrial cycle, manufacturing in its mills the rails, carriages and wagons for the railway which had created it.

The slaves may well have been free, but they and their children were still subjected to inhuman treatment. The post-Civil War policy of 'separate but equal' – segregation – meant that they ate and drank in separate establishments, travelled on different transport, and had to send their children to different schools. For 'segregation', read 'racism'. However, a century after the end of the Civil War, the South had become a different place, due to the success of the Civil Rights movement.

In April 1963, Martin Luther King was imprisoned for his part in the Birmingham campaign of non-violent protests and sit-ins, which were designed to confront, but by peaceful means, the racist laws. King hoped that mass arrests would clog up the system, to the extent that eventually the point would be made and negotiations would then have to open to allow equal treatment for blacks.

King was deeply saddened when he read a newspaper, smuggled into the prison by a friend. The article in question was the 'call for unity', an open letter from local white clergymen, which demanded that Civil Rights protestors should use the courts to settle their grievances, rather than assemble and protest in the streets and other public areas. But it was the sentence 'protests led by outsiders' which most hurt King because, being based in Atlanta, it referred to him.

He immediately started to scrawl a response in the margin of the newspaper's front page. These words would soon become the famous 'letter from Birmingham jail', a crucial text for the Civil Rights movement. Its premise was that the main stumbling block on the road to the black man's freedom was not the Ku Klux Klan but the white moderate who was devoted to order rather than to justice. It ended with the words: 'injustice anywhere is a threat to justice everywhere'.

Because of the abundance of mining in the area, Klan members had ready access to explosives. The city quickly gained the nickname 'bombingham', as those people set against the emancipation of the black man dynamited black people's homes and the meeting places they frequented. Among these was the 16th Street church.

On Sunday 15 September 1963, the Klan planted a bomb under the church's steps which was timed to go off as the congregation arrived. It killed four little girls – an atrocity which is difficult to imagine. However, this was the catalyst for events which culminated in the triumph of the Civil Rights struggle. President John F Kennedy had already called for a reform of the race laws. After his assassination three months later, his successor Lyndon Johnson signed off on the new legislation. Martin Luther King had won.

Inverness Alabama is in Shelby County, a suburb of Birmingham. That morning I had risen early and had given Inverness a perfunctory exploration as I drove to do something I'd always wanted to in the South. I chose the Vineyard Church, one of fifty or more churches along a tree-lined avenue just off the town's main drag, simply because I liked the name.

'We're over here, buddy,' came a voice to my right. I was walking towards a crowd of people standing at the door of a new church, pale grey in colour with two ornate columns either side of a dramatic front stairway. It had a simple wooden spire with a cross atop. Behind it rose a gentle slope, green in the bright Sunday morning sun and alive with all manner of trees.

'I'm here for the church service,' I said, weakly. It was foolish of me to assume that the church service would actually be in the church.

'Today we're in here,' said the man, pointing behind him with his thumb towards a dull steel shed, which looked like a factory. There were even more people milling around there. 'I'm Dave,' he said, thrusting out his paw. He was in his fifties, and wore ragged jeans and a shirt, untucked. I assumed he was a janitor. By the time I got inside the Vineyard church, another dozen or so people had pumped my poor mitt.

The church sported rows of seats, as opposed to pews, and at the far end was a beautifully lit stage. Scattered around were guitars on stands, keyboards and mics. In the corner was a small booth with the top of a drum kit just visible. Now it resembled more closely a concert venue than it did a factory, but it still didn't look like a church. There was a large white projection screen bolted to the far wall behind the stage, presumably for song lyrics. Music from U2 blared from the PA system as people crowded in.

I was struggling to come to terms with the fact that I was in a church at all, as the lead guitarist opened the service with a rock riff which would not have been out of place at Glastonbury. People flooded in as the first number continued, and soon the hall was filled by several hundred people: black, white, old and young. I looked around. I was the most formally dressed man there, and I was only in polo shirt, jeans and a blazer. All were casually attired, while some were downright slovenly. Many wore ripped and faded jeans or shorts, and most wore trainers or flipflops. Few, it seemed to me, had made any effort at all.

I had expected music in the shape of a few hymns and a handful of prayers, but I had not expected such charismatic drama. The clapping started, the hands began swaying in the air, and soon the emotion was flooding back through the doors and into the Alabama Sunday air. I could not help but get carried along with it.

As the first rock number ended, there were shrieks of approval, thunderous applause and more hand waving. 'Don't sit down, don't sit down,' bellowed the lead singer. 'Introduce yourself to three people you don't know before you sit down.' So we all did. It was at this point that I noticed that Dave, the janitor who had guided me away from the church to the factory, was playing the lead guitar.

The second piece of music was slower, but not by much. These were modern songs, and this was more like a rock gig than a church service. I looked around at the full hall. Some swayed silently, others sang, and many held their hands up as though they were at an auction or in a classroom trying to attract the teacher's attention. Neighbours held their hands out in front of them, palms upward. I assumed this was to receive God's grace or something.

I started to feel uncomfortable. These people were odd, mad even. But after twenty minutes I began to enjoy it. The atmosphere was intoxicating. It was a real lump in the throat time, and I had tears in my eyes. I began to feel really emotional. Yet I am not religious in the slightest.

'We praise you!' bellowed the lead singer at the end of his set.

'We do!' shouted some in the congregation. I was going to use the word 'audience' but I suppose, technically, they were a congregation.

'Amen,' said some more people. There was thunderous applause and then the pastor came on. At first, I thought he was the band's roadie because he was the most casually dressed of the lot. Bubba Justice wore distressed denims and a battered old shirt, once again untucked.

His sermon touched on racism and injustice which was still prevalent in Alabama. I was shocked. Still?

The pastor of Inverness Vineyard church rejoiced in the splendid moniker of Elgie 'Bubba' E Justice Junior. He was in his forties, and had worked as an accountant before he joined the ministry. Clearly, he too didn't believe in dressing up. He didn't believe in shaving either, as he was sporting the beginnings of a straggly goatee beard. He had been a military policeman with the United States Air Force National Guard and was mobilised, although he used the word 'activated', to go on Operation Desert Storm, the mission to remove Iraq from Kuwait in 1991.

'I got as far as Birmingham airport, and spent the war there!' he laughed. 'But the USAF paid for me to go through college.'

I don't have much time for religious types, but I have to say I instantly took to him and his wife Melanie. After the service, they treated me to lunch at a rib restaurant to show me some Southern hospitality. They were knocking at an open door there, because ribs are quite possibly my favourite food in the world.

'Lord, it is an honour to be with Mike today. Please grant him the wisdom, strength and patience to complete his project.'

This was the grace Bubba said for me and my trip as we sat down. I was touched. I looked outside to the rib cooker. It was in the car park next to the kitchen, and looked like it could be towed by a large lorry. On it was a steel chamber with two thin chimneys. The chamber had two orifices: one for the meat and the other for the hardwood fire. Piled neatly beside the trailer was a stack of roughly hewn logs, ready to be burned at the steak.

When I think 'barbecue', I think of standing outside with a beer in hand, and a little machine in the corner with a gas cylinder inside, and sausages and steaks sizzling away. Here in Alabama that is called 'grilling', and is somewhat frowned upon by those who enjoy their food. A barbecue is something else entirely. Here, a barbecue is where meat is slow-cooked over hardwood smoke for several hours. The precise number of hours is the subject of great debate, usually requiring several beers or whiskies. It can be anything from eight to twenty-four hours to get the meat to have the required smoky taste. I'd rather have my meat taste of meat than anything else, but that's the USA for you.

As I've said, ribs are probably my favourite food, and I had long abandoned the knife and fork to tackle the beauties in front of me. My hands were glistening and I had rib juice drizzling from my chin as I listened intently to Bubba.

'As a pastor I deal with all strata of society. We have millionaires and homeless people worshipping together. I spend a lot of time preparing for Sunday worship – I never have a day off – and we do a lot of mission work. I have been to every continent, with the exception of Antarctica. I've spent a lot of time counselling people with problems ranging from marital problems to financial difficulties.

'My main effort is trying to help children. We have a number of children in the area who don't eat from the time they have lunch at school on Friday until the lunch they have at school on the Monday. That is tragic and we can't have that. We spend a lot of time and energy trying to get food to these children.'

I stared at my remaining ribs, and said nothing. The point was made. I asked him about his sermon and the mention of racism.

'To me, the racism people are dealing with these days is based on socio-economic factors rather than colour of their skin. The poor and the things that go with being poor, the gangs and the drugs and one parent families and the terrible home environment which leads to a poor educational experience, all means that people find themselves being separated from those who have two parents in their homes. That situation usually falls along racial lines. It creates a prejudice against African-American people who live in areas which white people are reluctant to go into. But if you send African-Americans into a white community, the children have the same standards of education and if there's a two parent home, there's not the same prejudice against them simply because of their race.'

At the service I had just attended, a black man and a white woman had brought their baby daughter to be blessed by Bubba. Was that such a big thing here? Was I racist for even noticing?

'There is a hesitancy for people to deal with racial issues here, especially if there is a mixed marriage. My generation was the first here to go to integrated schools. And by the time I reached sixth grade, schools were fully integrated. But people who are older than me and who grew up in completely segregated schools, they find it very difficult. I am still old enough to remember black people not being allowed to go for certain jobs because of the colour of their skin. For this generation it's not an issue. Both of my daughters have had African American friends come on vacation with us. In their mind it's not an issue whatsoever. I find myself in a sandwich generation.'

I looked at Bubba. He was a big man with an open, honest face. He spoke with that lovely Southern drawl and I knew that he would be a good friend. He was brought up in the Woodlaw area of Birmingham, near the airport – a predominantly black neighbourhood. As we chatted, I casually mentioned that I love a pint of Guinness. There was a silence, a tumbleweed moment. Bubba had never had a drink. We moved on.

'The population here in Inverness is 45% white and 45% African American. The other 10% is Hispanic and other racial groups. But the churches are not like that. They are not divided up along these racial lines.'

I asked him why. There were black people at the service that morning, young and old. I don't see religion as a particularly healthy thing, but I would have thought it should bring together people of the same religion. Apparently not.

'There are very distinct differences. Worship style is one thing. There are differences in musical tastes and I think that has more to do with it than anything else, more than the differences in the teaching. There is a way many of the African American pastors preach and there's a distinct way white American pastors preach. We like to dress casually, they dress up. But the main thing is where the churches are located. Communities tend to be very segregated. So the more integrated a community is, the more likely you are to see a mixed race church.'

I hadn't been here very long, but it was clear that Inverness Alabama was predominantly white and predominantly middle class. There couldn't be much for him to do apart from the odd wedding, funeral and christening. Could there?

'People are people and they struggle with very different issues. I am never off duty. I can get called out at eleven at night and there could be someone in hospital or someone struggling with a marital issue. People make mistakes, they are not machines. They are individuals, and helping people get through their lives is my biggest challenge.'

Bubba was a darling man and I could have talked to him for hours. Personal faith is a wonderful thing but I detest organised religion and what it makes people do. I wanted to tell him this, but thought I'd better not.

This Inverness was not how I imagined it. There was no community feeling, the church excepted. As I left Bubba and Melanie, they told me there are 1,000 churches in the general Birmingham area. Maybe it needs them.

I drove up and down the main drag, which is in reality Highway 280, looking for something that vaguely resembled a community. I could be driving to this day, and I doubt I'd have found it. Business straddled the highway. There were a Lowe's DIY centre, a Michael's craft shop and a Hobby Lobby. Dick's Sporting Goods is a favourite of mine, and it was across the way from the IHOP, the international house of pancakes. The shops were all on the east side of the road while the office blocks and banks were all on the west. I'm not sure if there was any geophysical reason for this, but it was interesting.

There were newly built houses up on the hill overlooking the town, and I took the Chevy for a spin up there. Obviously expensive, some were massive, with wide, ranging lawns and four garages. They were red brick but had tiles that didn't look particularly strong, and I wonder how these dwellings would fare in a hurricane. Winters here wouldn't amount to much, but they would have to have serious air conditioning to cope with those steamy Southern summer nights.

These houses were pretty enough but the area was sterile. There were a few cars dotted around but not a single living person to be seen, like the place's namesake in Illinois. Wealthy people lived here but must spend their free time indoors or elsewhere. What saddened me is that there were no signs of children, no bikes or toys lying around in the yards, no balls on the lawn and no basketball hoops in front of the garages.

I was looking for the real people, so I drove back down to the main drag but there was nobody around. It was like a ghost town. The church was full and the rib restaurant was busy, but nobody walked the streets or was sweating on a mountain bike. This may have been because it was now uncomfortably hot, or that this part of Inverness was a business rather than a residential area. It was also Sunday.

Inverness Alabama looked like a new town. All the shops, banks, and motels appeared to have been built in the last twenty years. On my first full day here, I got the distinct impression that the people who worked here didn't live here, and the people who lived here didn't work here. Those posh houses up on the hill probably indicated that most residents had good jobs in Birmingham.

The car parks were busy, so I stopped for an hour and wandered around the shops to encounter some actual human beings. The malls were very expensive by usual American standards and I noticed, with some sadness, that the staff were almost exclusively black. The only thing that made me smile was driving past the Edwards Chevy dealership on the way back to my motel.

I bought an iced coffee and chatted to a couple who were playing with their toddler in the kids playpark outside one group of shops. Beneath his Southern drawl, I heard a familiar brogue fighting to get out.

'Musselburgh,' he laughed. Wherever you go in the world you'll find a Scotsman. Stuart Morris was a big man. He must have been about six feet four. And he was big out the way, as well. I don't mean to be unkind but he was, well, large. It was 95 degrees and he was wearing the uniform t-shirt and cut-off baggy jeans. His arms and legs were like tree trunks. While I'd happily have gone for a run with this lad, I certainly didn't want to arm-wrestle him.

'I got to a career dead end in Edinburgh in 2005 and because my wife Mandy has dual US and British nationality, we decided to go west, young man,' he said. 'I was running tournaments in Scotland for a card game called "Magic, the gathering," and mutual friends introduced me to her while she was studying at Edinburgh University. She was only eighteen at the time. She thought this was weird, there we were playing this unusual game with odd cards. So I introduced her to it and gave her a deck to play with. I told her there was a tournament in a few weeks, one of the first I'd ever run. She went along and when I opened the question and answer session, she was the first to put her hand up. I thought she was cute and she thought I was nice. After 18 months of being friends and 18 months of engagement, we were married.

'We sold our house in Edinburgh in 2005 for £109,000. It was 880 square feet. Our house here in Inverness, which we bought in Spring 2006 is 3200 square feet and we paid $170,000 for it. So a three times bigger house cost us much the same price and we also have a garden which is humungous. Comparing the cost of living with Edinburgh, which is my home and somewhere I still have a lot of affection for, to this place – well there is no comparison. This is my future.'

We were interrupted by his toddler son, exhorting his father to retrieve a football from behind a wire mesh fence at the playpark. Secretly I was delighted that the child was playing Scotland's game rather than the bonkers American football which is surely an aberration and deserves to be removed from the folder of activities described as 'sport'. Or worse, 'sports' as the Americans call it.

'We both work in IT.' There was a pause. That figured. Fantasy card games and computers. I'll bet he doesn't like sport, I said to myself. What a geek.

'Yeah I know what you're thinking, I'm a geek. We work for the biggest employers in the state. That's not Verizon, that's not Microsoft – it's the UAB, that's the University of Alabama at Birmingham. That's the tail that wags the dog of the state's economy, that's 19,000 people who work there, spread across an area of eighty city blocks, that's a lot of people and a lot of salary money. It's federally funded to the tune of half a billion dollars a year – and don't forget the contribution of the cash spent by 17,000 students. That's a lot of beer!' he laughed. 'The university fundamentally shapes the economy of the city and the state.

'People here put the wrong emPHAsis on the wrong syllABLES. They call it BirmingHAM. I keep telling them they do it wrong, but then people here laugh and tell me I talk cute.'

I wanted to tell him that I was none too impressed with Inverness so far, but I stowed it. He was a big lad, after all. He has nice soft features and lovely doe eyes. But he looked to me like a slow burner, and these guys can be tasty.

'So what's it like to live here?' I asked, lamely.

'Life is good. A quarter of the population of the entire state lives in the general area of south east Birmingham. In many ways it's like any major north American city But there's a strange difference in psychology here. It's easy to get to know Americans casually, but it's hard to get to know them deeply. Generally in the UK and the further north you go in Scotland it's the other way round.'

'So are you a hibbee or a jambo?' I asked. You couldn't have lived in Edinburgh most of your days and reached your forties without being one or the other.

'I'm neither. I don't like sports.'

Inside my head, I could hear the jackpot wheels turning and the coins spill out of the machine. Told you.

'I do like beer, though.' I could sense this was a hobby of Stuart's. Here we were standing in the baking sun talking of beer rather than drinking it. I could feel my palate cracking in the heat.

'When I got here in 2005 I went to the supermarket and I looked around. I was amazed by the severe lack of choice. American beer, let's face it is the punchline to a joke. Bud, Miller and Coors. Corona is Bud with a silly hat, Heineken, Stella and Amstel are imported and these are really Bud with a silly hat and a strange accent. I kept asking myself, why is there nothing here. Eventually the frustration welled up in me and I started ranting about it to one of my colleagues. He introduced me to a group called "Free the Hops." This is a grass roots and non-profit organisation dedicated to the cause of changing Alabama's beer laws. I looked at it and thought it was something I could get interested in, paid my $25 membership fee, started going to meetings, got more and more involved and got so involved I took over as president.

'The two big issues we were formed to fight were ABV and container size.' Stuart was a nice lad and I genuinely liked him. In the short time we had spoken, I realised he was a genuine big guy who loved his wife and family. But I was losing the will to live here. I steeled myself. I like trains, I told myself, each to his own. Go on Stuart, you were saying?

'Alabama law capped beer at six per cent and capped container sizes at 16 US fluid ounces and we were constantly told we would never change that law. In 2009 we changed the ABV law. So instead of six per cent being the cap, it's now 13.9 of alcohol by volume.' There are things that are way more important than beer (but, right there and then, I couldn't think of any. But go on, Stuart.).

'The Alabama constitution is the longest constitution in the world. It is taught in political science classes as how not to write a constitution. Why beer? Because beer is quality of life. It also gives you an insight into how that country or state perceives its role in the modern world. The more restrictions you have on something which is legal and enjoyed by millions of people and raises a lot of tax and duty money, the more liberty is taken away. Alabama has a bad reputation which isn't deserved. It's a great place to live, people are really friendly, the food is something else entirely. We in Free the Hops took on this beer law thing and we did the ABV last year, the big one and the hardest one to change. Beer is the one part of the economy which has stayed good during the recession. Craft beer grew last year by 37% and that was in a recessional economy. That's more opportunities for entrepreneurs, they're having to take on more staff to meet demand and that ripples out through the economy.

'The anti-beer lobby and the legislators come out with their usual bleat, think of the children, which is a kneejerk reaction from people who have no argument against you. The answer is, we do. The Alabama state beer tax goes into the state beer fund.'

Mandy turned up to meet her husband and son. He was still playing happily, although not with the football. She was petite, dark-haired and bespectacled. We chatted and I told her about my church experience. Mandy knows Scotland.

'This is the only place where you come to Birmingham, but go south to Inverness to go to church.'

That afternoon, I drove around trying to find some of the places Bubba was talking about. But my eye was caught by a massive fountain, and I drove off the main drag until I found it. It was in the middle of a man-made lake surrounded by neatly manicured, but rather sterile, lawns and a mile or so square. There were people here, and at least a few were pluckily peching around it but, given the heat, I'd rather stay in the Chevy with the AC on a notch or two.

A few hundred yards from the fountain stood a grey marble obelisk with 'Inverness' in gold lettering on the side. Nearby was a huge building belonging to the Aliant bank, a big player in the south. Other corporate headquarters abounded but, it being a Sunday, it was all very quiet. The most charming thing about the place was the couple of hundred Canada Geese who were acting as guards.

The next day was a different matter, and I stumbled upon real people very early. I was looking for somewhere to have breakfast and, by sheer accident, saw a row of shops and diners I had driven past several times the day before but had totally missed. The sun was cracking the sidewalk, despite the early hour, and I took the opportunity to enjoy some shade and air conditioned cool. After my usual breakfast of scrambled eggs on rye toast and a gallon or two of coffee, I felt much more positive about things.

From a distance it looked like the gas station in the film 'Deliverance' and, for a moment, I thought I could hear duelling banjos as I drew in for petrol. Despite all this time in the USA I still can't bring myself to call it 'gas.' The thin roof was supported by two pillars clad in pieces of stone, and the forecourt was littered with things to buy along with your fuel, such as succulent plants and cases of fruit and vegetables. Some of the tomatoes were nearly as big as footballs. At the side stood a refrigerated ISO container, in front of which was a rusting axle from a horse-drawn something and a sign which exhorted me to buy minnows, worms, crickets, pecans and ice. This unlikely combination said everything I needed to know about Perrin's gas station and grocery, which was a real piece of the South thriving among the soulless concrete and reflective blue glass.

I filled up the tank and bought a packet of pistachios to munch while I sat in the shade and watched the world go by. This was way more like it. The staff knew every customer who came and went, and the service was the American way with a Southern smile and drawl. Down the street was a barber shop and, feeling the heat somewhat around my curly bonce, I trotted over to see about a trim. Going for a haircut at home is a mixed blessing. I crave silence, and I like nothing more than sitting down for twenty minutes in peace and quiet for a number three all over. I have tipped barbers handsomely for switching off the TV or whatever music they have on and, when asked how I want my hair cut, I invariably reply, 'in silence.'

Happily, my barber back in Glasgow knows my little quirks, and hits the mute button on everything, including himself, when I rock up to his shop. He knows that if I open the conversation, then fine. Until I do, it's silence please. I don't mind the 'something for the weekend?' chat or even the 'getting away yourself this year?' line of inquiry. It's just the MTV on full tilt that does my head in. Life is stressful enough. He is Algerian and sometimes we speak French. His barbing is always exquisite and I tip him handsomely.

My heart had sunk a little when, on entering, I saw the red and gold of the United States Marine Corps flag on the wall, and I predicted all kinds of martial music blaring. But it was first thing on a Monday morning, I was the only customer and, once I got chatting to him, he killed the music without even having to be asked. Big tip coming your way, buddy!

Greg Crauswell was a Marine and still looked fit enough to be one. He wasn't tall but had that immediately noticeable strong and capable way of the ex-military. I explained to him that I didn't want a military haircut: just enough of a trim to keep the sweat off my scalp would be fine. He laughed.

'This is a dying trade, Mike,' he said, as he applied an unusual pair of clippers to my barnet. It had a hose attached which was linked to some vacuum affair and sucked all the loose hairs away to the bin and not down my shirt.

'Inverness is depressed. There's just no money here now, especially in this business. It's all salons or sportsmen's shops now where you get the same treatment as the ladies or you can sit and watch the ball game. There are very few places like this any more – men's barber shops which are traditional in every way bar the singing!' I cringed. Barber shop singing is all good and well. But…

'Here we do lots of cops and military cuts which are still asked for by loads of people and we get regulars, mostly businessmen who aren't keen on sitting in a hairdresser's salon and would prefer a proper barber shop.'

Greg was about to head for the till when I realised I just had the quickest haircut of my life. I endeavoured to slow him down because I enjoy sitting in peace and quiet, and anyway the shop was empty of customers bar me.

'I've been here for eight years. It used to be good. Lots of people sold up elsewhere to come and live here because the property prices were so low and they got more bang for their buck than they did up north. I have twelve chairs and they're usually empty, but I'm very busy on a Saturday.'

I told him about my job and how I spent hours with a cameraman, and we generally know more about each other than do our partners. Greg agreed.

'Sometimes it's like a confessional. Guys will tell you what's on their mind. You get the stories like a bartender does and I was a bartender for twenty-two years but I guess it's a little different. I've prayed for people here. I'm a Christian. I don't push it on anyone but if they want to talk, we talk,' he said, sombrely.

Greg was an M60 gunner in the Marines and said he was a 'Semper Fi,' man all the way. This comes from 'Semper Fidelis,' the Latin motto of the Corps meaning 'always loyal'. Looking at him, I can quite believe it. And while I'm all about loyalty and the military, I hoped he wasn't giving me the USMC haircut, ie all off.

'No man,' he laughed. 'I'm giving you a three on the side and a little off on top but it's still way too long for the Marines. Man it's too long even for the Air Force.' We both laughed.

*   *   *

Many journalists had expertise in sport or politics. Mine was the military. For more than a decade, I had bent the ear of the RAF's press officer in Scotland about a special story I wanted to cover. He always said it was unlikely, but one day out of the blue he called my mobile with the best possible news.

'Mike, you've heard of 617 Squadron? The Dambusters? Be at RAF Lossiemouth next Tuesday at 10am. If you pass the medical, you'll fly in a Tornado twenty-four hours later.'

And what a medical it was. I don't think I've ever been poked and prodded so much. The whole thing lasted an afternoon. For a while, I was panicking that I might be grounded because of the dizzy attacks from which I sometimes suffer, due to an inner ear problem I've had since childhood. The RAF Lossiemouth doctor assured me that all was fine with my ears. But then came the acid test. She took a metre stick and measured my upper leg. I frowned.

'You can't fly in a Tornado if your femur is too long,' she explained. 'If you have to eject, your legs tend to get cut off on the way out.'

With that sobering thought ringing in my ears, I was taken to the quartermaster and measured up for flight kit. The first layer was a set of thermal long johns and special socks. On top of that was a drysuit: a bulky rubberised nylon one-piece garment which you had to climb into, before closing it with a shoulder-to-navel zip.   The weather was still cold enough to warrant this precaution, in case we had to ditch in the sea or Loch Ness. On top of that went a flame retardant flying suit, on top of that a waistcoat which incorporated a lifejacket, and then flight boots and special gloves.

On my head went the bone dome helmet, which was specially adjusted to fit my napper. The last embellishment was a pantaloon affair, like knee-length shorts with an open front, which went over the top. Protruding was a flexible pipe with a fitting on the end designed to plug into something. These were special trousers which would be pumped full of compressed air to grip my legs and to stop the G forces draining blood away from my brain.

It took twenty-four hours to prepare for a forty-minute flight and, after the medical and kit issue, the rest of the day was taken up with briefings. As a serving officer in the military, I was deemed competent enough for the role of changing radio frequencies, and I was also asked to prime the bombs which we were scheduled to drop on the Tain bombing range. It was an absorbing day.

The pilot for the sortie was a young Flight Lieutenant called Jim Freeborough. I was surprised that the first question he asked me when we met in the briefing room was where it was that I wanted to go. We were about to jump into a multi-million pound supersonic jet warplane, which costs the taxpayer thousands of pounds an hour to operate, and he asked me where I wanted him to take it. He saw my quizzical expression.

'Relax Mike. If I wasn't going somewhere with you, I'd be going with someone else. It's cool. Where do you want to go?' he asked again.

I told him I was from Inverness and would like to overfly the town. He nodded. I added that, when I was a child, my parents would take me to Dores beach on Loch Ness, to this day one of my favourite places on the planet, and that I had been mesmerised by the fast jets which flashed down the Great Glen at supersonic speeds, only a few feet above the water. He smiled, and said this was fine. We huddled over a desk littered with PCs, charts and flight manuals. The route we would take was projected onto a screen on the wall, as Jim pored over the detail, explaining every step to me.

Noise over residential areas had to be taken into consideration. Air traffic in and out of Inverness airport was one factor, and we also had to avoid Gordonstoun school because there were ongoing exams there. Also, there was a bird reserve at Corrymony which was out of bounds. I watched as he plotted our flight on the computer, calculated the fuel required, and assessed the meterological reports and bomb load.

All my preparations, including the medical, were being filmed for a piece I would cut for the news later that week. But Jim ordered Danny Livingston to switch off his camera and leave the room when I was given the briefing on the ejector seat. It was too important, he said, for me to be thinking about producing a piece of television when I should be concentrating on my survival.

Jim said he'd rather I didn't pull the yellow-and-black handle between my legs, because that would fire the rocket-propelled ejector seat and I'd be chucked out of the Tornado at a great rate of knots, before fluttering to earth on a parachute. But if, for whatever reason, I did this, he said it wouldn't fire his seat and he'd stay with the aircraft and return to base. However, he told me that, if there was a genuine emergency, he would pull his handle to eject us both. I told him I had no intention of leaving the jet on my own.

'What happens if you have a heart attack and we start spiralling earthwards?' I asked. 'If I pull the handle, you'll be stuck.'

'I'll take that chance,' said Jim.

Sleep was a commodity which was very hard to come by that night and I felt like a wee laddie on Christmas Eve. Flying in a fast jet was surely every boy's dream. I'd flown with the RAF many times before, but only in their transport planes and helicopters and never in a Tornado.

The original Dambusters were the men of 617 Squadron, who in 1943 had carried out a courageous bombing mission in specially adapted Lancaster bombers to unleash a secret weapon, the bouncing bomb, against dams in western Germany. The weapon had been invented by Barnes Wallis, a man who had offices at Craig Dunain Hospital in Inverness for a time. The munition was designed to imitate a skipping stone on water, and bounce over torpedo nets protecting the dam.

At a high cost to the RAF crews, eight aircraft were shot down and fifty-three men killed, but the Eder and Mohne dams were breached. This disrupted German hydro-electric production, and it was also a resounding propaganda victory which had a devastating effect on German military and civilian morale. Wing Commander Guy Gibson led the mission with courage and skill and won the Victoria Cross for it.

The raid was the subject of a celebrated black-and-white film which I loved as a child. But I never thought for a second I'd come into contact with the Dambusters for real. As I sat in the aircrew mess room at RAF Lossiemouth, I noticed a cabinet in the corner, which was regarded as the holy of holies by the men of today's 617 Squadron. It contained Guy Gibson VC's peaked cap and a copy of the script, signed by actor Richard Todd who played Gibson in the film. Before we walked out to dispersal for our flight, Jim opened the cabinet and handed the cap to me. I felt incredibly privileged to hold a piece of history.

The back seat of a Tornado is a snug fit. Ground crew strapped me in, pointing out the yellow-and-black ejector seat handle between my legs and warning me once again not to touch it unless I absolutely had to. At my left and right elbows were banks of switches and, in front of me, were what appeared to be two large TV screens. Beneath them were more dials and switches. My checklist of things to do for Jim had been printed out, and placed neatly in the transparent flightsuit pocket on my left thigh. A small map of our route was in the corresponding pocket on my right thigh. Secured by Velcro to the instrument panel in front of me was a video camera, the pictures from which I would use for my report.

My helmet contained earphones and my oxygen mask a mic, but I sat quietly in the back and only spoke when Jim spoke to me. I listened as he went through his pre-flight checklists and watched as groundcrew swarmed over the aircraft. We sat for nearly an hour in preparation, and I still can't believe that so much effort went into such a short flight.

There was a low murmur, then a growl, then a whine. Seconds later, the sequence was repeated as the two Rolls Royce jet engines sparked into life. The canopy came down and locked into place, and now I could barely hear anything other than Jim on the radio. I could feel my heart racing with excitement. This was something I'd always wanted to do.

Suddenly, the Tornado rolled forward and taxied out into the bright sunlight. The weather was clear and calm. I saw Danny with the camera to his eye filming us, then I watched as he was ushered into a Land Rover which sped off to the end of the runway, where he would film the take-off. Just before we joined the runway, Jim came over the radio.

'Mike this is it. This is your go/no go for take-off. If you don't want to fly, you have to tell me now and we will go back to the hangar. Once we go onto the runway it'll be too late,' he said calmly.

'I'm absolutely fine Jim,' I said, my voice cracking with excitement, 'let's go!'

'OK, Mike. We're about to take off. It'll be fast and noisy, so stand by. If there's a problem after a certain point I'll take it into the air and deal with it there. If there is an emergency, please do exactly as I say. Do you understand?'

'Yes sir,' I said.

There was a grumble from the engines as he upped the power and we rolled out onto the runway. I heard him ask for and receive clearance for take-off from the control tower, then there was a few seconds of silence before he spoke again.

'Three, two, one, left afterburner, right afterburner and Lossie five-five is rolling ... now!'

Somebody kicked me twice in the small of the back, and we sped forward. There was an ear-splitting noise as the engines spun up to take off power, and we gathered speed. The afterburners pumped raw fuel into the scorching hot exhausts, and this gave the aircraft a hefty kick in the pants. The grey and green of the buildings and hangars quickly became a blur and, after what seemed like only a couple of seconds, Jim lifted the nose and we blasted off the runway. The landing gear retracted into place beneath us, and we turned steeply to the right and headed for Inverness.

I'm ashamed to say that, when I replayed the tapes back at STV the next day, I had shouted 'This is fucking awesome!' at take-off but, a few moments later, I added a more broadcastable 'Yeeha!'. Due to noise regulations, we had to overfly Inverness at altitude, but the weather was at its best and I could see my home town in all its glory from the most unexpected of platforms. Then Jim warned me to hold tight, and I'm glad he did.

The Tornado was now much lower, and there was water below me and green high above me on either side as we entered the northern end of the Great Glen. We seemed to be going much faster, and I looked out of the aircraft on the left to see Dores beach flash past in a fraction of a second. Loch Ness felt so close that I could almost reach down and touch it as we barrelled down at supersonic speed. This was epic!

On the left, the red sandstone of the Abbey School at Fort Augustus appeared and then, just as quickly, was gone, and the pantaloons gripped my thighs as we shot heavenward. All around was blue and I could hear myself breathing heavily. Jim flipped the Tornado over and we pirouetted on the left wing, causing me to retch involuntarily. Thankfully, my mask remained unsoiled, and that was as airsick as I got. On my right-hand side, the Skye Bridge was visible for an instant, before the sea was replaced by the land and we were racing northwards.

Right, then right again and, down at low level, we weaved between the hills. We were again over water, but I guessed it was fresh water and that we were screaming down one of the many lochs in the Highlands.

'Dam ahead,' said Jim, as we dropped even lower. 'Loch Shin, stand by.' A strip of straight concrete loomed ahead, then vanished in a heartbeat. They loved their dams, these boys. A longer, straighter overland leg, then we passed Helmsdale and rocketed out over the North Sea.

Pirouetting on the right wing, we dived again, and Jim told me we were approaching the Tain bombing range. He referred me to my checklist, and I found the two switches I needed to press on his command to prepare the munitions for release. Another 'three, two, one,' from Jim and I did as I was bid. A moment later, I heard a clunk and felt a slight jerk as the bombs were released. It's obvious that anybody you've just bombed isn't going to like it much, and will be pretty keen to shoot you down, so Jim threw the jet into a series of aerobatic manoeuvres and dived to avoid ground fire. I felt the pantaloons grip and release my thighs again as we screamed low across the Moray Firth, bobbing and weaving to evade the fictitious enemy around Tain.

Then we were heading for home. There were a few more things on the checklist for me to complete prior to landing, and I was busying myself with them when I heard Jim's voice in my headset. Beneath me was the glassy blue green of the Moray Firth, above me the crystal blue sky, and on either side of me the dun grasses of Sutherland and Moray. In an instant it all changed, as Jim flipped the Tornado on its back.

'Sorry, Mike. Flying upside down is one of the rules when there's a guest in the back seat,' said Jim. My guts churned. I felt the trousers grip my thighs again as the blues of the sky and sea were confused. My arms were heavy, and I felt myself hanging against the straps of the ejector seat. I was trying to get my head around the new arrangement when Jim flipped us the right way up.

All too soon, I felt a rumble as the landing gear was dropped and the blue of the water was replaced by green. Then a strip of grey concrete flashed beneath us, and we were down. One of the greatest days of my life was over.

But I was soon to exchange supersonic speed in the blue sky over the Highlands for the murky depths of Scotland's waters in another fearsome killing machine.

Just as I had pestered the RAF press officer, so was I a similar nuisance to the Royal Navy's media man. He and I came into frequent contact when I covered stories about the Trident submarine fleet based at Faslane. Every time we met, I would hassle him for any exclusives that would give us the edge over the BBC. Submarines are mysterious and very televisual, especially the Vanguard boats which carried the controversial Trident missiles, so they always made good topics for stories.

To celebrate the centenary of the submarine in Royal Navy service, a host of events was scheduled for Faslane, and I made sure I was sent to cover them. I had to pinch myself on the first day, when I watched the crew of a Russian Kilo class submarine goosestep past Princess Anne on the dais. Afterwards, we were ushered along to the Faslane berth where the submarine was tied up. No sooner had the camera rolled, when a hatch popped and a sailor emerged wearing the familiar Russian uniform of a blue-and-white striped shirt. He eyed us suspiciously, before questioning me in a broad Russian accent.

'Do you have permission to make your movie?'

'Cheeky bugger,' said the Royal Navy Petty Officer escorting us. The old salt nodded towards the vessel's unusually rounded Soviet-era nose protruding from the Gare Loch. 'If we'd seen that bloody thing come up the Clyde a few years ago, we'd have torpedoed it.'

The Navy's PR man phoned me up out of the blue a couple of days later, and told me to be at the Navy pier in Kyle of Lochalsh at 10am the following Wednesday for a special exclusive story which gave us unprecedented access. Cameraman David Lees and I packed our kit, and headed off with an air of expectancy. This was going to be great fun, and it was getting it right up the Beeb.

We were met at the pier by a Swedish sailor with the standard bushy red Viking beard and biceps the size of Bournemouth. He helped us onto a ridiculously small Gemini rubber boat with the biggest outboard motor I've ever seen. Soon we were zooming out towards the Skye Bridge, bumping over the waves with the spray cold and fresh in our faces.

'I am Lars and it is my duty to take you to the Swedish Navy submarine *Gotland* which is just over there,' he shouted in excellent but heavily accented English.

Cameramen have excellent eyesight, which is just as well, and David saw it immediately. But I craned my neck and squinted into the sunlight, expecting to see a long black glistening submarine. Nothing. Then I caught it. But it was not what I was expecting. Bleached grey-white by the salt water and sunlight, a small object hove into view. I regarded her intently as we got closer, waiting to see the crew drag out a gangway or a ladder.

Instead of slowing down as we approached the Gotland, Lars started to accelerate and the Gemini bounded across the water. Still no men on the casing of the submarine, still no ladder or gangway, still we accelerated. Then a tiny door opened in the conning tower, and a huge sailor, with an identical Viking beard, stuck out his head.

'Stand by!' shouted Lars above the deafening outboard, and we hammered towards the submarine. Just yards away from the Gotland we again accelerated, and my knuckles were white as I clung to the ropes on the side of the Gemini. An instant later, we rammed the submarine, and our bow mounted the Gotland's casing and started to ride up towards the conning tower. The sailor on board leant out and proferred his hand to me.

'Now!' shouted Lars and, after a pause of a second or two to consider my mortality, I launched myself towards the sailor's outstretched hand, trying not to look down at the frothing sea beneath. He dragged me on board as if I was a rag doll, propelling me into the conning tower where his other hand was wrapped round a stanchion. David and the kit followed, and then we were in the cool, calm, dimly-lit control room, where we were greeted by the Captain.

Jonas Haggren was a very young man to be the commander of a submarine, but he clearly knew his stuff. He made us feel welcome and told us that, after a long time at sea, the prospect of visitors was something he and the crew much welcomed. The Gotland was small, and exactly the size and shape of the vessels you see on war films. She was cramped, and the men who crewed her had that salty, swarthy appearance and demeanour of their forebears. I barely had time to drink in the atmosphere, when Jonas spoke into the PA system via a telephone handset and the crew sprang into action.

David instantly lifted the camera to his shoulder and started to film. Klaxons sounded, bells rang and men ran to their positions. Then there was a decided lurch for'ard as the ballast tanks were blown and filled with the cold water of the Sound of Raasay. I watched as dials twitched, and the attitude indicator pointed downwards to show that we were diving. I felt a really odd sensation, one I'd never experienced before, as we slowly sank 500 feet to the bottom. There was a gentle bump as the Gotland reached the seabed. Then all was quiet.

Submarine warfare is about being invisible and silent. After we hit the seabed, everything was done very quietly, lest it be picked up by enemy sonar. But today's exercise, which we had secured rare permission to film for STV News, was not about taking lives but saving them.

We were aboard the Gotland for an hour or so when we felt another bump, this time aft. There was much rushing to and fro by the crew, and then David and I were ushered to a ladder and hatch behind the engine room. Having joined the submarine in unusual circumstances, we were shortly about to leave her in a similarly unconventional manner.

Exercise Sedgemoor happens every two years, and it was particularly apposite this time round, given that the Kursk tragedy had happened less than a year earlier. The navy had invited the media along because it wanted the world to see how NATO submariners could be rescued in the event of an accident, an option not chosen in time by the Russians. Aboard the Kursk, the fuel had ignited inside a practice torpedo, resulting in the detonation of live warheads and a catastrophic explosion and fire which sank the vessel and killed 118 people. Our scenario saw Gotland as the stricken submarine which was lying incapacitated on the seabed.

The bump we felt was the Renfrew-based LR5 rescue minisub attaching itself onto the casing aft of the conning tower to rescue the crew. Another day at the office turned into a day I'll never forget, in a week I'll always remember.

David and I scrambled up the ladder into the tiny minisub where, despite severe claustrophobia, I had the sense to do a quick interview with the pilot, as well as a piece to camera lying next to him at the controls. There was more room there in his cockpit than anywhere else on the vessel, which carried sixteen men sitting facing each other in extremely cramped conditions. However, being uncomfortable for a few minutes was a small price to pay if the alternative was a cold, dark and lingering death. As I started to feel most uncomfortable, there was a clang of a hatch closing and a lurch to indicate that we were free of the Gotland.

Heading up to the surface, I could just see out of the pilot's tiny window as we passed over the dark mass of the submarine. This was just an exercise and, of course, it made great television for us, but it was an sobering thought to imagine how it must feel to be nearing safety in this vessel after a calamitous accident.

At the surface, where the mother ship dropped a line from an A-frame at the stern and lifted us out of the water, we lurched and bobbed for a few minutes and, with no window other than the pilot's tiny porthole from which to look out at the horizon, the claustrophobia I felt was suddenly mixed with nausea. I don't think I have ever felt so miserable. With my eyes screwed shut, I struggled hard to concentrate on our story: how men who were rescued for real might feel. Not nearly quickly enough there was a bump, as the A-frame winch dropped us on the afterdeck of the mother ship.

The adventure didn't end there. Another Gemini took us off the mother ship back towards the Skye Bridge. From a distance, the dark shape of a Royal Navy Trident submarine appeared between the concrete spars. Just as the Gotland had been tiny, HMS Vanguard was a Leviathan. There was no arm-wrestling with a sailor in order to board. Instead, a net ladder had been thrown over the casing for David and me.

Commander Karl Evans was also a young man, young in years perhaps but obviously not young in experience or intelligence. To command a capital ship is one thing, but to command one which can fire sixteen Trident missiles containing 200 nuclear warheads, each with the power of eight Hiroshima bombs, is quite another.

However, despite the sensitivity of the submarine and the weapons she carried, we were allowed to film anything we wanted. The crew even carried out a Trident missile launch drill for us, which I found both fascinating and chilling, and I did a piece to camera holding the trigger, closely resembling a Scalextric handset, which would release a Trident nuclear missile.

Only four people on the submarine ever know precisely where she is, these being the captain, his executive officer, the navigator and the weapons officer. In a high-tech environment, with the power to end the world many times over, there is still a prosaic way of doing things.

When a missile firing command is received by radio from London, it is printed off and carried aloft through the submarine so that everybody knows what is happening. The officer carrying it then enters a little shack in the control room, which is closed off by a curtain, where the four cognoscenti open the safe which contains the authentication codes. They check that the launch command is genuine and has not been sent by a terror group or the enemy. While this is happening, a burly Navy policeman stands outside the curtain with his truncheon drawn, to deter any crewman who has had a change of mind and wants to disrupt the launch. This was all very dramatic stuff, which Karl and I chatted through over dinner in the wardroom that evening.

Everybody in the military, even sailors and airmen, does a job which is out of the ordinary. Regardless of their service, everybody in a uniform receives basic weapon handling instruction, is taught how to shoot, and given the most rudimentary of infantry tactics training. Everybody in uniform, therefore, has the capacity and training, even at the most fundamental level, to kill. The crew of a Trident submarine has that power several millionfold. What strikes me about them all is their apparent ease with that burden.

'Most of us are family men and we have no intention of doing anything other than going home to our wives and children after each patrol,' said Karl. Despite being on a submarine, we sit in a surprisingly spacious wardroom fitted out with comfortable armchairs, a big change from the Gotland and LR5.

'We have no qualms about firing the missiles, that's what we are here for. That's our job', he said. 'We are always clearly aware of that and totally focused. When a message comes through, we let the training take over and we go through the drills. God forbid it ever happens for real. This is a deterrent. Just having these weapons sends a message.'

The Cold War is long over, but there remains a potential threat faced by the UK from terrorists and rogue states. So Trident submariners still believe their weapons are vitally necessary. They are based at Faslane, which is a huge boost to the local economy although their removal is a central plank of SNP policy. Karl didn't even go there. As a serviceman, he wouldn't get involved in politics, even though Trident is a political weapon with only the Prime Minister able to give the order to fire. He told me that he welcomed the peace camp, which has been outside Faslane for decades, because it demonstrates that Britain permits freedom of speech and expression of opposition.

Shortly before we left Vanguard, Karl gave me an on-camera interview. I didn't spare him.

'So with no Soviet Union to worry about, where are your missiles aimed? North Korea? Syria?' With barely a pause, he body-swerved the question with ease.

'I can't tell you that, and you wouldn't expect me to. But what I can tell you is that we carry far fewer missiles and they have been de-targeted, to the extent that the time taken to programme and fire them is now days rather than the hours it took previously.'

Karl let us climb up through the vast conning tower into the crow's nest, where David was able to film some stunning footage. We were now under way at sea, and were passing Skye *en route* to Faslane. We would submerge during the night well off the north tip of Lewis and surface again at the foot of the Firth of Clyde, before dropping into the armament depot at Coulport either to arm or disarm (Karl wouldn't say which) and then return to base. We weren't allowed to be aboard for the Coulport part, so we would be transferred onto a small tender and dropped off at Helensburgh pier.

I was sound asleep in a comfortable bunk when we slipped beneath the waves, and was still in a deep slumber when we surfaced and rounded the Mull of Kintyre. I had one last request and Karl gave me the nod. David and I donned lifejackets and clambered up another ladder onto the casing. David positioned himself as far astern as he could go without getting his feet wet, and set up the camera on his tripod. I was fifty yards away at the foot of the conning tower as we slid up the Clyde and, once he was happy with sound and light, I walked towards him while delivering probably the most dramatic piece to camera I've ever done.

'Beneath my feet are the hatches covering tubes containing the Trident nuclear missiles which have the power of nearly 2,000 Hiroshima bombs ...'

A week later I was back at work. Celtic had beaten off very stiff opposition to face Porto in Seville in the forthcoming UEFA Cup Final but, beyond this being a great news story, I didn't think it would have anything to do with me. But my backside had barely touched my seat back at STV when my boss called me in to his office and told me that I would be going to Seville to tell the supporters' story.

Celtic were the first British team to win the European Cup, famously beating Inter Milan in Lisbon in 1967. They reached the final again in 1970, but were defeated by Feyenoord in Milan. The Seville final would be their third and a huge achievement. Such was the occasion, fans were scheduled to fly in from all over the world and would flood the city, despite very few of them having any chance of finding a ticket for the game.

My brief was to chart their journey for the evening news and gather material for a special documentary programme called 'The Bhoys from Seville,' to be broadcast a week after the game. My only restriction was that I was not allowed to fly, because that would be too easy and wouldn't make for good viewing. In the days before the exodus to Spain, I found a pub in Glasgow's Gallowgate which had organised a bus trip to Seville, and I managed to secure seats for a cameraman and myself.

We boarded the bus on the Saturday morning before the match, and set off down the motorway towards England. We got as far as Leeds airport where the boys were flying direct to Spain. Airliners were not part of our brief, so we carried on over land, hoping to find Celtic fans making their way to the game. We were not to be disappointed.

We caught the train to London and then the Eurostar to Paris. The number of supporters grew with every pace we took in the French capital, and there were so many Celtic fans that the overnight train from the Gare de Lyon to Madrid could have been from Glasgow Central to

Dalmarnock. The mood was joyously expectant, and rich with colour and atmosphere, as we filmed and vox-popped the night away.

At Madrid we changed trains and joined the service for Seville but, because there were no seats left in standard class, we went first class. This was no hardship, I assure you, and even though it was still mid-morning we were served with a glass of ice-cold sherry before breakfast. We weren't the only ones to have imbibed and, when we arrived in Seville, it had already been taken over by a merry army of Celtic fans.

We met people who had travelled from New Zealand for the game. We met people who had never before been on an aeroplane but who had gladly put their fear of flying to one side. We met one man who had been at the games in Lisbon in 1967, Milan in 1970 and who was here to see Celtic in their third European final. We met some families who had put themselves in serious debt to pay for the trip. We met several men who didn't want to be filmed because they'd told their partners they were working offshore. And we met others who didn't want to be interviewed because they were unemployed and thought their benefits would be stopped if they were seen in Seville.

When people asked me how I thought Celtic would do against Porto, I told them all the same thing. I said that Bobo Balde would be sent off and cost Celtic the game. I took no pride in the fact that this prediction came true. Henrik Larsson scored two goals, including a header which defied the laws of physics, but Celtic were beaten 3-2. The bold Bobo was red-carded, as I forecast, and Celtic had to play with ten men during extra time.

I had neither a ticket nor a press pass, but that didn't matter. The story I was telling was that of the fans and their experiences. The cameraman and I would patrol the streets of Seville while the game was in progress, and discover how those supporters without tickets watched it. We were also primed in case there was any trouble but, despite a narrow defeat in controversial circumstances and the consumption of vast amounts of alcohol, there was none.

During and after the match, tens of thousands of supporters partied like there was no tomorrow, and there was not a single arrest, far less a riot. We stayed in Seville for a couple of days afterwards to hoover up the reaction and atmosphere, then we flew home to Glasgow, coincidentally from Porto. I spent the next four days in an edit suite making my documentary – 'The Bhoys from Seville' – which was one of the highlights of my career.

The documentary was a great success. The viewing figures went through the roof, and merited a repeat showing at Christmas that year. To this day, people stop me in the street to and tell me how much they enjoyed the programme.

Five years later, STV sent me to Florence for the UEFA Cup semi-final where, if Rangers beat Fiorentina, we were set for a re-run of the Seville story, albeit in the less glamorous location of Manchester. Rangers despatched the home team and, within minutes of the full-time whistle I was broadcasting live from Tuscany, where excitement was already starting to climb to the same dizzy heights as in 2003.

I was again assigned to tell the fans' story, and we set about making plans for the short trip to Manchester where Rangers would play Russian side Zenit St Petersburg. The game was on the Wednesday night and, on Sunday morning, cameraman Steve Kydd and I drove south.

Virtually opposite our hotel was a Russian restaurant. Early on the Monday morning I was knocking on the door, asking to speak to the manager. With the media arriving hourly in the city, this little restaurant wouldn't stay our secret for long. The cleaners confirmed that the manager was Russian, but he lived in Liverpool and had taken to his bed with manflu. Undaunted, I leaned on the cleaners and stressed how important it was that I spoke to Vladimir.

Within the hour, a heavily-accented man croaked down the phone to me. By noon, realising there was no such thing as bad publicity, he was perched, sweating and quaffing paracetamol, in front of Steve's camera and telling me how much he was looking forward to serving borscht to both Rangers and Zenit fans. In return, I promised him we would eat and drink in his gaff until we left. Our piece with Vladimir was on the news at 6pm that night. The papers got to the story on the Tuesday. Result!

Steve and I had a really good week. Fans were appearing in Manchester from all over the world. There was blue everywhere, and everybody had a story to tell. We took a trip out to Old Trafford and filmed some young Rangers fans kicking a ball about beside the 'United trinity' statue, depicting Denis Law, Bobby Charlton and George Best. We visited a campsite in Cheshire which had been inundated by fans who were sleeping in caravans, tents or under bushes. It was all great value, and my pieces for the news each night were full of faces, humour and colour.

The day before the game, I did a piece with the senior police officer who would be the match commander. I was astonished that there was no alcohol ban and told him my views, but he didn't seem in the slightest perturbed. He said that having two premiership clubs in the city with large stadia and huge supports, meant that the police were well prepared for any eventuality. I told him what I thought would happen and, once more, my prediction came true. I said that, win, lose or draw, there would be trouble with Rangers fans, alcohol would be a factor and it wouldn't be pretty.

Match day dawned. Again, I had neither a ticket nor a press pass, but again that wasn't an issue and I would spend the ninety minutes patrolling the city and telling the story of how those fans who were not at the game would watch it. My producer was a cracking lad from Coventry called Tom Lowe, who had been overwhelmed by the strength of the Rangers support. He had his eyes well and truly opened in Manchester that day.

On the morning of the game, he handed me a match ticket which his friend had lent him so we could do some filming with it. I thought this was very trusting, and I felt a bit scared in case I was mugged for it. But I stood in the centre of town holding my prop up to the camera and uttering the lines: 'the rarest and most valuable piece of paper in Manchester tonight, worth many thousands of pounds.'

The atmosphere in the run-up to the game was electric, and although I've followed Scotland to two World Cups, I don't think I have ever before seen supporters drink so much alcohol. People were pushing supermarket trolleys around stacked with crates of beer and, by kick-off time, many were in an advanced state of inebriation. Screens had been set up in Picadilly Gardens and Albert Square for fans, and crowds gathered in their tens of thousands. Steve and I headed there.

In Seville I had shouted for Celtic, but that night in Manchester I was firmly rooting for Rangers. Although I thought they were just short of enough quality to win the game, if it went to extra time and penalties, then they had a chance. Seconds after kick-off it was clear that Zenit were no slouches.

It was a beautiful Spring evening and Albert Square was crammed with thousands of singing and dancing Rangers fans. I love European football and I was wallowing in the occasion. All that was required was a Rangers win. To add spice to the occasion, if any was needed, Zenit were managed by former Ibrox boss Dick Advocaat. He was clearly out to prove a point and, from the start, Zenit began to turn the screw.

As things were getting tricky for Rangers on the field, events involving their fans were taking a nasty turn off the pitch. The screen in Picadilly Gardens failed and, when engineers turned up to try to repair it, they were pelted with missiles by drunken, outraged fans. Riot police then waded in, and things grew ugly. Fuelled by drink, and angered at not being able to see the game, supporters started making their way to the second screen in Albert Square. Soon our party atmosphere changed as more and more drunk and frustrated fans crammed in.

As long as the game remained goalless, Rangers were still in the fight. However, it was no surprise when Igor Denisov scored the opening goal for Zenit in the 72nd minute. In a heartbeat, Albert Square turned from being a happy, optimistic place to a seething sea of despair. Rangers had to equalise quickly to force the game into extra time, where they had a chance of stealing something, but that goal never came. Instead, Zyryanov scored a second deep in injury time, and it was all over.

Just before the second Zenit goal went in, the missiles started flying. Bottles, cans, stones, chairs – you name it – came crashing down. Filming anything became impossible, as the missiles rained in, so we took cover behind the screen, which was only marginally safer.

A bottle came zinging out of the crowd and crashed onto my temple. I have half a memory that it struck something nearby during its trajectory, which took some velocity out of the equation, but it was still travelling at a fair old rate of knots. Thankfully, it did not shatter. Shocked and dazed, I fell backwards, and landed in a heap on the ground. I was surrounded by shards of broken glass and puddles of beer, vomit and urine, but luckily I was unscathed – apart from a growing Tom and Jerry lump on the head. I stood up and, grabbing Steve by the collar, we ran for cover.

The air was soon heavy with police sirens, as crowd trouble erupted all over the city centre. I was feeling pretty woozy but Steve and I tried our best to film, in safety, some of the ugly scenes. One supporter took objection to our filming, and ran towards us shouting and swearing. As he approached he launched himself into the air and arched his body like a javelin thrower to spit at us with as much power as he could muster.

We joined a cluster of TV crews and stayed together, believing there was safety in numbers, as events continued to descend into carnage. Riot police waded in and broke up large groups of fans intent on trouble. These were Rangers fans fighting among themselves and with the police, targeting hapless passers-by or trashing property. There were no Zenit fans to be seen anywhere, which was just as well. Precious few had come to Manchester because of issues with visas, and those who had made the journey stayed in the stadium to see their heroes lift the UEFA Cup. Afterwards, they were herded onto their coaches by the police and escorted straight to the airport for the flight home. To go into town that night would have meant big trouble for Zenit fans.

There was an increasing police presence and the streets were steadily cleared of drunken supporters. In the days and weeks that followed, many Rangers fans complained of police heavy-handedness. Hand on heart, I have to say I saw none. As we later walked around the city centre, the streets were almost knee-deep in broken glass and crushed beer cans, and were swimming in urine and vomit.

Bizarrely, given the mayhem just a few streets away, the Russian place was still open and nearly empty when we got back to the hotel late that night. After a hot scoff and a few beers, and with a throbbing head where the bottle had hit, I dropped gratefully into bed in the early hours. I was scheduled to return to Glasgow the next lunchtime, but such had been the scale of the trouble that I didn't leave Manchester until the Saturday night.

Prime Minister Gordon Brown described the scenes as a disgrace, and Glasgow Council leader Stephen Purcell apologised to the people of Manchester on behalf of the city of Glasgow. CCTV pictures released by Greater Manchester Police revealed the extent of the trouble. One horrific sequence showed a gang of fans separate an officer from his colleagues, throw him to the ground, and kick and beat him. Luckily for him, his protective equipment prevented anything more serious than a few bruises. I interviewed him the next day and, in that stoic way of policemen, he said he hadn't been badly injured. When I interviewed the match commander again that afternoon, I had to bite my tongue to stop myself saying 'telt ye.'

Some people may think that I say these things because I have an agenda against Rangers or am Celtic-minded. That is not true. I have no axe to grind either way. I simply say this. I saw both teams play in the UEFA Cup Final and watched their fans in defeat from very close range. Seville was an amazing experience and one I will never forget for its colour and happy atmosphere. I will remember Manchester for all the wrong reasons and, even if I ever do manage to erase it from my mind, the scar on my forehead is a constant reminder.

The big news stories came thick and fast, and no two days were the same. I covered many high-profile murders, from the crime scene to the court room. And while Tobin's killing of Angelika Kluk had been bloody and brutal, and his trial a lengthy piece of theatre, the Lockerbie bombing remains to date the biggest mass murder on Scottish territory.

I spent many days in Lockerbie after the bombing, and I felt the same sense of local resentment at my intrusion which I had experienced in Dunblane when I returned there after that tragedy. But, while some locals were aggressive in their refusal to be interviewed, others were happy to air their views on camera. Some of the cameramen I worked with hated going to the town, because they had been there on the night of the disaster and remembered all too well the stench of aviation fuel and the horrific vision of children's bodies in the trees.

Twelve years after Lockerbie, Abdelbaset Al-Megrahi was convicted by three Scottish judges, sitting in a special court in the Netherlands, and sentenced to life imprisonment for the bombing. I had stood and watched as the helicopter bringing the Libyan to Scotland dropped over the east end of Glasgow and landed inside Barlinnie. It never entered my head that, years later, I would stand outside Greenock jail, to where Al-Megrahi was transferred from Barlinnie in 2005, and see his motorcade leave for Glasgow airport where he would fly back to Libya. He had been released early from his sentence because he was terminally ill with prostate cancer.

That day in Greenock I was chatting to a policeman who was part of the perimeter guard. He told me about the night he had just come off duty and was sitting at home, when his sergeant phoned him and told him to come back to the station because a plane had crashed on the M74. He went through events with the clarity of a policeman's memory and, when he finished, I asked on the off-chance whether he'd mind repeating on camera what he had just said to me.

Serving police officers are usually very reticent, and seldom speak to the media unless they've been cleared to do so in advance by their superiors. He thought about it for a moment before agreeing. Trying not to alert the crowd of journalists standing outside the jail, I gestured for the STV cameraman to come over.

Just as we finished the interview, other cameras and mics appeared as reporters spotted what we were doing. The policeman agreed to do the interview because he said watched me on TV every night and he trusted me. He added that, as the next day was his last day in uniform after thirty years, he knew his bosses could do nothing to punish him for speaking to the media without authorisation. On camera, he told me about the trauma of the night of the bombing. Once he'd finished, he refused to do any other interviews. This was a great scoop.

I covered the stories of many killers, but none who aroused as much fierce condemnation as Ian Brady. The Moors murderer had been born and raised in Glasgow and, although he moved to Manchester and committed his dreadful crimes there, we had a firm angle on the story.

STV sent me to Manchester Crown Court to cover a tribunal which was hearing Brady's application to return to the mainstream prison population. There, he would be treated like any other prisoner, and he could go on hunger strike and die naturally, as he wished, rather than be force-fed as he was in Ashworth Hospital in Liverpool.

Along with his partner Myra Hindley, Brady had been jailed for life in 1966 for the appalling murders of five children and dumping their bodies on Saddleworth Moor. Four of the victims were recovered and given proper burials, but the body of twelve-year-old Keith Bennett was never found.

I sat in grim silence as Brady gave his evidence. He was being fed through a naso-gastric tube. His voice was shaky as he gave his evidence, but it still held traces of a Glasgow accent. He spoke of mixing in jail with infamous British criminals, such as the Kray twins and the Great Train Robbers. The killings which he and Hindley had committed were an 'existential exercise', he said. It was the only time he had ever spoken in public since his trial.

The tribunal rejected his application, meaning he would stay in Ashworth and never be heard from again. I guessed from his appearance that he did not have long to live. When I returned to Glasgow the next day, I wrote to Brady in the hope that he would tell me something that he had never told anyone before, which would make captivating viewing for STV News.

My letters asked him questions about his crimes and what his life had been like in prison. I repeatedly asked him about Keith Bennett and what he had done with the poor boy's body. I asked if he would ever give Keith's family any relief, or if he had a message for them or an apology to make.

I couldn't believe it when he replied. He told me much about his life in Durham jail's special unit where he had worked in the kitchens with Reggie Kray in the 1960s. He also told me about mixing with the Yorkshire Ripper Peter Sutcliffe in jail in England in the 1970s. But my questions about Keith Bennett were ignored. Instead, he referred me to a book he had written about the killings and their supposed 'existential meaning'.

Upon his death, I used a letter as a prop in a piece to camera in the Gorbals area of Glasgow where he had grown up. I said that, when he replied to my letters, what he hadn't written was more important than what he had, and that he had taken to his grave the secret of Keith Bennett's final resting place.

My beat was the courtrooms of Scotland, and I covered dozens of high profile and gruesome trials.

I was a young reporter when I covered the murder of Indian waiter Surjit Singh Chhokar in the street in Wishaw in 1998, in a dispute over a stolen giro cheque worth only a few pounds. But I was in my fifties when I covered the trial of Ronnie Coulter for the killing. He had earlier been acquitted of the murder but, after a change in Scotland's so-called double jeopardy law which meant he could be retried for the same crime, he was convicted. The programme which carried the emotional interview I did with Surjit's family when Coulter was jailed for life, was nominated for another RTS award.

Alcohol and the blade are a deadly combination. All too often I have seen post-mortem pictures of the result, and interviewed on the courtroom steps the shattered family of the victim. I have also covered cases of matricide, patricide, fratricide and infanticide. Lisa Brown was pregnant when she battered her mother Anne to death with a heavy torch after an ongoing family argument, and then threw her body into a burn near Dunlop. Jailing her for life, the judge said it was a crime which had wrecked three generations of one family.

My police contacts were once again so good that I broadcast sensitive information about the killing on TV the night after the murder, which led me to be interviewed under caution by detectives. They quickly eliminated me as a suspect but demanded I tell them my source. Of course, I declined.

Alarmingly, men on occasion murder their fathers and brothers, often fuelled by alcohol and for the most petty of reasons, usually as a result of family feuds. But among the most common murders of all are those where husbands kill their wives, and I have frequently sat in court and listened to these men trotting out the most flimsy and contrived of defences.

Probably the most cunning and duplicitous of them all was a nurse called Malcolm Webster. In 1994, less than a year after they married, he and his wife Claire Morris were driving along a country road near Aberdeen, when he suddenly swerved into the verge. He leapt out and doused the car with petrol from a container in the boot, and set fire to it.

Two sets of passers-by stopped to help him, and he told them that he had been the only occupant.

It wasn't until firefighters arrived that Claire's body was discovered. He told the police that he had swerved to avoid a motorcyclist, and the car had burst into flames. Incredibly, his story was believed, and he collected more than £200,000 in insurance payouts. Already a rich man, Webster set out to acquire more wealth to fund his lavish lifestyle. He moved to New Zealand, remarried and, in 1999, tried the stunt again on a motorway in Auckland, but this time his wife Felicity Drumm survived.

It transpired that he had been systematically drugging her since they married and she believed that, on honeymoon, she had slept for thirty-six hours after drinking a cup of tea he had made. He even drugged her while she was pregnant. His scheme unravelled when it was discovered that he was due to inherit a quarter of a million pounds from his wife if she died. As it was, he fled the country after the accident, cleaning out Felicity's bank account *en route*.

His crimes came to light only by chance. Felicity's sister Jane was the director of a domestic violence prevention organisation, and had flown to the UK for a conference. She was chatting to a senior police officer, and told him her concerns about Webster and the similarities between what had happened to her sister and to Claire Morris. A major police inquiry was launched, and it took a second set of forensic tests on a tiny piece of Claire's liver, still held in the police laboratory more than a decade after her death, to reveal that Webster had also been drugging her. On the night of her death, she had been too incapacitated by Temazepam to escape from the burning car.

By the time the police caught up with him, Webster had moved back to Scotland and was about to marry a nurse in Oban. Her father was a wealthy consultant surgeon who had set up a sizeable trust fund for her, and detectives said they had no doubt that her life would have been in danger from Webster. He was a smooth talker, and had fooled a string of rich women into relationships across the world with the sole intention of stealing their money. He even shaved his head and eyebrows and lost weight, before telling several of them that he was suffering from cancer. But the jury at the High Court in Glasgow weren't fooled, and I reported how they found him guilty him after only a few hours of deliberations. He was jailed for thirty years.

Over my quarter of a century in front of the cameras, I've reported how some criminals have been jailed, served their sentence and were released to re-offend. Among the people I've seen jailed twice is an odious pair of paedophile murderers whose total number of victims will probably never be known.

In 1998 I covered the trial of Charles O'Neill and William Lauchlan for appalling crimes against children, aged between nine and fifteen, who were lured to a house in Skelmorlie where they were plied with drink and drugs before being abused. I watched as the pair, who were cousins as well as gay partners, were jailed for eight years for a catalogue of thirty-one crimes against the boys. But they were released early, and continued to commit more crimes.

O'Neill abused a teenager in Irvine upon his release, then the pair abducted a boy in Spain and tried to drug and sexually assault him. Police launched a surveillance operation against them when they received intelligence that the cousins were grooming a six-year-old boy for sex.

It then transpired that they had been involved with a woman called Alison McGarrigle on Bute. They had befriended her but, when they learned that she was about to give evidence against them in a trial where they were accused of the abuse of a boy, they killed her and dumped her body in the Clyde. It has never been found. I sat in court to see the pair jailed for a second time: on this occasion both received life sentences.

The most satisfying part of my job is the variety. I never know where I will go on any given day nor which story I will be sent to cover. Every year I used to run the newsdesk for six weeks over the summer to cover for people who were on holiday. And, while that was challenging in its own way, I realised that I'd much rather not work in an office.

I sometimes do sports stories and I sometimes do politics stories, but these subjects have their own correspondents and it usually falls on experts to cover the issues of the day. I've done features, I've made documentaries and, all too often, I've found myself doing the 'and finally': the story about the footballing nun or the speaking cat. As you can imagine, these are usually a lot of fun.

Generally, the day begins with a conference at 9am, when staff gather to discuss the previous night's programme and to look at the day ahead. Reporters and correspondents are mated up with camera operators and satellite trucks, and I spend the first hour of the day on the phone trying to trace people and asking them to do an interview on-camera for my story. Usually, we'll head off to do these interviews and related filming, then return to the studios to edit a package for the lunchtime news, before heading off again to do more filming in the afternoon. Depending on the story, the plan is to return to the studios to cut a package for the Six o'clock News in the late afternoon, but sometimes I have to head off again to the scene to do a live report from the satellite truck. I'm usually not home before 7pm, and often much later.

There has been quite a lot of politics to report on over the past few years, and I've had my fair share of big stories to cover. On the night of the 1997 general election, STV sent me to Dingwall for the count in the Ross, Skye and Inverness West constituency. Sitting Lib-Dem member Charles Kennedy was up against Donnie Munro, the lead singer of Runrig, who was standing for Labour.

It was a great experience and one I much enjoyed, not least because these were men for whom I had respect and admiration, in different ways. I'd met Charlie many times down the years. He had been a staunch ally during the *P&J* strike but I had also been to loads of Runrig concerts! This promised to be interesting, challenging and great fun. And so it was.

Donnie Munro had long been a Labour man, and the polls showed that he had a good chance of a shock result against Kennedy, a local favourite who had represented local people since 1983. The 1997 election was the famous night which saw Tony Blair sweep to power, and thereafter New Labour would run Britain for thirteen years. But, as Tories were losing their seats all over the UK to a huge Labour swing, Charlie Kennedy was hanging on to his, despite a fine campaign which saw Donnie Munro whittle the majority down to just 4,000 votes. Two years later, Kennedy was elected Lib-Dem leader.

This was before the emergence of the SNP as a major electoral power. In those days it was all Labour in Scotland, and one of the key planks of Blair's policy was Scottish devolution. As this was unfolding, I found myself spending a lot of time covering stories with Donald Dewar, the Glasgow Garscadden Labour MP who would be Scotland's first First Minister and a man of whom I grew very fond. He always seemed to be scatty, but underneath he had a razor-sharp mind and a dry sense of humour.

My favourite Dewar story is about his new researcher going to his office in the House of Commons one morning, and opening the door to find papers strewn everywhere, briefcases lying open on the floor and books dangling off shelves. Horrified, she called the police. Some time later, Dewar arrived to find at the door a policeman, who told him that his office had been ransacked. The bold Donald took one look inside and said 'what makes you think that?' I was in Jordan on exercise with the Army when I heard on the BBC World Service that he had died, and I went for a walk out into the desert with a lump in my throat. Sadly, Charlie Kennedy is no longer with us either. Two good Scotsmen taken far too soon.

I've been friends with many MPs, among them Tom Harris, a fellow Napier journalism graduate. From memory, all Tom spoke about at Napier was politics, and it was no surprise when he was elected as the Labour member for Glasgow Cathcart in 2001. He invited me to dinner in the House of Commons one night, and afterwards showed me around all the nooks and crannies the public don't see. We went to the terrace bar for a nightcap and, glass in hand, I peered over the wall to the murky waters of the Thames below.

'This isn't very secure, Tom,' I said. 'Terrorists could throw a rope up here with a grappling iron on the end, climb up and shoot the lot of you.'

As I turned towards Tom, my eye caught a slight movement in the shadows. I peered into the dark and could just make out the shape of a policeman standing there, a machine gun strapped across his chest and a pistol on his belt. He stepped out into the light and smiled patiently at me.

The public exposure of my job means that I am stopped in the street quite a lot and asked to sign autographs or pose for selfies. The majority of people are pleasant and polite but you get the odd comedian. Occasion-ally, I get a menacing look from someone in a pub, and once or twice I've had the 'are you looking at my bird?' opener.

The variety of my job means I go to work every morning not knowing what I will do, where I will go or who I will meet that day. People often ask me who, of all the celebrities I've met, was the nicest. It's a hard one. The celebs I've had dealings with have mostly all been perfectly polite and nice to me, but that's because they generally have to be. I only meet them for a few minutes and, if they're punting a book or a new album, the last thing they want to do is piss off a journalist.

When I met two famous sons of Glasgow, both of whom are knights of the realm, I was touched that they both seemed as genuinely pleased to meet me as I was to meet them. I was surprised when Sir Alex Ferguson thrust out his hand to me in a crowd at Glasgow City Chambers during one charity function and said 'good to meet you'. And Sir Billy Connolly did much the same shortly after he laid flowers outside the Clutha bar in the aftermath of the police helicopter tragedy. It's clear both men still spend a lot of time in Glasgow and stick the news on every night when they're at home.

Most impressive, however, are the ordinary people who have been caught up in extraordinary events. I enjoy meeting them and hearing their stories most of all. Diana Baird was one stand-out and Alfred Anderson another.

Diana's father, a Helensburgh man called John Logie Baird, invented television and gave the world one of its greatest technical advances. She spoke of her childhood and how her father was driven to succeed. She said that he had built a television set out of an old hat box and the lenses from bicycle lamps, and that he had once received a massive electric shock but sustained only a few burns. However, the electrical surge had fused the entire apartment block in Hastings where the family lived, and the man who changed the world was asked to leave by the landlord.

In 1927 he transmitted a television signal down phone lines between London and the Central Hotel in Glasgow and the new age of television had arrived. I was touched by her tales of watching her father work on something which we all take for granted and to which now virtually everybody on the planet has access. It has also given me my livelihood for twenty-five years. The STV outside broadcast unit when I joined was a massive lorry with a studio control room in the trailer. Painted on the door of the cab was the name 'John Logie Baird.'

Alfred Anderson lived alone in a neat little flat in Alyth near Perth and, when I met him, he was 108 years old. Neil McLaren and I drove up from Glasgow to do a piece with him about the ninetieth anniversary of the Christmas truce on the Western Front, which he had witnessed. When we got to Dunblane, I phoned him to make sure everything was still on for our visit.

'Don't bother coming. I don't want to talk about it,' he said. 'I'll be going for a long walk.'

I was flabbergasted and not a little worried because all the arrangements had been made and we were nearly there. But this was obviously a very sensitive situation so I phoned his daughter, a lady in her late seventies, to tell her the news. She was nonplussed.

'Oh don't you worry about him,' she said. 'He'll be right as rain by the time you get there.' And so he was. The daughter had obviously gone round and given the poor man a row! But the way he said 'I'll be going for a long walk' still haunts me. I wouldn't want to talk about such carnage either.

In one of the longest interviews I have ever done, Alfred spoke about his amazing life. He had been in the Territorial Army, and in 1914 had gone on summer camp to Comrie. But instead of returning home to Dundee, his Black Watch battalion was mobilised and sent straight to France. Could you imagine that happening today?

He said that all his pals were with him, and everybody was happy because they were together and going off on a great adventure. He said he'd never had a foreign holiday before and was looking forward to one. But things changed when they reached France and became involved in early heavy fighting.

That Christmas Eve he was in the trenches, and spoke movingly of the moment when he noticed that the shelling had stopped and there was a brief and unofficial truce all along the Western Front before the carnage started all over again. I chanced my arm a bit and asked him about life in the trenches and his memories of that time, but he would only say so much and nothing of battle.

He returned from the War and resumed working in the family joinery business. When World War Two broke out he was too old to join up, but he served in the Home Guard in Dundee. When Neil and I left, we gratefully shook hands with Alfred in the hallway. Bizarrely, he started to apologise.

'I'm sorry about earlier. I can't really concentrate just now. My son is unwell and I am worried about him. He is eighty-five and in a nursing home in Perth.'

I didn't know what to say. It was humbling. This remarkable man, who had lived through so much, wanted to apologise to us for not being on top form. At 108! I walked to the end of his path and, at the gate, turned. Of course, neither of us was wearing uniform but I stamped noisily to attention and threw up my best salute. I thought it was fitting but his comment totally disarmed me.

'Aye, that was very good,' he said, laughing.

*   *   *

As something of a homage, I diverted away from Inverness Alabama briefly and drove into downtown Birmingham. On the corner of 6th Avenue and 16th Street stood the imposing red brick structure of an icon of the South and the Civil Rights movement.

The 16th Street church loomed over the junction like a giant, and its blue and white Art Deco sign was like a beacon. The church was built in 1909 and was the biggest in the city for black parishioners. In later years, it was the HQ and focal point of the Civil Rights movement, which battled against prejudice in the South generally and in Birmingham specifically.

As I mentioned in the previous chapter of this book, the deaths of the four little girls murdered here in the Klan bomb plot of 1963 are widely regarded as the tipping point in the struggle. Nearly half a million dollars was raised by unsolicited donations to repair and rebuild the church. Among the donations was a stained glass window from Wales, depicting Christ as a black man. I paused for a while, and the noise and heat of the busy, bustling city seemed to disappear. All this happened shortly before I was born.

That morning I had gone through the 7am ritual. The unspeakable motel chain I always use in the USA is ubiquitous, basic and very cheap, but it has all I need. I am usually so tired from driving all day that I want to collapse into a clean bed, watch a bit of TV and have a hot shower in the morning. I have no need for hairdryers, no need for irons and no need for room service. The best thing about the chain is that, because of its cheapness, it attracts all sorts of waifs and strays, most of whom are on long cross-country journeys to start new lives. I have frequently spent ages chatting to them and enjoy their stories.

Its only indulgence is that it serves free coffee in the lobby from 7am, and I am usually the first guest in line. My tactic is to place a couple of cups in an ice bucket and carry a third. The cups are thimble-sized at best. If you do the ice bucket thing, you can get a decent mouthful although the third cup is always a shade lukewarm by the time you get to it. I staggered, bleary-eyed, into the bright lobby. The Alabama morning was already well under way, and the raging sun was cracking the sky in the east. I was due to hit the road again that day.

'How are you enjoying your stay with us?' She was short, blonde and built for comfort, not speed. She was also the lady who checked me in at reception. Her smile had been bright and breezy and made me feel welcome.

'It's been great,' I said, 'but I'm moving on.' Three days in this Inverness would surely have got me a reward in heaven.

She asked where I was from, and I said Scotland but not Inverness. That would have opened a whole can of worms. I have a well-rehearsed story which I trot out whenever I am asked what I am doing in the US but frankly, at Christ o'clock in the morning, I didn't really want to engage in conversation. But she did.

'I'm from Birmingham, but I'm a relief manager and the company sends me anywhere they want. It can be fun. but it can be a challenge.'

'Yes, it's quite a place,' I agreed, thinking about some of the characters I had seen on this trip.

'You can say that again,' she went on, 'and the police don't even care here. We phone them up and they say "what do you want us to do about it?"' This grabbed my attention. There was a police car in the car park beside the lobby the night I arrived.

'Drugs are dealt from the rooms, prostitution goes on here. I even caught a couple having sex in the pool yesterday,' she said, shaking her head disapprovingly.

I saw children playing in the pool the night before, I remembered, and hoped the chlorine levels were high. Back at the motel on San Francisco Bay, I saw what could only have been a room full of what are now called 'sex workers,' preparing to ply their trade. 'Hi, honey, want some company?' one had screeched from her open door as I hurried past.

She went on. 'I told them they had ten seconds to get out of the pool, or I would call the cops. The guy looked at me sheepishly and said "sorry ma'am, I just got caught up in the moment". I tried not to laugh. 'They just don't understand. They don't get it at all. On 4 July we had forty-nine cars in the car park that didn't belong here. One person rents a room and then thirty people turn up to party.

'When I was on my management course in Tulsa,' she went on, getting into her subject, 'we went out for dinner one night and one of the guys at my table was approached by a woman, obviously a call girl. She handed him her card and suggested he call her. Of course, he had no intention of doing so. It wasn't until we got back to the motel that night that he noticed the number on the card was the number for the motel he managed.'

She sounded exasperated. She told me that she couldn't stand it much more, and that she wanted the company to move her on quickly. The motel had been through four managers in four years at this location. I kind of sympathised.

'They just don't understand, these people,' she repeated, 'they just don't get it.' I frowned. I wasn't sure at that stage what she meant by 'these people'.

Something clicked. Something Bubba had said just fell into place. When I checked in the other night, she had been very welcoming. She had been all over me like a rash, in fact. I thought it might have been my witty, debonair personality, my rakish good looks and my chat. In truth, it was something far more prosaic than that.

She was the white manageress of the hotel and I was the only white guest. We were the only white people for a country mile. And she hated it.

CHAPTER FIVE

Inverness, Florida

Create myself down south,
Impress all the women,
Pretend I'm Samuel Clemens,
Wear seersucker and white linens.

Tom Petty

The gold dome of the Georgia state capitol glistened on the horizon in the evening light, as the sun set away behind me. Looking in the Chevy's mirror was painful on the eyes for a while, but I was more interested in looking forward. Atlanta. At last.

Bubba had been a lovely host, and I had enjoyed meeting Stuart and Greg, but I was glad to have left my fourth and penultimate Inverness. The racism I'd heard so much about in the South was still alive and kicking in Alabama. I departed at lunchtime, and headed up to Birmingham, where I latched onto I-20 and headed east.

My mother aroused my interest in Atlanta through her passion for *Gone with the Wind*, a 1936 book made a few years later into a film, both of which had been an important part of her childhood. I love the film, too, but for different reasons. She often spoke of how, when she first read it, she had been a young girl, full of hope at a time when Europe was plunging headlong towards another war. She loved the fashion of the stars' elaborate costumes and, of course, the dashing Rhett Butler, even though he didn't give a damn.

I saw the film in adulthood, and I was moved more by the scale of the production and the intrigue of the plot than I was by the dresses. Rhett Butler, though, was quite a boy, and I'd have loved to have met him for a drink. Born in 1900, the novel's author, Margaret Mitchell, was also something of a character. Interested in writing since early childhood, she went on to work as a reporter with the *Atlanta Journal*. She was engaged five times, and the best man at her first wedding would be her second husband. She also had a passion for erotica which was, to say the least, daring for a woman at that time. She collected volumes of what we would nowadays call 'soft pornography', and it was around the height of her interest in this genre that she wrote *Gone with the Wind*.

I cut off the freeway and nosed the Chevy along Peachtree Street, the city's most famous thoroughfare, to the house where she wrote her masterpiece and which is now one of the most popular museums in the USA. It is a traditional red-brick building which would not look out of place in suburban London. A popular student squat for a time, it was more than once badly damaged by fire. The area around it has been redeveloped down the decades, and is now a thriving business district with office blocks, apartments and shops. Yet somehow the house, set back from the road behind a lush green lawn, does not look at all out of place.

The room where she worked on her manuscript is furnished in what today we would describe as the Victorian style, with velour sofas and chintz-shaded standard lamps. Her tiny desk has an ancient typewriter sitting on top, and papers and books are neatly piled on the window shelf behind. I paused for a few minutes to enjoy the moment. It was special to be in such an atmospheric space, where one of the twentieth-century's greatest works of popular literature was created. More moving for me, though, was the link the place had with my mother, and the joy which the words written at that desk had given her.

Margaret Mitchell's life was cut short at the peak of her success. Crossing the road outside her home, she was knocked down by a drunk driver. She was taken to hospital but died five days later without regaining consciousness. She was forty-nine years old.

Although I had earlier on this trip visited the Lorraine Motel, the scene of his assassination in Memphis, such was my unbounded admiration for Atlanta-born Martin Luther King Jr that he was my main reason for stopping in this city on my way to my last Inverness.

In the morning, I would indulge myself in one final session of homage to my hero. Tonight I would spend the night in another of my unspeakable motels, in the suburb of Decatur. Tired after a long day behind the wheel, I had a hot shower and nipped across the road to a diner for a steak and a beer. I was the only white man in the joint but nobody batted an eyelid, least of all me.

King and his father were both christened Michael King, and the 'Martin Luther' was added after King Senior travelled to Berlin in 1934 to attend the Baptist World Alliance Conference. It was there that he studied the life and work of the eponymous German, a leading figure in the sixteenth-century European Reformation, and adopted the name as a tribute.

Young Martin followed his father into the ministry, and was immediately swept up in the Civil Rights movement. Not yet thirty years old, he formed the Southern Christian Leadership Conference, and was thrust into the forefront of campaigning as America approached a momentous period in her short history. From then until his assassination, his life's work was to secure the emancipation of African Americans, many of whom were suffering from the most blatant and degrading segregation and discrimination.

Although subjected to brutal treatment from the police and white supremacists, King's movement was committed to non-violent protest. This culminated in the March on Washington, when in August 1963 an estimated quarter of a million people travelled across the USA to converge on the capital. The day ended with King's 'I have a dream' speech.

President John Kennedy had agreed to meet King and the other organisers, but would only do so when the event had finished. It was deemed too politically sensitive for him to speak from the same podium at the Lincoln Memorial, so he invited them to the White House afterwards.

I nosed the Chevy down Auburn Avenue and found a parking spot close to the Ebenezer Baptist Church, which is synonymous with the King family. King Jr was baptised in the church and his funeral was held here. It was from the church that his coffin was borne, symbolically, by a farm cart pulled by two mules to a nearby cemetery.

He and his father were once the church pastors, and King Jr delivered his first sermon here, aged just nineteen. Externally, with two large windowed towers, the red brick building is smaller than, but a similar structure to, to the 16th Street church in Birmingham I'd visited the day before. Inside, it looks like any other urban American church and, if you didn't know the history of the place, you'd be forgiven for feeling underwhelmed. Built in 1914, it has a congregation today of around 6,000. It is understandably popular in the community, and is known locally as 'Sweet Auburn'.

I sat in silence on a pew, pondering the many humanitarian changes which had grown from the seeds first planted in this church. The congregation here had played a critical role in this, and many powerful orations were delivered here by great men: among them, of course, both Kings.

There were choir stalls behind the altar, and the potential number of worshippers was boosted to more than 1,200 by a first-floor balcony. On the wall, on either side of the choir stalls were two banks of pipes for the organ, which sat at right-angles to the altar. Martin Luther King's mother Alberta was murdered as she sat playing this organ in June 1974, six years after her son was assassinated. Her killer was a young black man called Marcus Chenault, who had intended to shoot Martin Luther King Sr but he told police that he shot his wife because she was closer.

He said Christians were his enemies, and that black preachers posed a threat to black people. In a stance so typical of the King family, they pleaded for the assassin not to be sentenced to death. He did receive the death penalty but this was commuted to life imprisonment, and he died in jail in 1995 aged forty-four.

Next door to the church were the museum to King's life and the mausoleum where he and his wife Coretta are interred. It was this, more than anything, that I had come to see. I stood and reflected by the glass case containing the suit King wore the day he was assassinated. It wasn't a moment of voyeuristic bad taste, which I feared it might be. Rather, I was captivated that such an important piece of history was only a few inches away.

Outside in the sunshine I sat again for a time at the pool, in the middle of which is a large white marble sarcophagus resting on a small red-tiled island. It contains the remains of King and his wife, who died in 2006 after a period of ill health. It is beautifully tranquil. The only thing you can hear is the fluttering of the eternal flame which burns just a few feet away.

It is an extraordinary oasis of cool sanctuary in the middle of a bustling city.

The heat in Atlanta can be oppressive, but the air conditioning in the Chevy did its job. The city hosts the global HQ of CNN but, as the last place I wanted to visit was a TV studio, I gave it a miss. Atlanta is also home to arguably the world's most famous brand, and I spent a few hours following the story of Coca Cola.

Like Birmingham, Atlanta sprang up from virtually nowhere because of industry. It was a vital railway junction in the early nineteenth century, and it grew as the iron road drove further west and the country plunged into the Civil War.

The Coca Cola museum is in a huge complex of buildings situated in what used to be the city's railway marshalling yards, and is understandably very busy. It charts the history of the drink from its unusual origins to the present day. Confederate Colonel John Pemberton, a pharmacist, became addicted to morphine after the drug was used to treat a sword wound to his chest, which he sustained at the battle of Columbus. Desperate to kick his habit, he began experimenting with various plants, and eventually came up with a tonic wine which developed into the brand we know today.

The museum houses the vault, which keeps the top-secret Coca Cola recipe safe behind a massive circular steel door. On the way out, you can sample the real thing, and its many derivatives, from a series of taps protruding from a neon-lit wall. Some of the cherry and lime variants I will leave for others to judge.

I had one more stop to make in Atlanta before I left Georgia and crossed into Florida, the last state on my swing across the US. Martin Luther King is Georgia's most famous son and, among other luminaries, such as Ray Charles and Oliver Hardy, the state produced another American political figure whom I grew up admiring. From downtown Atlanta, I gunned the Chevy onto I-75 then I-20, and then off down a tree-lined avenue to the Jimmy Carter Presidential Library.

Carter, a Democrat, replaced Republican President Gerald Ford, and came to power in 1977 after the Watergate scandal which had destroyed Richard Nixon. The Watergate affair enthralled me as a child in the early 1970s, and in later years 'All the President's Men' fuelled my urge to be a journalist. I wanted to be Bob Woodward or Carl Bernstein, I wanted a contact like Deep Throat. I've had many good contacts, but none who stood in the shadows of deserted nocturnal car parks and anonymously fed me the kind of information which forced an American President to resign.

Carter's background as a Georgia peanut farmer won him wide public support across the South, and his laid-back style was popular. His Presidential Library, in a 1980s building not dissimilar to the Martin Luther King Museum a few miles away, tells the story of his single term in office and his astute policies and attempts at negotiating peace around the world. His term spanned momentous events. He was behind the Camp David accords to try to find a solution to tensions in the Middle East, as well as being closely involved in the SALT II nuclear arms reduction treaty with the Soviet Union.

But he was dealt crippling blows by the Soviet invasion of Afghanistan and by the Iran hostage crisis. The latter led to a disastrous and fatal military attempt to rescue diplomats taken hostage by radical students

inside the US embassy in Tehran. Carter's hopes of a second term lay
in flames, alongside the wreckage of the Hercules transport planes and
Sea Stallion helicopters which collided at the secret airfield, codenamed
Desert One, in Iran.

The Carter Library highlights the remarkable Camp David accords
he negotiated in 1977 between President Anwar Sadat of Egypt and the
Israeli Prime Minister Menachem Begin. The resulting Egypt-Israel
Peace Treaty saw the demilitarisation of Sinai and the end of the state of
war which had existed between the two countries since the Arab-Israeli
conflict of 1948. The two leaders shared a Nobel Peace Prize in 1978.
Carter would receive the same honour in 2002 for the work carried out by
the Carter Centre, which adjoins his Presidential Library, in peace negotiations, election monitoring and disease eradication across the world.
The museum is geekily fascinating and holds homely artefacts, such as
Sadat's pipe from the Camp David talks.

Heading south on I-75, I left Atlanta with something of a heavy heart. I
can't remember what CD I slid into the Chevy's slot or what radio station
I dialled but, whatever they were, all I could hear was the powerful theme
from 'Gone with the Wind'. As I glanced into the rearview mirror, the
setting sun was bouncing off the windows of the buildings downtown,
making it look, for a second, like the scene in the film where retreating
Confederates torched their remaining supplies so they wouldn't fall into
enemy hands and, by so doing, set the city alight.

After taking Atlanta, Union General William Sherman conducted his
'march to the sea' and, by the time his victorious army reached the coast
at Savannah, it had destroyed military targets as well as civilian infra-
structure, primarily the railway, along a sixty-mile-wide swathe. He also
freed thousands of slaves, with the promise that each would receive forty
acres and a mule. At Savannah, Sherman turned north again and, six
months later, the war was over.

As I drove, I couldn't help but smile to myself because I was now
on the American Civil War route I had planned to take all those years
before, when I had cut short my holiday to return to Scotland for the job
interview with Grampian TV.

I followed in Sherman's footsteps on his 'march to the sea' as far as
Macon, then I swung south. Little more than 150 miles later I'd cross into
Florida, where lay my last Inverness and my journey would end. Although
I've always enjoyed visiting the Kennedy Space Centre, from where those
moon missions had been launched, it pleased me that I would avoid the

usual tourist traps in the Sunshine State. You couldn't pay me enough to go to Disney, and anyway Florida has other things to enjoy. I'd been to the Florida Keys. In the Everglades I'd been on an air boat, one of those flat-bottomed craft with a huge propellor encased in a cage at the stern. And Miami Beach's art deco quarter is a favourite of mine.

But this trip was all about Inverness.

If you watch what you're doing, you can drive from the coast to Inverness and bypass Orlando without using a toll road. This is a important for someone as parsimonious as I. It's around 100 miles from Cape Canaveral, home to the Kennedy Space Centre, to my last Inverness and, with a mixture of childish excitement and a heavy heart because I knew my journey was nearly over, I pulled into town.

On the right-hand side as I hit the outskirts, lay the 'cooter pond', a large boardwalk-lined lake named after the cooter turtle which thrives here. The pond is also home to an unknown number of alligators, and I made a point of remembering to double-lock the door of my unspeakable motel that night. Just in case.

The cooter pond is also home to several railway wagons which ended up in the water after a train derailed here in the 1930s. The wagons held canned ham and a sizeable consignment of women's clothes. Apparently, locals dived on the wreckage to recover as much booty as they could but were fought off, not by railway officials or police but by the alligators.

Inverness Florida looked like a big town. But it had a small-town feel and, although the rain was lashing down, the streets were busy with people. There was a mixture of architecture, from ante-bellum to modern. Some buildings were quaintly named, and the Chevy took me past Community Oxygen and Medical, Ace Hardware and Advance Auto Parts.

Maybe it's because I spent so much time covering local government stories in the one true Inverness as a young reporter that I have a fixed image in my mind of what town clerks look like. They are male, in their fifties, and use Brylcreem in their hair. They wear checked jackets or crumpled suits and always have pens in the handkerchief pockets. They are single, and drink two pints of dark beer before going home at night. Invariably, they have a copy of *Sporting Life* in their raincoat pocket.

Younger members of staff, especially females, find these men daunting, if not positively scary. Yet they are invaluable. Their experience knows no bounds, they can quote the city ordnances by heart and, after just a cursory glance, can tell you a retaining wall's life story and the circuitry of a streetlight.

In my time I have come across many such at the Town House in my Inverness. But when I met city clerk Debbie Davis at the government centre in Inverness, she flummoxed me. She was blonde and glamorous and wore an executive suit and heels. I spent a considerable amount of time with her during my visit, and it was clear from the very start that she wasn't a *Sporting Life* kind of gal.

I think the term 'City Clerk' here in the USA means something quite different from the 'Town Clerk' I am used to in Scotland. From spending time with Debbie, it was clear that she was more like the Chief Executive than the guy who tells you where and how deep to lay your drains.

'I'm not elected, but I am appointed. I am still a servant of the city, one of the two charter officers and if the council don't like me then it's out I go.' She kicked towards me with a shapely leg.

She was no slouch either because, when I met her, she had a reporter and photographer from the local squeak there ready to do a piece on my visit for the next day's paper.

'You should have been here to see our ice last week,' she said, with something approaching pain in her voice. 'The temperature was way down in the teens!'

I tried to counsel her about the temperatures in the one true Inverness but I don't think she would have got the point. Florida last saw snow in 1972, and I have little doubt that trying to get people's heads round the kind of winters we have in Europe would cause them to keel over.

'I've lived here since 1978 – that was before we even had a McDonald's – and I've seen this city grow from having just a two lane road to being something much more. People want to come here to live now,' she said proudly.

We sat in her smart office in the city government building, a kind of town hall, newly built in grey/brown. It was clean and new, but also cold and empty. There was still building work going on, and presumably more offices to move in. Across the road was the Hooper Funeral Home and Downtown Affordable Muffler.

Debbie introduced me to Frank Di Giovanni, one of these annoying people who can eat what they want, and in whatever quantities they want, but still not gain a pound in weight. Frank was about six feet three tall and rake thin. He was dark, and his Italian eyes sparkled when he got into his subject. His subject was, of course, Inverness. He was the city manager and, I am guessing here, he was higher up the tree than Debbie. The two of them were formidable. And talk about efficient: not only was I interviewed for the local paper, I was also down to attend its editorial conference the next day. It dawned on me very slowly that my visit must be quite a news story.

'Our business is old people,' said Frank as we walked to the meeting. 'In most places people are out all day working and the services provided by councils like ours don't really kick in until the evenings and the weekend. Here we provide services all day long and at night and at the weekends. Also, people here are retired and have time on their hands. In other towns people don't have time to pay bills. Here they do it in person because they want someone to talk to. Paying for your electricity in Inverness is a social event!'

We ambled past the Brannen Bank and Van Allen Insurance and trotted up the steps of the Old Courthouse. The original was burned down in the 1800s by a band of miscreants. The people who threw up the new building weren't stupid: they placed fire hydrants at each corner. It sat in the centre of a quaint old square and looked not dissimilar to the town hall in 'Back to the Future,' with a large white clock in the domed tower on a red tiled roof and two sets of white columns flanking the steps up to the main door.

Inside, it was identical to every American courthouse I had ever seen on TV. In fact, I fully expected Perry Mason or Petrocelli to confront me. It was oak-panelled, and came complete with a little wooden fence with a gate in it to separate the public from the officers of the court. The judge's bench was high above the rest of the room, and there was a cardboard cutout of Elvis Presley in the corner.

Hang on.

A cardboard Elvis?

'It's a tribute to the film he made here in 1961,' said Charlie Brennan, the *Citrus County Chronicle* editor, and a double for Bill Gates, gripping my hand and ushering me through the gate. I almost felt compelled to ask the judge's permission to approach.

'It was called "Follow That Dream" and the courtroom scenes were done here.' He gestured expansively around the room.

'Is that so?' I replied. I tried, vainly, to suppress a giggle. Elvis looked a tad out of place in his gold lamé suit.

'Elvis played a character called Mike Edwards in one of his films,' I told the assembled board. There were nods of 'really? really?' as I sat down.

They didn't know it, but I had a more meaningful reason for enjoying the atmosphere. It was in this very room that my man Tom Petty met Elvis Presley while he was shooting 'Follow That Dream' in 1961. Petty's uncle was working on the film as a producer and took the eleven-year-old Tom to meet 'The King.' That night, Tom went home to his house in nearby Gainesville and told his father that he wanted to buy a guitar and become a rock star. My favourite musician started on the road which gave millions of people such pleasure after he got the bug from Elvis in this very room.

I have been to more editorial conferences in my time than I care to think about. I have also been inside many courtrooms in my time. But the twain have never met, until now. This was local government going to the media. In Scotland, it would happen the other way around, without a fraction of the bonhomie I felt here.

There were a dozen or so people around the table which sat beneath the judge's bench. All were executives, of one sort or another, of the *Chronicle* group of newspapers. There was a single female. The men all wore small town outfits, uncomfortable suits with pastel shirts and incongruous ties, jeans and chinos. There were coffee cups and yellow legal pads around, and people doodled while they listened.

I was still big news. Frank introduced me, and explained who I was and what I was about. Good old Frank, sporting a colourful red-and-black shirt and tie combo, was most impressive. He was quizzed on water and sewerage and power supplies and the cemetery, and he fielded every question with ease. He rattled off facts and figures and plucked estimates seemingly from nowhere. He didn't have a single note in front of him.

As the meeting went on, I noticed the jury box where twelve good men and true would sit. Then I glanced up and saw the area set aside for black people back in the day.

Afterwards I was taken to lunch as guest of the paper to Stumpknockers, a bar/restaurant on main street. It was one of those places that tried awfully hard to be from bygone times. There was a kind of 'pub in Star Wars' moment when the room went quiet as I entered. People stopped what they were doing, forks hovered in mid-air and heads snapped round. I overheard 'he's the writer from Inverness, Scotland'. I sat down with my back to the room, and the hubbub of a weekday lunchtime in Inverness resumed. I tucked into my staple of ribs.

Gerard Mulligan, the *Chronicle*'s publisher, was one of the number wearing an odd shade. His salmon pink shirt and silver tie blended well with a healthy honey-brown tan. I just couldn't imagine him getting up early to put on his galoshes and scrape snow off his car.

'The biggest employer here is the hospital. Around 1,200 people work there but I guess that isn't a surprise when you think of the number of old people who live in the area. Why, there are 25,000 military veterans here alone. People like to retire here,' he said.

Someone else chipped in with a fact that didn't sound like it was something he was altogether proud of, like biggest statue or smallest tax or widest road junction.

'The second biggest nuclear power station in the USA is just up the road,' he said. 'It's called Crystal River and beside it are another four coal, oil and gas plants. Security is very tight up there, especially since 9/11.'

The *Chronicle* was like every other newspaper on the planet and was feeling the pinch during a global economic bellyflop. Its titles were full, though, and there seemed to be plenty of advertising. In my time there, it covered meaty issues like 'Shepherd of the Hills Episcopal Church in Lecanto is putting out a food pantry SOS' and 'Denny's gives away free grand slam breakfasts' and, of course 'Inverness, Sco reporter visits all five US Invernesses.'

But what about the real stories, what about the biggies? I think of my time in the business in Scotland and remembered that, in six months of 1988 alone, I covered the worst terror attack and industrial accident in UK history: Lockerbie and the Piper Alpha disaster. What was the local equivalent?

Charlie Brennan and I stepped outside into the rain. They get quite a lot of rain here, but rarely any snow. 'I moved here from Tampa, thinking it would be much quieter than the big city.' As Charlie spoke, I tried not to stare. He really was a doppelgänger for Gates. He could have got the gig as the former Microsoft man's body double, if the *Chronicle* went down the tubes.

'One of the first stories I covered was a quadruple murder. That was in 1990. We don't have many murders, but when we get them they are big news.'

He wasn't kidding. I quickly scanned my mental data bank. I can't remember covering a quadruple murder, if you exclude the Dunblane tragedy. In thirty-plus years in the business, the biggest death toll I've encountered in a single homicide was three, in an episode in Govanhill on the south side of Glasgow. Standing there in the genteel drizzle of a

Florida lunchtime, I just couldn't imagine Inverness outgunning 'the no mean city' of Glasgow.

'It was a botched love triangle insurance job. The husband wanted the wife dead because she would make a million from their divorce. He hired a hitman and the hitman went to the house looking for her. There were workmen restoring the roof and when he couldn't find the woman, the hitman freaked out and killed the four workmen with a ball hammer instead.'

Out the back of the town hall and across the square from Stumpknockers sat the Sheriff's office, and Scotty Roush gave me a warm welcome. He'd been part of the Inverness Sheriff Department for thirty years, and his office was like policemen's offices the world over: shelves and cabinets full of hats, badges and shields from other forces. There were pictures, too, of him and his son standing beside recently shot deer, deep in the wilds somewhere.

His hair was the regulation policeman short, and he had a moustache of two-day stubble. He was stocky and very strong. His Sheriff's Department shirt was puffed out by the stab-proof vest he wore beneath it. But even without that, I got the feeling he was muscular and not the kind of person you should mess with. Inverness seemed an unlikely place for anyone to stab a policeman, but I guess it only needed to happen once.

On the rear wall of his office was a cabinet, inside of which was a medal. I have many medals for army service in Iraq and Afghanistan. You got the impression that Scotty won his for getting involved.

'It's the Medal of Valor,' he said. He saw I was about to ask why he got it, and there was a pause for a second or two, before he grabbed his keys off the table and ran for the door. 'Come on and I'll show you where it happened.'

'Doesn't this mean you need to make me some kind of Sheriff's Deputy?' I quipped, as we walked out to his green-and-white patrol car. 'Don't I get a badge and a gun?'

He zapped open the boot and talked me through his kit. First to catch my eye was a riot shield and helmet: riot gear here? Beside it was a CBRN (chemical, biological, radiological and nuclear) suit and respirator in a rucksack. If Inverness wasn't the kind of place where a cop would get stabbed, and it was hard to imagine a riot here, imagining the moment when you might require a CBRN outfit was beyond my ken. Terror here? In Inverness? Would Al Qaeda plant IEDs on the Withlacoochee trail?

Would they drop Sarin into the cooter pond? Then I remembered the nuclear power plant up the road.

The car, a Ford Crown Victor, was big and powerful, the same as Ray's taxi back in Oakland, a lifetime ago and a continent away. We pulled out onto Highland Boulevard.

'Centre, this is ten-eight,' said Scotty into his radio handset. I looked around as he chatted to his HQ. In front of me was a laptop computer with access to a huge database of cars and criminals. Above it were switches controlling all the lights and sirens, a mammoth searchlight and a radar for lassooing speeding motorists. Locked to a bulkhead behind us was Scotty's CAR-15 assault rifle, and below it was a webbing belt crammed full of magazines of extra ammunition. Already on his belt was a Glock pistol, a Taser stun gun and a baton. I felt safe with Scotty.

'Centre this is ten-eight, now ten-twelve,' he said. We had become something else just a moment or two after leaving the car park. '"Ten-twelve" is the car code meaning I have a passenger,' he informed me. Secretly I hoped Centre would send ten-twelve to a two-eleven. I must point out here that I have no idea whatsoever what a two-eleven is, but it always heralded some action in episodes of 'Hill Street Blues', my all-time favourite TV programme.

But an icy hand suddenly touched my heart. Years before, I did a feature piece for STV about the Royal Navy's search and rescue helicopter at HMS Gannet on the Ayrshire coast. As we took off, the pilot informed me that, if there was a genuine emergency, he would land the Sea King and drop us off so they could attend the call. How we would get back to the world in this eventuality was not made clear. I remember spending the entire flight panicking, in case the aircraft was diverted to rescue a woman about to have quins and we would miss the story because we were stranded in some remote field on Arran.

'I drive past here daily and I think about it every time,' he said as we passed Walgreens and entered a shopping mall car park. Scotty stopped at a precise spot with a Winn Dixie supermarket to our left and a pharmacy ahead of us. He pointed over the steering wheel to a pair of buildings.

'That used to be a pizza parlour and I was called here one day to investigate a break-in,' he said. 'I heard her screaming, that was what caught my attention. At first I thought it was a domestic. I saw him drag her towards her car by her beautiful long hair. I ran towards them. I was just planning on jumping him and getting him on the ground. Then I saw he had a gun to her head.'

I could feel the drama. Policemen are generally quite well paid and an old Glasgow bobby told me once they weren't paid for what they did, but for what they might have to do. I don't think they're paid nearly enough.

'I drew my pistol and levelled it at him. For a split second I thought we were going to have a gunfight, right there in the car park, with all these people around. Instead, he ran off.' Scotty gestured towards the trees behind the mall. 'I chased him up there into those woods. By this time I had radioed for back-up and another officer and I captured him in the trees. Who knows what he was thinking – a sexual motive no doubt.'

The attacker was called Smith and was, of all things, a prison guard from Miami. Whatever was his motive, he would have had plenty of time to ponder his life choices in one of his own jails. A couple of blocks away from the mall was the town's cemetery. As if out of respect, the police car slowed to a roll as we approached.

'In 1984 Inverness had a tornado. It was one of the worst things I have ever had to deal with,' said Scotty. 'It picked up a car containing a family and carried it a mile or so and dropped it right here in the cemetery. At the start there had been a mother, father and two kids inside. Only the children survived. It was really sad.'

We drove back to the office and ten-twelve became ten-eight again. Centre hadn't despatched us to a two-eleven, far less a nine-eleven, and I handed back my imaginary deputy's badge and gun, trying not to show my disappointment. This may have been something of a sleepy town, with not much happening in the way of major crime, but it was a big town and the biggest Inverness so far. It clearly had its moments, and I understood that Scotty thoroughly deserved his Medal of Valor.

Scotty's last anecdote before we parted company was about his bike patrols. He told me how he had been pedalling quietly through the woods one afternoon when he came across two four-by-fours backed up to each other with their tailgates down. He waited until he got closer and his suspicions were realised. Then he radioed for back-up. He drew his pistol and arrested the two men who were working in a mobile drugs factory. They were convicted, and a significant quantity of highly-addictive crystal meth was confiscated.

I just couldn't imagine somewhere like Inverness being the kind of place where a mobile drugs factory would locate itself. But I could imagine cops on bikes here. In fact, that would be typical of the place.

Talking of bikes, so efficient were Frank and Debbie – too damned efficient if I am being honest in this case – that they had organised for me a cycle tour of the town, courtesy of Charlie Wade, owner of Sun Coast Bicycles. I agreed immediately. I must have been tired or I must have dropped my guard for a nanosecond, for I agreed to it without thinking. Given the size of the place, it couldn't take that long. An hour maybe?

'You'll enjoy it,' Debbie said.

I was aware, if not fully conscious, of Debbie talking about Charlie Wade and how great a guy he was and how I could hire a bike from him. He ran a big bike shop and rental agency down on Lake Henderson, on the edge of town.

'It shouldn't take that long.'

I was thinking onwards, about other things, about the other charms of Inverness, about the other Invernesses, and about how my journey was nearly at an end.

'The tour is only about twenty miles.'

It would be an emotional moment, saying farewell to the final Inverness after visiting all the other Invernesses from coast to coast. Whoa! Twenty miles?

At least when I said farewell to the previous Invernesses, I had others to look forward to. But this was it.

Twenty miles on a bike?

After this one, it was game over, and I was heading for home to the one true Inverness.

'Sorry, Debbie, did you say twenty miles?' I asked, slowly.

'Weather permitting,' she said, smiled sweetly, and returned to whatever she was doing.

I was dumbfounded. I prayed that she couldn't see the look of stark terror on my face. For a kick-off, I couldn't imagine spending that length of time on a bike and, given the size of downtown Inverness, I figured you would have to cycle round it a dozen times to clock up twenty miles.

'Of course,' I said, quietly.

I said my farewells and went back to my unspeakable motel to start a raindance. You will be well aware by now, given my banging on about it wherever possible, that there is a railwayman inside me fighting to get out. So you will imagine my disquiet that this Inverness's railway line, which was lifted in the 1980s, was now a cycle path.

The railway bed now formed the quaintly named Withlacoochee Rails to Trails bike path, and placed strategically alongside it was Charlie Wade's bike shop. Thankfully, the day I visited him there it was at the end of a rainbow after hours of monsoon-like rainfall. My dance had worked. How it had worked.

'I weighed over 300 pounds and was living life to the full, if you get my meaning, from an alcohol and overeating point of view,' said Charlie. He was around sixty years old, and bore a passing resemblance to John Cleese. His red polo shirt was liberally bedaubed with logos of bike manufacturers and sponsors.

'I was in insurance and had built up a big business, but my life was out of control. I knew I had to change or I wouldn't be here today talking to you,' he said. He was a still a big man, but in the right proportions.

'So I got on my bicycle, although I could hardly ride round the block where I lived. But I stuck at it and slowly got my weight under control. I became an 8,000 to 9,000 mile a year cyclist and I would go all over the country. Cycling helped me get back to health and fitness and I quickly realised my hobby could become my business.'

Bikes aren't really my thing, but I asked him what was his drug of choice, in a bicycling sense.

'Oh, I like a road bike, a tourer,' he said, pointing to a machine among the hundreds in his shop. There were bikes of all shapes and sizes, road bikes, mountain bikes, racers. There were also a couple of those odd tricycles where you sat in a chair low to the road and held a joystick-type control column with the brakes and gears on it.

'I had one of them set aside for your tour today, but the weather is awful. It's such a shame. I heard you were really looking forward to it.'

There was an awkward silence.

We sat in the office, which took up a corner of his shop. The air was heavy with the smell of rubber from hundreds of tyres. When I walked in, that aroma immediately teleported me back to Junners bike shop on Greig Street in the one true Inverness, and the day I got my first bike.

My father had been a member of two social clubs in Inverness: the Caley Club and the Railway club. It may have been because he enjoyed the company, but I think it had more to do with the fact that beer was cheaper in a club than in pubs.

Each had a draw called the Hundred Club. This saw members pay a quid a week into an account, and every Friday night there was a draw with the winner picking up £100, second place £75, third £50 etc. I can't remember what happened to the rest of the cash, which may have gone towards a children's Christmas party. One Friday, he went into the Railway Club for a pint after work and discovered he'd won the top prize.

Being the generous type, he bought everybody a drink then headed for home. En route, he stopped at the Caley Club for a nightcap to find he'd won the top prize there too. In 1975 £200 was a huge sum of money for a railway clerk. My mum had the house redecorated and I got my first bike: a blue Raleigh Olympus racer.

'There is no such thing as a typical day in this business,' said Charlie. 'One day you could sell six bicycles, the next not sell a single one but do a ton of rentals. We do rentals here from all over the world.'

I shuffled my feet nervously. Charlie may well be doing a roaring trade in rentals, but he didn't get my business today. I glanced outside to see the rain still cascading down, and said a silent thank you.

'For some reason we're big in Germany. I am in some German travel magazine, although I don't know how, and they come here by the planeload. They must rent houses here. Of course you Europeans are great bike riders anyway, aren't you?'

"Except me, Charlie," I wanted to say. 'Except me.'

The stories got bigger. In recent times I woke to two of the biggest. As I slept one night, the controversial Donald Trump was elected to the White House. Trump wants to build a wall along the Mexican border and plans to stop terrorism by banning Moslems from travelling to the USA.

Another morning I woke to the news that Britain had voted to remove itself from the EU. David Cameron, the Conservative Prime Minister who called the EU referendum, and Nigel Farage, the right-wing politician who led a vociferous campaign for people to vote out, have both disappeared from office, leaving the country to get on with it.

The world never stops turning.

But my world stopped one day recently when I met the girl of my dreams and, as I left the fifth and final Inverness, I would be going home to my wife and our little boy. Emma and Pete are my world. My travelling days are nowhere near as important to me now as my days with them. The one true Inverness will always be my spiritual home. But now the road home leads to Emma and Pete.

I kissed Debbie and pumped Frank's hand. They had been so kind to me (the bike ride apart) and I was deeply grateful to them. They had gone out of their way to accommodate me, to make me feel welcome, to show me their town. Theirs was a corporate welcome, a polished political with a small 'p' welcome, but they wanted me to know how special they felt about their town.

In a way, all the Invernesses here had been like this, yet each place had been so different. The sense I got from all of them was the same: pride. Despite their obvious contrasts, the clear differences between the kind of people who lived in each one, the jobs they did, the cars they drove and the homes they lived in, each Inverness shared a golden thread.

We in Scotland, and I include those who live in the one true Inverness, will complain about the weather, work, the traffic, whatever. And while there is much about the Americans which annoys the hell out of me, they are all instilled with a deep-rooted sense of patriotism about where they live, pride in their job and belief in what they do. It's just how they are. There's not much about America that I would import to Scotland, but it is their pride I wish we could share.

All five visited, I was now ready to head back to the one true Inverness. This would be my final journey, a blast up I-95, the main north-south freeway on the east coast. At the top lay New York, Kennedy airport and the great iron bird back to Blighty. In London I would go to Euston station and, as a treat, board the Royal Highlander, the sleeper to Inverness.

It was a prospect from which I was already taking great comfort, as I hefted my battered old Samsonite into the Chevy's trunk, the steel briefcase onto the backseat and my ageing lapdog in its bag on the passenger seat beside me. I would be cosily tucked up between crisp white sheets and sound asleep, as the electric locomotive rocketed us through the night.

Some time in the early hours we would coast into Mossend yard and the electric loco would leave us, to be replaced by the two 26s which would muscle me over the hills and home. If I was awake, I'd be able to see the southbound train standing in the next siding, waiting for its electric traction to take it to London.

In a compartment on that train, his nose pressed to the window, unable to sleep because of the excitement of an impending adventure, there might be a small boy, his wanderlust setting in.

I padded the brake and slipped the shift into drive. It didn't take many revs to roll away from my last Inverness. I passed the Cinnamon Sticks bakery, the Chas E Davis Funeral Home and Crematory and paralleled the Cooter Pond before looking in my mirror to see a green sign saying 'ssenrevnI'.

I smiled. Then I gunned the engine, rolled out onto I-95 and pointed the Chevy's nose north.

About the Author

Twice a day, every day, for the last twenty-five years, Mike Edwards has entered into the homes of millions of people across Scotland.

Mike is Senior Reporter at STV News and, in his own inimitable and respected style, he has covered every story of significance to have broken over this period, including politics, sport, humour, personalities, crime, tragedy, travel and much more.

He is a Major in the Army Reserve and has served in Iraq and Afghanistan. He has also written a novel, *Friendly Fire*.

Mike was born and brought up in 'the one true Inverness' in the Scottish Highlands, and he currently lives near Glasgow.

Map of Journey

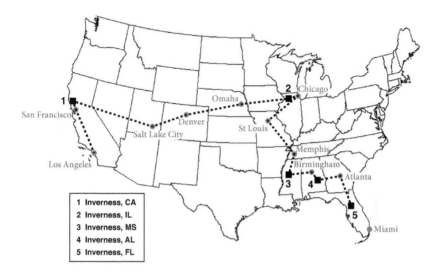

1 Inverness, CA
2 Inverness, IL
3 Inverness, MS
4 Inverness, AL
5 Inverness, FL

This map outlines the route which Mike undertook – by road and rail – when writing and researching this book. The USA is a vast country, covering over 6 million square miles and containing around 325 million people. It would be unhelpful, and perhaps confusing to the reader, to present a detailed map of the entire sub-continent, so this map concentrates solely on the main cities and states through which Mike journeyed, from California to Florida, an approximate distance of almost 4,000 miles in total. The five Invernesses are clearly marked, as is the route Mike followed on this arduous, frequently exhausting but ultimately fascinating and fulfilling experience.